ELECTING THE PRESIDENT: 1964

Chandler Publications in

POLITICAL SCIENCE

Victor Jones, *Editor*

ELECTING THE PRESIDENT: 1964

By *DANIEL M. OGDEN, JR.*

United States Department of the Interior

AND

ARTHUR L. PETERSON

Ben A. Arneson Institute of Practical Politics,
Ohio Wesleyan University

18324

 CHANDLER PUBLISHING COMPANY | SAN FRANCISCO

To
Val and Connie

Contents

Preface

Electing the President describes the process of choosing the chief executive officer of the United States. It reports the experiences of the two major parties in the 1960 election and examines the expectations for the 1964 campaign. It includes discussions of history and of constitutional and legal determinants in the detail needed to support its always practical emphasis.

Each of the authors writes from the combined knowledge of a practicing political worker and a scholar in political science. Both write from expert and intimate familiarity with the 1960 campaign, having been Faculty Fellows assigned by the Citizenship Clearing House to the National Committees of the Republican Party (Peterson) and the Democratic Party (Ogden). They also approach the 1964 campaign with the knowledge that flows from continuing attention to government and politics.

The writing plan for *Electing the President* has assured an objective book as well as a practical and accurate one. The work of each author was scrutinized by the other and also by the series editor and the editorial staff of the publisher. The result has been to develop maximum clarity and accuracy and to eliminate, to the satisfaction of two men with opposed party commitments, any statements challengeable as partisan.

THE PUBLISHER

ELECTING THE PRESIDENT: 1964

Chapter I

The 1964 Presidential Election

THE ADVANTAGE OF INCUMBENCY

An incumbent President of the United States usually can win reelection. Indeed, so great is his advantage that since 1900 only two incumbent Presidents have been defeated when seeking reelection. In 1912, William Howard Taft lost because his Republican Party split. In 1932, Herbert Hoover lost because the Great Depression turned many of his supporters into Democrats. Without such major political catastrophes, even a President of the minority party can win reelection, as Woodrow Wilson proved in 1916 and as Dwight D. Eisenhower confirmed in 1956.

A President seeking reelection has many advantages. Of greatest importance is his famous name. He is known worldwide. Whatever he says, whatever he does, wherever he goes, he makes news. People recognize his picture, listen to what he says, line the streets to see him pass. No challenger can buy enough advertising to match the attention the President gets just by being President.

The incumbent also has experience in being President. Only a former President can claim equal qualification, for the job is unique and solitary. No standard steps of ascent to the presidency have ever been marked out in American politics, as they have to the prime ministership in Britain. Only once in American history has a former President challenged an incumbent President—in 1892. Significantly, perhaps, the former President, Grover Cleveland, won.

The incumbent President shapes the issues of the campaign. His proposals for new laws are before the Congress for approval or rejection. The acts of his Administration are the subjects of debate. The programs he chooses to emphasize become major issues, by his choice. The statements he makes upon them are public policy while he lives in the White House. Singular indeed is the challenger who can create a major issue of his own, as Adlai E. Stevenson did in 1956 with his proposal to ban atomic testing. Most challengers have been content to exploit accumulated dissatisfactions by promising to take the country "back to normalcy," or to "end the Hoover Depression," or to "bring the boys back from Korea," or to "get the country moving again."

A united political party is another advantage for the President. Freed from a contest for his party's nomination, he is able to center his preconvention political activities upon creating party unity and securing good candidates to join him on the ticket. His status enables him to mediate or settle intraparty rivalries. His patronage summons the regular local party organizations to his cause. His programs attract his party's idealists.

Campaign funds, too, are available for a President. Only Harry Truman, in 1948, suffered for want of money. Yet this shortage turned to a flood of gold the morning after victory when many a lagging Democrat discovered that he had forgotten to mail his campaign check, which had been written several days before!

Support for an incumbent President's candidacy is provided by the entire Administration. His Cabinet officers are expected to deliver their home states and to campaign elsewhere on his behalf. Congressional leaders solicit his appearance on their behalf, and return the favor by using their personal organizations to assemble votes for them both.

Despite an incredibly heavy schedule of public work and political appearances, the President can keep abreast of events and can present fresh ideas in well-turned phrases. A large and experienced personal staff is always at his call, to brief him, to write his speeches, to do his research, to handle the press, to conciliate the Congress, to control the Administration, and to protect his time. Rare is the challenger who, with uncertain future, can assemble comparable talent to aid him.

One special advantage the President enjoys because of the office he holds. His every move is professionally planned and managed by the Secret Service, which commands the respect and cooperation of law-enforcement officers throughout the land.

One last advantage is drawn from human nature itself, as Thomas Jefferson noted in the Declaration of Independence. Mankind prefers the known to the unknown. The nation knows how the incumbent will perform. It has no such knowledge of the challenger. "Don't change horses in the middle of the stream" can be the President's convincing advice to the people.

JOHNSON STRATEGY IN 1964

Lyndon Johnson will get the vote of a lifelong Republican, a secretary in Crawfordsville, Indiana, "because he seems to know so much about how to be President."[1] This report goes to the heart of Johnson strategy for 1964.

No man has come to the presidency with greater national experience in high elective office. Having served three years as Vice President, eight years as Democratic leader of the United States Senate and a total of twelve years as a United States Senator, and eleven years as a United States Representative, at 56 Lyndon Baines Johnson has spent virtually all of his adult life in high elective office in Washington, D.C. First elected in 1937 as a New Deal Congressman from Texas, he has served close to the centers of power under Roosevelt, Truman, Eisenhower, and Kennedy. Moreover, Johnson's first moves were designed to demonstrate that such experience is the best training for the job.

The assassin's bullets which elevated Lyndon Johnson to the highest office in the land on November 22, 1963, also gave him the nation's sympathy and forbearance. The people's response to the tragic assassination of President Kennedy was to rally around

[1] Roland Evans and Robert Novak, "Inside Report—Johnson's Republicans," *The Washington Post,* February 3, 1964, p. A-15.

his successor. Stability and continuity had first to be assured. A firm hand was needed to guide public action. The new President deserved time to get the job in hand.

A month's moratorium on politics gave Johnson time to prove that he would be no mere caretaker. Promptly he moved to take over his Party, to preempt the center of the political spectrum, and to identify himself as a leader of all the people.

With the 1964 Democratic National Convention only nine months away, and wanting the nomination for President without a contest, President Johnson had no time to establish a political organization of his own which could preclude opposition within the Democratic Party. His only recourse was to embrace the Kennedy organization which held control of the Party machinery. He asked the Cabinet to remain. He asked Chairman John Bailey of the Democratic National Committee and his entire staff to stay at their posts. He added only a few of his personal aides to the White House staff.

Under the circumstances, no other political action would have been gracious or acceptable—or tactically sound. The only going political organization capable of offering resistance to a Johnson candidacy for the Democratic presidential nomination had been summoned to his cause. The Kennedy organization, in turn, had no other gracious or acceptable course of action than to rally behind the new President. He had loyally accepted the vice-presidential nomination in 1960 and had carried most of the South for the ticket. Without his help, Kennedy could never have won the presidency. Now it was the Kennedy team's turn to help Johnson and in its hour of crisis the Democratic Party expected it to do so.

While securing organizational unity, Johnson simultaneously moved for policy unity within his Party. He had been the leader of the South at the 1960 National Convention. Now he had to demonstrate that he believed in policies favored by Democratic liberals from the industrial Northeast, from the agricultural Middle West, and from the Far West with its economy based on natural resources. Addressing a joint session of Congress shortly after taking office, he enthusiastically adopted the Kennedy program and the Kennedy record as his own.

These acts were not enough. To occupy the political center, to reassure his Party's liberals, and to create an image as leader of all the people, Johnson had to demonstrate unique qualities of his own. The obvious path lay in a brilliant display of his legendary legislative leadership. Kennedy's program lay becalmed in Congress. By securing its enactment, or even by winning passage of several key bills, Johnson could establish his political policy posture, shape the issues for the 1964 campaign, prove his sincerity to the liberals of the North and West, and demonstrate his qualifications for leadership.

Action came first. Major appropriation bills for foreign aid, defense, agriculture, public works, and other purposes were still before Congress, with nearly half the budget year already gone. All were hustled to passage, the last on the very eve of Christmas by summoning some vacationing Congressmen back from their firesides.

Moves to occupy the political center followed. The $11-billion tax cut urged by former President Kennedy to stimulate economic growth had been moved through the House with a promise of government economy. Johnson took personal command of final budget preparations for the fiscal year beginning July 1, 1964. Cuts in funds and reductions in numbers of employees were ordered wherever possible. Significant savings were made by slowing the stockpiling of fissionable material and by closing obsolete military bases. Civilian programs designed to promote economic growth were given modest increases. In January, President Johnson offered Congress a budget for fiscal 1965 which was half a billion dollars lower than the previous Kennedy budget.

In January, with the opening of the second session of Congress, the tax-reduction bill came to life in the Senate Finance Committee, passed the Senate, went to conference, and before February ended was signed into law. Moderates and conservatives were greatly pleased. Senator Richard B. Russell of Georgia, long-time leader of the Southern bloc in Congress, announced his support for Lyndon B. Johnson for President and virtually precluded a Dixiecrat revolt in 1964.

Next came proof that Johnson would stand as a liberal and would be a national leader. The Civil Rights bill, a cornerstone of the Kennedy program, was called up by the House Rules Committee and passed February 11, 1964, after the longest debate in the House of Representatives in recent history. Promptly plans were laid to by-pass the Senate Judiciary Committee, headed by Senator James Eastland of Mississippi, and take the bill directly to the Senate floor for debate and early enactment.

Bolstering his appeal to liberals, Johnson sent Congress a vigorous plea to authorize medical care for the aged through Social Security. Long a goal of the labor unions and other liberal groups, it would be either a major Johnson legislative landmark or a major Johnson campaign issue.

A war on poverty widened his liberal program. On April 9, 1963, President Kennedy had established the President's Appalachian Regional Commission to attack the continuing problems of depression which plague that 10-state area. Within a month of taking office, President Johnson declared war on poverty generally, set up a task force to prepare an action program, and in early February appointed Sargent Shriver, a Kennedy brother-in-law, to head the attack. The Appalachian program, scheduled to be presented to the President in late February, 1964, seemed destined to be part of the larger effort.

Although he enjoyed all the advantages of an incumbent President, Johnson also strengthened his image by traveling widely in the preconvention period. He visited St. Louis, Missouri, in the heartland of the Middle West, to celebrate that city's 200th birthday and named Stan Musial, its most famous baseball player, head of the national physical-fitness program. He scheduled an extended swing through the West for late May to speak about conservation, reclamation, wilderness, outdoor recreation, and public power. Similar visits to New York, New England, and the Middle West were planned.

Everywhere he went, Johnson spoke of the national goals of the United States, of the national problems, and of the nation's responsibilities for world leadership. All that remained of his sectional past were his Texas accent and his homey phrases, which he could not and would not change, for they make him real and keep him close to the people.

Such a strategy, designed to establish an image of great experience and a capacity for action while retaining the loyalty of the conservative South and serving the needs of the liberal North and West, seemed by early spring to be working. As the Johnson image sharpened into focus before the public eye, the President's coat tails lengthened. Democratic congressional, state, and local candidates began to see in him a most welcome leader of the ticket who, like Franklin D. Roosevelt, might carry one and all to victory in November. The rush to board his bandwagon added to his momentum. Democrats, with the hopes of victory high, eagerly turned to the 1964 campaign.

To win election safely, Johnson needs to lengthen the Kennedy margin of 1960. At any event, as one wag put it, he has to do at least as well. John F. Kennedy polled 34,227,096 votes. He carried but 22 of the 50 states with 303 of the then 537 electoral votes. Nixon, with 34,107,646 votes, received 219 electoral votes from 26 states.[2]

Johnson tactics for 1964 must be based upon holding all of the1960 Kennedy states and also carrying states which narrowly went for Nixon. Attention will center upon adding states in the South and Far West and keeping key states in the Northeast and Middle West.

Nixon, like Eisenhower before him, successfully raided the "Solid South," carrying Florida, Kentucky, Tennessee, and Virginia. These 45 electoral votes plus 7 from Mississippi are prime prospects for Johnson in 1964, even though some may be beyond recall. Together, however, they could barely offset the loss of one big state like New York.

Other fields must therefore be cultivated and the Far West offers several excellent prospects. California went for Nixon by a mere 35,600 votes, less than ½ per cent of the 6,484,000 cast

---

[2] Alabama gave 6 of its 11 votes, Mississippi all of its 8 votes, and Oklahoma 1 of its 11 votes to Senator Harry F. Byrd of Virginia, who was not even a candidate. There will be 538 electoral votes in 1964. See Chapter II.

for President. With 40 electoral votes, a Democratic Governor who defeated Richard Nixon in 1962, and a Democratic legislature, California will be a prime target for President Johnson. The state of Washington, likewise led by a Democratic Governor, two Democratic Senators, and a Democratic State Legislature, presents a similar picture. Its 9 electoral votes went to Nixon by only 30,000 votes in 1960. Alaska, too, though it casts but 3 electoral votes, must be counted a prime target, for Nixon won it, with only 1,100 votes—a margin of less than 1 per cent—and the state is led by Democrats.

The other most promising states for Johnson gains are Montana, which Nixon carried by but 7,000 votes, and Wisconsin. In Montana a strong Democratic ticket is in the making with Senator Majority Leader Mike Mansfield seeking reelection and Assistant Secretary of Agriculture Roland Renne, former President of Montana State College, running for Governor. Wisconsin, though traditionally a Republican stronghold, now has a Democratic Governor and two Democratic Senators and cast but 51.8 per cent of its vote for Nixon in 1960.

On the other hand, keeping the Northeast and the Middle West will not be easy. Kennedy carried Illinois by but 9,000 votes out of 4,700,000. With its 26 electoral votes it will be a major battle ground, for it is in the heartland of traditional Republicanism. New Jersey was also close, with a difference of 22,000 votes out of 2,750,000 cast, although these 17 electoral votes will be more difficult for Republicans to capture. Two small states also gave razor-thin leads to Kennedy: Hawaii's 3 electoral votes went to him by a mere 115 votes; Delaware's 3 by but 3,000!

President Johnson counted two further advantages which he hoped might be decisive. The Democratic Party is clearly the majority party in America today. Repeated polls by responsible scientific survey research organizations reveal that more than 50 per cent of the American voters identify themselves as Democrats while less than 35 per cent call themselves Republicans.[3] Other

[3] Angus Campbell and others, *The American Voter* (New York: John Wiley & Sons, Inc., 1960), p. 124.

things being equal, Johnson would need only Democratic votes to win.

In 1960, other things were not equal. John F. Kennedy was a Catholic. The Survey Research Center's study shows that Kennedy clearly lost the votes of at least 6.5 per cent of the Democrats, apparently primarily for that reason.[4] Johnson, a Protestant who loyally supported the Catholic President, would face no religious issue.

One strategic move yet remains for Lyndon Johnson—a move he will leave until after his nomination by the Democratic National Convention in August, 1964. He has to select a running mate who will strengthen the ticket. The tragic loss of President Kennedy has made imperative the selection of someone who obviously is qualified to step into the post. The need to carry the Northeast and Midwest makes a vice-presidential candidate from those sections a likely prospect.

To Democrats, at least, the sum of these considerations seemed clear: Lyndon Baines Johnson looked like the odds-on favorite in the 1964 presidential race.

REPUBLICAN STRATEGY IN 1964

Republicans looked differently at the coming presidential election. They did not see the odds as prohibitive nor the President as a likely winner.

Instead, some Republicans felt that 1964 could be a year of surprise, as was 1948. Beneath the surface of American political life they detected uneasiness, uncertainty, and apprehensiveness which could lead the American people to seek a change in administration. They saw 1964 as a period of crisis rather than "normal" times and they knew that an incumbent President who cannot meet national crises can be headed for defeat.

The expected Republican strategy will be to exploit the Johnson administration's weaknesses and make constructive counterpropo-

[4] Philip E. Converse and others, "Stability and Change in 1960: A Reinstating Election," *The American Political Science Review*, LV (June, 1961), 269-280.

sals. Republican hopes for recapturing the presidency rest on finding over-all positions on major policy issues which more accurately reflect the deep feelings of the majority of American voters than do the policies and leadership patterns of the Johnson administration.

In late winter, 1964, civil rights seemed likely to be the most troublesome and explosive issue of domestic politics in the 1964 campaign. By early March, Republican leaders had clearly indicated their belief that the Johnson administration had misread the feelings of the majority of the American people on the issue. Though the Republicans historically had fostered civil rights legislation and had provided the crucial margin of support necessary to pass a strong civil rights bill through the House of Representatives in early February, a growing difference began to emerge between their position, as a whole, and that of the northern Democrats.

Speaking in Cincinnati on February 12, 1964, Richard Nixon stated what may be the essence of the Republican position. He agreed that if a civil-rights law is passed and effectively administered, it will be a great step forward for equality of opportunity for all Americans. Then he continued:

> But much of the good that the law may do will be destroyed if the irresponsible tactics of some of the extreme civil rights leaders continue.
>
> A law is only as good as the will of people to keep it. The hate engendered by demonstrations and boycotts have set Americans against Americans and have created an atmosphere of hate and distrust which, if it continues to grow, will make the new law a law in name only.
>
> It is time for responsible civil rights leaders to take over from the extremists.
>
> In this election year Republicans will be urged by some to out-promise the Johnson administration on civil rights in the hope of political gain. I am completely opposed to this kind of political demoguery. Making promises that can't be kept—raising hopes that can't be realized—are the cruelest hoaxes that can be perpetrated on a minority group that has suffered from such tactics for a hundred years.
>
> I think that the Republican party should stand forthrightly on these principles:

We are proud of our record from the time of Abraham Lincoln to the passage of the first civil rights legislation in a hundred years under President Eisenhower.

We shall continue to lead the fight for equality under the law for all Americans, including not only our Negro citizens but other minorities who because their numbers are less are sometimes overlooked —the Puerto Ricans, the Eastern and Southern Europeans, the Central and South Americans, the Mexicans, and our American Indians.

But we are a party that was founded on the principle of the rule of law. Abraham Lincoln led the nation to war to maintain the rule of law in our land. The encouragement of disrespect for law through mass demonstrations, boycotts, and violation of property rights, in the long-run, harms rather than helps the cause of civil rights.

We disapprove of the spectacle of public officials lending the prestige of their office to extra-legal pressures on the part of any minority or majority group. This encouragement of disregard for law and for the rights of other people and other minorities will plague the cause of better understanding among the American people for years to come.

We stand for the rule of law and reject mob rule.

The only rights worth having are the rights created in the law, by lawful means, and which exist for all Americans equally and equitably.[5]

Republican belief that most Americans favored orderly change at "all deliberate speed" and disapproved of the extreme demands and more militant actions of some civil-rights groups was founded on the reactions of urban and suburban centers which have traditionally supported the Democratic Party. In February, 1964, riots developed in the heavily Democratic Italian wards of Cleveland, Ohio, over Negro insistence on ending alleged de facto segregation in the city's schools. That same month in Cincinnati, similar resentment appeared in white "labor" wards. As some Democratic leaders became identified in the public mind with the militants, Republican leaders saw an opportunity to gain support by identifying their cause with law and order.

At the same time, Republican National Chairman William Miller

[5] *Columbus Dispatch,* February 16, 1964, p. 34A.

was testing the usefulness of an attack upon President Johnson's voting record on outlawing the poll tax. Said Miller:

. . . President Lyndon Johnson issued a statement following the ratification of the 24th Amendment to the Constitution by the South Dakota legislature, an action which outlawed the poll tax as a requirement for voting in federal elections.

Here is what the President said:

"As majority leader of the Senate, I personally urged the banishment of bars to voting. This triumph now of liberty over restriction is a proud moment for me."

. . . When he tries to establish himself as a leader in the movement to abolish the poll tax, he is asking for an answer.

The record is there for anyone to see, and the facts are that Lyndon Johnson voted against abolishing the poll tax over and over again. Between 1942 and 1960, while he was a member first of the House of Representatives and then of the Senate, he voted against legislation to outlaw the poll tax not once, not twice, but twelve times.

His effort to claim any small share of credit for the 24th Amendment is downright effrontery. . . .

These efforts had great potential significance. The urban centers are the heart of Democratic strength in those industrial states which can make or break a presidential campaign. In 1964 a presidential candidate will win if he carries the eleven most populous states plus the District of Columbia.

A second domestic issue also seemed in the making: corruption. Senate investigation of the fiscal dealings and alleged influence peddling of President Johnson's former Senate aide, Robert G. Baker, suggested the makings of a scandal with potential campaign appeal. Remembering past public reactions against expensive gifts to Truman administration officials, Republicans explored the usefulness of the new revelations to win support from voters who might otherwise support a man of Johnson's background and style.

In foreign affairs Republicans will aggressively challenge the Democratic record. Recognizing that President Johnson will have to defend the Kennedy foreign policies and that many situations are not to America's advantage around the world, Republican leadership began early to point out "weaknesses" and "failures." The continuance of the communist Castro regime in Cuba with its latest affront to the naval base at Guantanamo, the Panama Canal crisis, the unsatisfactory hostilities in South Vietnam, the strife on Cyprus, the uneasy truce in Laos, French recognition of the Chinese Communists, the erection of the Berlin wall and the danger of violence there, even the heavy continuing burden of arms offered ready targets for attack.

The Republicans will press all of these negative points to full advantage. They will charge that the Johnson administration is an administration of press agentry rather than substance. They will insist that the election of their ticket and the implementation of their alternative policies will best serve the interests of the United States in the years ahead. And they will likely make every effort to outline policy differences between the two parties.

In January, 1964, shortly after his appointment as Chairman of the Resolutions Committee for the 1964 Republican National Convention, Congressman Melvin Laird announced that the Republican platform would not contain a catalog of legislative proposals, but that it would set forth clearly for the voters a choice between the two major parties.

The sharpness with which those differences would be defined seemed likely to rest on the political philosophy of the Republican presidential candidate. In announcing his candidacy in early January, Senator Barry Goldwater said:

I have not heard from any announced Republican candidates a declaration of conscience or of political position that could possibly offer to the American people a clear choice in the next presidential election.[6]

Appearing on a television program (*Meet the Press*, NBC-TV) on January 5, Goldwater said that if he were President he might withdraw recognition from the Soviet Union and that he would continue to oppose the public-accommodations section of the Civil

[6] *Congressional Quarterly Weekly Report*, Washington, D.C., Vol. XXII, No. 2, p. 39.

Rights Bill. On January 6, Goldwater told a Republican fund-raising dinner that "Democrats cannot be beaten by a 'me too' in reverse—a Republican posture that attempts to out-liberal the liberals.[7]

Governor Nelson Rockefeller, on the other hand, will differ with the Democrats less on policy objectives than on methods and procedures. At a January 3 rally in Portsmouth, New Hampshire, Rockefeller said:

I did not enter the race for the Presidency of the United States to "stop" anyone else within my own party, and I certainly am not among those who view the worth or importance of the Republican nomination any differently today than I viewed it six weeks ago. . . . I am in this race all the way . . . because I want my party, the Republican party, to be a strong, dynamic and responsive force for good government in America. I am neither a "summer soldier" nor a "sunshine patriot" of the political wars; neither am I the foe of any other Republican. . . . I want to help build a Republican party whose doors are open to all men in the broad mainstream of American life and thought, and without regard to race, color, creed, national origin or economic status, . . . a Republican party which appeals to the best in people—not the worst, . . . not their fears, . . . a Republican party that rejects the extremism of both the left and right, . . . a Republican party that does not flinch from the real and pressing human problems of the very people whose confidence we seek —a party which takes the initiative in facing up to these problems and offers sound and sensible and workable solutions. America will not— and it should not—respond to a political creed that cherishes the past solely because it offers an excuse for shutting out the hard facts and the difficult tasks of the present."[8]

Other potential candidates, including former Vice President Richard Nixon, gave promise of policy positions somewhere between the two active candidates. Charging the Johnson administration with inconsistency, uncertainty, and the appearance of weakness, Mr. Nixon suggested that the nation dedicate itself to a policy of defending and extending freedom abroad, restoring confidence in our policies at home, and regaining respect for America overseas. On civil rights, he added:

[7] *Ibid.*
[8] *Ibid.*

We need a national program which will increase understanding among our people, the will to obey that law and other laws, and which will reduce the hate fomented by professional extremists and political demagogues.[9]

Whoever the Republican candidate is in 1964, he seems likely to display less concern for his national image and more concern for a national consensus on civil rights and foreign policy than his predecessor did in 1960. He also seems likely to give more attention to the conduct of the campaign. The combination of an effective exploitation of the Johnson administration's weaknesses and a dramatic presentation of reasonable, constructive alternatives to the Johnson program is likely to be his campaign formula.

The question which remains to be answered is which party, which leader, and which policies best reflect the contemporary American consensus. The electorate will give its judgment on November 3 when it elects the next President.

[9] *The Columbus Dispatch*, February 16, 1964, p. 34A.

Chapter II

Constitutional Foundations of Presidential Campaigns

The strategy of presidential elections was set in 1787 by the Constitutional Convention at Philadelphia. The Founding Fathers made two crucial decisions which have shaped both the nature of presidential campaigns and the nature of American political parties.

First, the drafters of the Constitution provided a chief executive who would be elected independently of the legislature for a term of four years. Such a guarantee of stable, one-party control of the executive branch effectively limited to two the major national political parties which could make a serious bid for power and destined both major parties to be "arenas of compromise"—decentralized, semipublic associations of many different sorts of people united primarily by the desire to win public office. Stands on public issues have had to be a product of compromise within the parties. Political philosophy has not been a useful basis for party association.

Second, the drafters of the Constitution provided that the President would be chosen by electors, especially selected for that purpose in such manner as the legislature of each state should prescribe. Each state was to be entitled to "a number of electors, equal to the whole number of Senators and Representatives to which the State may be entitled in the Congress." In 1962, the Twenty-third Amendment added three electoral votes for the District of Columbia.

THE ELECTORAL COLLEGE

To win election, a candidate for President must receive a majority of "the whole number of electors appointed." Should no one receive such a majority, selection falls to the House of Representatives, where each state is given but one vote, to be cast as the majority of its representatives shall determine.

The drafters of the Constitution imagined that the electors would be men of high station and independent judgment who would exercise <u>their choices</u> in what they believed to be the best interests of the nation. The device reflected the influence of Montesquieu's praise for the British system of divided powers— as he understood it—with the democratic, aristocratic, and monarchical elements represented in the Commons, Lords, and King respectively. The electoral college was to be a way of designating the chief executive which would obtain for a republic the separation from the passions of the moment that is insured for monarchies by hereditary selection.

Accordingly, the drafters innocently provided that each elector should cast his votes for *two* candidates for President. The candidate receiving the largest number of votes would be President, the candidate having the next largest number, Vice President.

All went well while George Washington was the leading candidate for President, because all electors voted for him, then scattered their votes for second choice. But after John Adams became President in 1797, the system quickly displayed its faults. When Adams sought a second term in 1800, Thomas Jefferson challenged him. Rallying the widely scattered rural, laboring, and frontier elements of the nation against the trading and financial interests which Adams championed, Jefferson laid the foundations for the party system of today. To assemble a majority coalition, he accepted as his vice-presidential candidate Aaron Burr of New York, an ambitious politician who later was to kill Alexander Hamilton in a duel, to conspire to set up an independent empire in the Mississippi valley, to be tried but acquitted of treason, and to die in disgrace.

Jefferson and Burr set about assembling slates of candidates for elector in each state who were pledged to vote for them.

Their success was phenomenal: they won overwhelmingly, but the result was a tie. Both Jefferson and Burr received 73 electoral votes. The decision fell, therefore, to the House of Representatives, which was still controlled by a majority of Adams' supporters. After prolonged negotiations, Hamilton threw his influence behind Jefferson and the intended presidential candidate was elected President. The Constitution was promptly amended to provide that electors would henceforth vote separately for President and Vice President.

The election of 1800 set a pattern for the behavior of electors which has been followed ever since. Each candidate for President arranges to have fellow partisans in each state nominate a slate of electors who are pledged to vote for him for President. The procedure varies according to state laws. Most of the states authorize state conventions of the political parties to nominate electors. Nine of the states allow the state central committees to designate them. Arizona nominates electors in the primary election. In Pennsylvania the presidential candidates themselves nominate their electors.

The presidential candidates then campaign, technically, for the election of their electors, because all states now provide that the electors shall be chosen by the people at the general election. But so routine has the role of presidential electors become that two-thirds of the states now provide by law that the names of electors shall not appear on the general election ballots. Instead, the ballots contain only the names of the candidates for President and Vice President to whom they are pledged. All other states but three list on the ballot both the electors and the candidates to whom they are pledged.[1]

Moreover, several states now further require by law that the electors cast their votes only for the candidates to whom they are pledged. Indeed, when the Oregon legislature tried in 1939 to

[1] Richard D. Hupman and Eiler C. Ravnholt, *Nomination and Election of the President and Vice President of the United States* (Washington: Government Printing Office, 1964), pp. 170-235. A complete, state-by-state exposition is set forth. See also United States Congress, Senate, *Nomination and Election of President and Vice President,* Hearings before the Subcommittee on Constitutional Amendments of the Committee on the Judiciary (Washington: Government Printing Office, 1963), pp. 103-104.

repeal the state law requiring electors to pledge when nominated to cast their votes only for the candidates of their political party, the voters in a referendum repudiated the legislature's change and retained the compulsory requirement. Presidential electors in the United States are not expected to exercise independent judgment.

However, a few states in the South do not oblige the electors to vote for the candidates to whom they are pledged. Alabama even provides for slates of electors with no reference to the presidential candidates. Mississippi permits unpledged as well as pledged electors. As a result, some southern electors in every presidential election since the close of the Second World War have cast their electoral votes as they have pleased, without reference to the people's choice or to the implied pledges contained in their use of a national party label.

In 1948, one Tennessee elector, pledged to Truman, voted for a third-party candidate. In 1956 an Alabama elector, pledged to Stevenson, did likewise. In 1960 one Nixon elector in Oklahoma cast his vote for another candidate, and six Alabama electors who were supposed to vote for Kennedy voted instead for a man who was not even a candidate for President! This sort of irresponsibility on the part of individual electors has occasioned considerable criticism. It could easily be remedied by state laws deleting the names of electors from the ballot and obliging electors to vote only for the candidates nominated by their national political party.

Some southern states have deliberately encouraged elector independence in the hope that enough votes could be wasted on a third-party candidate to throw the election into the House of Representatives where southern leaders have hoped to wield especially effective bargaining power. The most serious attempt of that kind occurred in 1948, when Strom Thurmond of South Carolina was advanced as a candidate for President on a States Rights ticket. Given the official Democratic label instead of President Truman in Alabama, Louisiana, Mississippi, and South Carolina, Thurmond was able to carry them but was unable to prevent Truman's election. A similar maneuver in 1960 carried only Mississippi for the third-party effort.

THE STRATEGY OF ELECTORAL MAJORITIES

The device of providing slates of pledged candidates for elector has had a profound effect upon the strategy of winning the presidency. Only one slate can win in each state. No states now permit the selection of electors at the congressional-district level, which could result in a divided electoral vote.

Accordingly, each major-party candidate for President starts his campaign with certain "safe" states where his party's voters normally are in a majority. Counting on winning all or most of these electoral votes, he next calculates those states in which his party seems to have a good chance of victory. Ordinarily these will be states which his party's presidential candidate carried in the last election and in which his party holds a number of key offices such as Governor, United States Senator, and United States Representative. Lastly he will look to the "doubtful" or "swing" states which from past performance, the division of party success, and the indications from current public-opinion polls appear likely to go to either candidate.

In 1964 there will be 538 electoral votes: 435 to equal the number of Representatives, 100 to equal the number of Senators, and 3 for the District of Columbia. A successful candidate must have at least 270. Traditionally, Democratic candidates have been able to count on the electoral votes of the Southern States, Republican candidates on the votes of New England and Middle Western States. As the Civil War has faded into history and modern industrial problems have shifted the patterns of party identification, however, the large urban centers of the North have tended to swing toward the Democrats, the urban centers of the South toward the Republicans. Two-party competition has now developed to the point that only a handful of states can still be regarded as reasonably "safe" for their traditional party. Republicans still usually can count on Colorado, Indiana, Iowa, Kansas, Maine, Nebraska, New Hampshire, North Dakota, South Dakota, and Vermont. Combined, they have 59 electoral votes. Democrats usually have been able to depend upon Alabama, Arkansas, Georgia, Louisiana, Mississippi, Missouri, New Mexico, North Carolina, South Carolina, Texas, and West Virginia with 114 votes. Rumblings of defection from the traditionally "safe" southern states largely disappeared with the succession of President Lyndon B. Johnson of Texas. With its 25 electoral votes, Texas has long been the keystone of the Democratic bloc. It is no accident that Democratic Vice Presidents and Speakers of the House, Garner, Johnson, and Rayburn, have come from Texas.

The center of attention, then, becomes the "doubtful" states. The reason is twofold. The most "doubtful" states also happen to be the states with the largest number of electoral votes. Chief among them are New York, 43 votes; California, 40 votes; Pennsylvania, 29 votes; Illinois, 26 votes; and Ohio, 26 votes. Any candidate like Franklin D. Roosevelt or Dwight D. Eisenhower who carries all five of these states with their 164 electoral votes is virtually certain to win the presidency. Without them it is virtually impossible to win. Indeed, only Woodrow Wilson, in 1916, has been able to win the presidency by carrying just two of them —and he won election with but 11 electoral votes to spare. Every other victor in a close election has had at least three of these "pivotal" states in his column. In 1960, Kennedy carried Illinois, New York, and Pennsylvania; in 1948, Truman carried California, Illinois, and Ohio.

Emphasis in a presidential campaign therefore centers on carrying these five key states and other large states like Michigan, 21 votes, and Texas. Appeals must be made to their interests and needs. Indeed, both parties ordinarily prefer at least one of their candidates for the presidency and vice presidency to be from these five pivotal states, in the hope of improving their chances to carry them. In the past 40 years, only the Democrats in 1960 and 1948 and the Republicans in 1940 have dared to violate this rule. No one has been nominated for President in recent times who hails from a state with as few as five electoral votes, such as Arizona.

Can the electoral college system designate a President who actually has received fewer popular votes than his opponent? Yes, it can; and it has, twice. In 1876, Samuel J. Tilden, the Democratic candidate, polled 4,284,757 votes while Rutherford B. Hayes, the Republican candidate, received 4,033,950. Hayes received 185 electoral votes, Tilden, 184 after a bipartisan commission had decided on a strict party-line vote that the electoral votes of several disputed southern states should go to Hayes. This "stolen" election was the most serious strain the electoral college system has received. Again in 1888 the incumbent President, Grover Cleveland, a Democrat, received 5,540,050 to his opponent's 5,444,337 votes. However, the Republican candidate, Benjamin Harrison, received 233 electoral votes to Cleveland's 168 and was readily acknowledged the winner.

Despite its quirks, the electoral college has a major advantage which has more often proved its worth. Because of its winner-take-all characteristics in each state, the electoral college was able to produce a clear majority for the most popular candidate in 1860, 1912, and 1960 when no candidate had received more than half of all the popular votes cast. Especially in 1860 and 1912, when major third-party candidates were in the field, this quality insured constitutional stability for the United States.

The electoral college system is unlikely to be changed in substance, even though the office of elector may someday be abolished and the votes be cast automatically by a designated official in each state, such as the Secretary of State. The present system permits the small states to cast a vote far in excess of their proportionate share of the total population. Voters in these states will not soon relinquish such an advantage. The very large states, for their part, are equally unlikely to forgo the advantage of being courted. Because the two major parties are of nearly equal strength in all the pivotal states, direct popular election of the President, or even proportionate division of the electoral vote, would wipe them out as decisive factors in the election. A vote would then be a vote wherever it could be won. Now a single popular vote in New York may not count proportionately as much as a single popular vote in Nevada, but that single New York vote can decide all 43 electoral votes and hence is worth a great deal more in the politics of the electoral college.

THE CONSTITUTION'S IMPACT UPON POLITICAL PARTIES

The two major American political parties are unique institutions in the politics of the free world because of the American constitutional system.

The political parties are unique first because, for all practical purposes, there can be only two of them. No law imposes such a restriction. Its most important cause is that only one party can gain control of the executive branch. Opposition to the leading candidate must unite behind the candidate with the next best chance to win. To support the candidate of a third party is to waste one's vote, for the third party candidate has no chance at all and a vote for him only destroys the voter's opportunity to determine who will be President.

This winner-take-all arrangement for the presidency is duplicated in every state for the governorship and also prevails in the election of members of both houses of Congress. Moreover, most state legislators, even those chosen from multi-member districts, are selected on the same winner-take-all basis, for the customary American practice is to permit the citizens to cast as many votes for the state legislature as there are members to be elected from their district, rather than to cast one vote each and have the election officials distribute the seats by some form of proportional representation, as in Europe.

Other causes of the two-party system have been suggested. Among them are the two-party tradition stemming from the earliest days of the Republic; widespread agreement among the American people on such potentially explosive issues as separation of church and state and the outlawry of special privilege such as a titled nobility; the division of attitudes between those who favor action by the federal government to achieve public goals and those who advocate preservation of states' rights; and the representation system used in Congress which obliges a political party which would control both houses to hold strength in both the large industrial states of the Northeast and the sparsely populated states in the West and South.

American political parties are unique, second, because they are arenas of compromise—associations united to elect and appoint fellow partisans to public office in order to advance as much as possible the varied goals of the many special groups within their ranks. Both parties are semipublic, decentralized, multi-group associations.

They are semipublic associations, not private clubs, in that every state regulates party organization, qualifications for party membership, the nominating process, and party finance. Yet in every state both major parties retain many private attributes. They take stands on issues as they please, must raise funds privately, and may select their own officers.

Both major American political parties are decentralized in that power rests with the state and local party organizations and principally with the county central committees. National party committees and national political leaders are unable to compel conformity on issues or oblige local organizations, leaders, or elected officials to support them in campaigns.

Both major parties also are multi-group associations. They are united essentially by a willingness to support common candidates for office. No central philosophy unites the members of either party. Individuals identify themselves with a major American party for a wide variety of reasons. Family preference, sectional tradition, occupation, policy issues, social status, race, and even religion have been important factors in choice. Identification is voluntary. Neither party votes people into membership, imposes dues, or requires any act of political loyalty, even that of voting for its candidates. Yet the members act together, voluntarily, for the penalty for failure is that other groups, dominant in the opposing major party, will win and use their public advantage in their own interest.

Public policy goals—party platforms—are a product of compromise within each party, not the application to a particular election of the party's principles. Policy goals are brought before each party by special-interest groups which seek party approval for their objectives. In the bid for votes for its candidates, each party tries to find "official" positions which will please each group without needlessly offending others. The parties thus act as a first stage in the political process of recognizing the legitimate needs of special groups in society for policy action from government. Groups do not expect policy *pledges* from the political parties, but rather an expression that the group's objectives are in the public interest and deserve serious consideration by elected officials. Party platforms, then, are guidelines, not pledges of action.

Some American political scientists, gazing uncritically at the British political system, have imagined that ideally political parties should be associations of people who share a common political philosophy. Such associations would unite to nominate candidates dedicated to the party philosophy. Once in office, the party members would stand together to enact the party program into law and to carry it out. Such parties are said to be "responsible." The voters are presumed to be able to choose between party programs and thus to give a mandate to one party to carry out its philosophy. Individual office holders are viewed simply as agents of the electorate whose task is to translate the party's promises into law. The public would not participate in shaping the parties' programs, but would only choose between them. Competition between such political elites is presumed to be sufficient to protect the public interest. To be effective, such parties would have to be private associations, centralized, and like-minded. The advocates of this "party-responsibility" theory have therefore proposed "reforms" to make American political parties more like parties appear to be in a unitary, parliamentary system such as the British.

American politics long ago developed a quite different rationale, which can be called the "arena of compromise" theory. American politics rest upon the premise that in a representative democracy the people freely elect public officers in whom they have confidence. Issues of public policy are then debated by such public officers in full public view and decided each on its own merits. The American people do not expect competing disciplined political elites to offer them comprehensive programs of political action for their blanket acceptance or rejection at an election and do not conceive of their political parties as seeking or being given mandates to enact comprehensive policy programs based on a body of political theory.

These American attitudes toward the making of public policy, as well as the "arena of compromise" characteristics of the major American political parties, stem from two fundamental characteristics of the American constitutional system: the separation of powers and federalism.

The separation of powers both shapes and reflects the American concept of policy formation. Election of the legislature separately from the executive stems from the conviction that the legislature should act independently from the executive. Public policy issues are to be determined by free votes cast by the legislators following public debate. But the same separation also removes the partisan political question of which party will hold executive power from policy debates in the legislature.

Policy making in American legislatures consequently is a bipartisan or even a nonpartisan affair. Only on a few highly controversial issues are party lines significant, and even on these party lines seldom hold.

Since policy questions have no necessary relation to political power questions, policy questions can be decided on their own merits. Members of both parties of all shades of opinion play a real part in making final decisions.

Accordingly, candidates for public office take personal stands on issues primarily to prove that they are able to exercise independent judgment. Ordinarily they discuss safe issues in which there is widespread interest but a clear public consensus. Occasionally, when it appears profitable, they take vigorous stands on particular controversial issues. But, as often as not, the part of wisdom is to display competence without making commitments which might offend as many voters as they please.

Presidential candidates play this game of winning personal confidence as vigorously as any candidate for Congress. The discussion of issues in a presidential campaign, therefore, often dismays those "party-responsibility" advocates who believe that the campaign should be a formal confrontation of political ideologies. The candidates, quite logically, are seeking votes, not debate honors. They may not emphasize or even discuss the same "issues" at all!

With policy decisions really left to Congress, another test of presidential capacity to lead, and thus an important campaign appeal, is ability to work constructively with Congress—on a bipartisan basis—to secure laws in the public interest. In the months following his succession to office, President Lyndon B. Johnson moved rapidly to demonstrate that his rather considerable reputation as a legislative leader could be carried with him to the presidency.

The separation of powers also reenforces and makes profitable the decentralization and heterogeneity of political parties. With an independent executive who does not need to have a majority in the legislature to win election or a disciplined majority to stay in office, neither party has an effective political whip to compel its elected legislators to vote for the party's platform or to follow the leadership of the President or of a state governor. The set term of office for legislators as well as for the President and governors further supports such independence. Knowing when they must face the voters and knowing they must face them on local issues, members of Congress and of state legislatures serve the needs of their states and districts unless national or party goals are truly overriding.

Federalism also makes American political parties arenas of compromise because it divides political power between the national government and the governments of 50 states. Elections are conducted by the states and won in the states. Only the presidency and vice presidency are filled by putting together the votes of several states. Thus the parties organize to win elections where they must—at the state and local level.

Each state and local party organization naturally reflects the particular needs and interests of the people within its area. In a nation as large and varied as the United States, differences may be very great. For example, the Democratic Party in Michigan may be intensely interested in labor relations in the automotive industry; the Democratic Party in the state of Arizona in water supplies for homes and farms; the Democratic Party in Philadelphia in urban renewal; the Democratic Party in Alaska in public development of natural resources. The national Democratic Party must therefore recognize and reconcile all these needs as best it can. Thus federalism is a basic cause of decentralization and heterogeneity in both major parties and is greatly reenforced as a cause by the varied social and economic interests of the nation.

PRESIDENTIAL CAMPAIGNING WITH "ARENA" PARTIES

Presidential campaigning is significantly affected in four chief respects by the "arena of compromise" characteristics of American parties.

First, with only two major parties in the field, each presidential candidate has bargaining power with the more extreme factions in his own party. Because in recent years the Republican Party has assumed a generally more conservative posture and the Democratic Party a generally more liberal one, very liberal Democrats and very conservative Republicans find themselves with no serious alternative if they disapprove of a moderate presidential candidate in their own party. In 1952, for example, conservative Taft Republicans were disappointed, but vigorously supported the moderate Republican nominee, Eisenhower, when the alternative was the liberal Democrat Stevenson. In the 1964 campaign, some very liberal Democrats may be critical of the moderate record of President Johnson, but the serious alternative is a more conservative Republican candidate who is far less acceptable to them.

Second, decentralization and heterogeneity oblige each presidential candidate to deal with a myriad of independent state and local party organizations. In some states, the state central committee will be so well organized that all dealings can be handled through its leaders. In others, some key county central committees will be traditionally independent and important. There the presidential candidate and his representatives will have to work with many separate units. Situations change from election to election, but, for example, the party organizations in the cities of New York, Philadelphia, and Chicago usually must be treated separately from their state organizations.

Some organizations will be so opposed to the presidential candidate that he will be unable to trust them. In that event, he will have to consider establishing separate "Citizens" or "Volunteers" committees to handle local vote-getting and campaign appearances for him.

Other state and local party organizations will prefer to center their efforts upon the election or reelection of candidates for Congress, state-wide office, or even county office. Holders of those offices commonly control the local organizations and are able to offer them important rewards in the form of policy decisions they want, jobs, and contracts. Somehow the presidential candidate must convince them that his election will serve their state or local interests, too. Fortunately, because he can easily attract far more attention, and thus far more votes, than can state and local candidates, he is usually able to keep their interest high, especially if it appears likely that he will win.

Third, campaign appeals must reflect state and local concerns and attitudes. For example, natural-resources development is important in the Far West, agriculture is vital in the Middle West, labor-management policy is of continuing concern in the industrial Northeast, and race relations are a major problem in the South. Even foreign policy and defense, though of interest everywhere, traditionally are of more intense concern on the East and West coasts than in the Mississippi valley.

Fourth, and most significant of all, the presidential candidate must convince the American people that he can lead the nation. He must establish confidence in his competence, honesty, judgment, and maturity. He must demonstrate warmth, human understanding, and concern about people. He must make clear his desire to solve pressing domestic problems of the day and must prove his ability to meet continuing international crises. But he does not have to promise his way into the White House. So long as he is somewhere in the great moderate center of the American ideological spectrum, he can appeal to reasonable men of all political views. His qualities as a person and as a leader are far more important on the whole than the stands he takes on particular issues. He needs to become, in the eyes of the majority of voters, "the best man for the job."

In our time, Franklin D. Roosevelt, Harry S. Truman, Dwight D. Eisenhower, and John F. Kennedy, in varying ways, all demonstrated these capacities.

Chapter III

Nominating the Candidate

American presidential candidates are nominated at national conventions of the major political parties. Customarily national conventions are held in the summer of election years. In 1964 the Republican National Convention will meet in San Francisco, California, from July 13 to 17; the Democratic National Convention in Atlantic City, New Jersey, August 24 to 28.

Theoretically, a national convention constitutes a representative assembly of rank and file party members. Acting in their name, it nominates candidates for President and Vice President, drafts the party program, adopts rules of procedure to conduct the party's affairs, and establishes the national committee and elects its members.

EVOLUTION OF THE NATIONAL CONVENTION

Political party conventions developed in the United States during the second quarter of the nineteenth century. The earliest method of candidate designation was by a caucus of party members who had been elected to Congress. Similarly, state legislators proposed nominees for Governor and other offices at the state level. This "legislative caucus" soon gave way in the states to a "mixed" caucus in which party organizations in those districts represented by a member of the opposition party in the legislature were allowed to select delegates to speak for them in the nominating decision.

30

The Congressional caucus held sway nationally until challenged by Andrew Jackson in the election of 1824. Poor attendance at the Republican-Democratic caucus and the defeat of the Republican-Democratic caucus nominee of that year, William H. Crawford, shattered confidence in the system. By 1832 the convention prevailed for both major parties.

Following the Civil War, party leaders and lobbyists so openly manipulated many state conventions that the system fell into disrepute. Between 1900 and 1910 most states provided by law that candidates would be nominated at a direct primary election conducted by the state. Only five states still permit conventions to nominate a very few important candidates for high office such as Governor and Congressman. All require nomination by primary for lesser offices.

The national convention has remained the system for presidential nominations, however, and state conventions are still used to select most delegates to the national conventions, to adopt state party platforms, and to conduct party business.

National nominating conventions have remained in style for sound political reasons. First, the convention really has but one nominating decision to make—the one for President. Public attention on that selection is so great that the unsavory practices which plagued state nominating conventions have never developed. The presidential candidate customarily is accorded the privilege of selecting his running mate. In recent times the only exception has been Adlai E. Stevenson's decision in 1956 to permit the Democratic National Convention to name the vice-presidential candidate. A hot contest ensued between Senator Estes Kefauver of Tennessee and Senator John F. Kennedy of Massachusetts. Kefauver won, but Kennedy was catapulted into contention for the presidency in 1960.

Second, a national presidential preference primary for each party would be prohibitively expensive. In 1960, the general election campaign alone cost the two political parties and their auxiliary committees an estimated $25 million.[1]

Third, the national conventions afford the state party leaders

[1] Herbert E. Alexander, *Financing the 1960 Election* (Princeton, New Jersey: Citizens' Research Foundation, 1962), p. 12.

their only real opportunity to gather together to organize for the presidential campaign. Since the election itself must be conducted separately in each state, winning control of Congress requires no interstate organization, or compromise. Without a presidential candidate to nominate, state party leaders would avoid meeting primarily to adopt a platform because a debate on issues followed by voting could only divide and embitter them. Thus the very ability to unite behind the candidate and to campaign success-fully for him turns to a significant degree upon the freedom of state party leaders to choose the candidate after face-to-face bar-gaining among themselves.

"AVAILABILITY"

At the heart of bargaining over the candidate for President is a quality long known in American politics as "availability." A man is "available" to be a candidate for President if he is ac-ceptable to the major groups in his political party, possesses cer-tain attributes which fit the temper of the times, and has personal characteristics which identify him with the broad majority of the people.

Foremost among the requirements of availability is experi-ence in high public office. In this century, only Wendell Willkie, Republican nominee in 1940, has lacked this quality. The Gov-ernor of one of the "pivotal" states fills this requirement especially well and adds a second: the probable ability to carry a large state. Cabinet officers and United States Senators and outstand-ing military leaders have occasionally been viewed as available. Ability to project a warm, attractive personality over the televi-sion and in personal contacts is a third element of being avail-able.

Philosophically, a moderate liberal for the Democrats and a moderate conservative for the Republicans usually fill a fourth requirement of availability. Thus conservatives such as Senator Richard B. Russell of Georgia, the southern preference in 1956, have no real chance to win a Democratic Party nomination.

Personal characteristics also are significant. The candidate has invariably been a man; white; preferably in his early fifties, al-though in 1960 both John F. Kennedy and Richard M. Nixon were younger; and preferably a Protestant. Kennedy is the only Catholic elected President and studies of the election reveal that he may have lost about 6.5 per cent of the Protestant Democratic vote for that reason, a margin which can be decisive in almost any presidential election.[2]

THE ALLOCATION OF DELEGATES

The strategy of winning nomination for the presidency at a national convention is greatly influenced by the varied and complex procedures which have developed for the allocation and selection of delegates. The allocation of delegates to both the Republican and Democratic National Conventions is determined by their respective national committees. No federal regulations are imposed, so each party uses a slightly different system.

Traditionally, both parties have assigned each state two delegates for each electoral vote. The Democrats adopted the practice in 1852. Since 1896, token votes also have been accorded the organized territories and the outlying possessions of the United States if a local party affiliated with the national party. Thus the District of Columbia, Puerto Rico, and the Virgin Islands are represented at both national conventions. The Democrats also allocate delegates to the Panama Canal Zone.[3] In 1964 Guam claimed a vote.

Apportionment of delegates based on the electoral college does not reflect the distribution of party strength, however. To remedy this disparity, both parties have resorted to additional provisions for the assignment of delegate strength. In 1913, the Republican National Committee adopted a penalty system to reduce the influence of the traditionally Democratic southern states in the convention. The move was prompted by the famous Republican Party split in the 1912 election which was occasioned, in part, when the incumbent President, William Howard Taft, won nomination over former President Theodore Roosevelt by controlling delegates from the southern states. Changed several times, the Re-

[2] Philip E. Converse and others, "Stability and Change in 1960: A Reinstating Election," *The American Political Science Review*, LV (June, 1961), 269-80.

[3] Clarence Cannon, *Democratic Manual for the Democratic National Convention of 1960* (Washington: Democratic National Committee, 1960), p. 21.

publican rule now obliges each state to "earn" delegates to represent its Congressional districts. A district which casts at least 2,000 votes for the Republican candidate for President gets one delegate, a district which casts 10,000 or more gets the customary two. Although the rule decreased southern representation by 76 votes in the 1916 Republican convention,[4] it is now obsolete. In the 1964 Republican National Convention only one Congressional district, in Mississippi, will be penalized one vote.

In 1940 the Republicans and in 1944 the Democrats turned instead to bonus votes to reward the faithful. Republicans award six to each state which casts its electoral votes for the Republican candidate for President or has elected a Republican Governor or Republican United States Senator since the last Republican National Convention. Democrats awarded four bonus votes for the same reasons until 1960. Having by that time permitted double bonuses and allowed states to retain representation lost in the 1950 Congressional reapportionment, the Democrats were discriminating against their key big states. They therefore abandoned bonus votes and allocated each state 2½ delegates per electoral vote plus one additional half-vote for each national committeeman and national committeewoman. Half-vote totals were rounded off to the next highest full number. However, no state was given fewer votes than it had enjoyed at the 1956 National Convention, so some overrepresentation continued.[5]

For the 1964 National Convention the Democrats changed standards once again, this time yielding to the demands of the big states to add bonus votes in proportion to the popular votes cast for the presidential candidate at the last election. A resolution adopted at the National Committee meeting of January 11, 1964, provided for a National Convention of 2,316 votes with a maximum of 3,052 delegates to cast them, some 800 more votes than had been provided at the 1960 Convention. Six rules determined the new schedule:

(1) Each state was assigned three convention votes for each electoral vote.

---

[4] See V. O. Key, Jr., *Politics, Parties, and Pressure Groups,* 5th ed. (New York: Thomas Y. Crowell Co., 1964), pp. 405-407.

[5] Cannon, *op. cit.,* pp. 13-19.

(2) Each state was given one bonus vote for every 100,000 popular votes cast for the Democratic candidate for President in 1960. Fractions over 50,000 were counted, but no state was to receive less than one such bonus vote. Only Alaska cast fewer than 50,000 Democratic votes for President in 1960. Alabama, which cast only 5 of its 11 electoral votes for John F. Kennedy, was counted as having cast only five-elevenths of its popular votes for him.

(3) States which voted for the Democratic nominee for President in 1960 were given an extra "victory" bonus of 10 votes. Alabama, however, received 5.

(4) Each state received two votes for its members of the Democratic National Committee, but no alternates can be appointed for them.

(5) No state was to have its representation reduced by the new apportionment system. Two small states, which had voted Democratic in 1948 but had forsaken the party ever since, gained by this provision. Montana, entitled to only 15 votes under the rules, received two more votes; Wyoming, entitled to only 12, picked up 3.

(6) For the first time in either National Convention, Guam was given representation, 3 votes. Since 1960, a Democratic Party had been established on Guam and had asked for affiliation with the national Party. The District of Columbia, able henceforth to earn delegates like a state, was given its electoral quota, two votes for its members of the National Committee, and half of the "victory" bonus.

All Republican delegates cast a full vote. Democrats, however, traditionally have permitted delegates to cast fractional votes, thus allowing more persons to participate in the Convention. In 1960 the Democratic National Committee provided that no delegate could have less than one-half vote. In 1964, to hold down the number of delegates, the Democrats at last adopted the same rule as the Republicans: only one delegate for each vote, but watered it down by permitting each state to send as many individuals as it had been permitted in 1960, in which case some delegates would have to be given one-half a vote. So generous was this rule that only Connecticut, Delaware, Hawaii and Maryland were

Republican National Convention 1964: Allocation of Delegates

State	Delegates	Electoral Votes	State	Delegates	Electoral Votes
Alabama	20	10	New Jersey	40	17
Alaska	12	3	New Mexico	14	4
Arizona	16	5	New York	92	43
Arkansas	12	6	North Carolina	26	13
California	86	40	North Dakota	14	4
Colorado	18	6	Ohio	58	26
Connecticut	16	8	Oklahoma	22	8
Delaware	12	3	Oregon	18	6
Florida	34	14	Pennsylvania	64	29
Georgia	24	12	Rhode Island	14	4
Hawaii	8	4	South Carolina	16	8
Idaho	14	4	South Dakota	14	4
Illinois	58	26	Tennessee	28	11
Indiana	32	13	Texas	56	25
Iowa	24	9	Utah	14	4
Kansas	20	7	Vermont	12	3
Kentucky	24	9	Virginia	30	12
Louisiana	20	10	Washington	24	9
Maine	14	4	West Virginia	14	7
Maryland	20	10	Wisconsin	30	12
Massachusetts	34	14	Wyoming	12	3
Michigan	48	21	*Territory*		
Minnesota	26	10			
Mississippi	13	7	Dist. of		
Missouri	24	12	Columbia	9	3
Montana	14	4	Puerto Rico	5	0
Nebraska	16	5	Virgin Islands	3	0
Nevada	6	3			
New Hampshire	14	4	*Total*	1,308	538

Democratic National Convention 1964: Allocation of Delegates

State	Convention Votes	Maximum Number of Delegates	Electoral Votes
Alabama	38	58	10
Alaska	12	18	3
Arizona	19	34	5
Arkansas	32	54	6
California	154	162	40
Colorado	23	42	6
Connecticut	43	43	8
Delaware	22	22	3
Florida	51	58	14
Georgia	53	66	12
Hawaii	25	25	4
Idaho	15	26	4

	Convention Votes	Maximum Voting Delegation	Electoral Votes
Illinois	114	138	26
Indiana	51	68	13
Iowa	35	52	9
Kansas	27	42	7
Kentucky	34	62	9
Louisiana	46	52	10
Maine	16	30	4
Maryland	48	48	10
Massachusetts	69	82	14
Michigan	92	102	21
Minnesota	50	62	10
Mississippi	24	46	7
Missouri	58	78	12
Montana	17	32	4
Nebraska	19	32	5
Nevada	22	30	3
New Hampshire	15	22	4
New Jersey	77	82	17
New Mexico	26	34	4
New York	179	228	43
North Carolina	58	74	13
North Dakota	15	22	4
Ohio	99	128	26
Oklahoma	30	58	8
Oregon	24	34	6
Pennsylvania	125	162	29
Rhode Island	27	34	4
South Carolina	38	42	8
South Dakota	15	22	4
Tennessee	40	66	11
Texas	99	122	25
Utah	16	26	4
Vermont	12	18	3
Virginia	42	66	12
Washington	35	54	9
West Virginia	37	50	7
Wisconsin	46	62	12
Wyoming	15	28	3
Territory			
District of Columbia	16	18	3
Canal Zone	5	8	0
Guam	3	6	0
Puerto Rico	8	14	0
Virgin Islands	5	8	0
Totals	2,316	3,052	538

obliged to send exclusively full-vote delegates. Four states, Maine, Mississippi, Montana, and Wyoming, and all the territories even retained the privilege of sending two delegates for every vote, except for their National Committee members!

Because some delegates always prove unable to attend the national conventions, both parties provide for alternate delegates. Each permits only one alternate for each full vote. Accordingly, the 1964 Republican National Convention will have a total of 2,616 delegates and alternates and the Democratic 5,260!

The great increase in Democratic National Convention votes was made for sound political reasons. The assigning of votes strictly in proportion to the electoral vote, even with a bonus for voting Democratic, did not reflect the number of Democratic voters in each state. Finding it less painful to grant votes than to take them away, the National Committee simply adopted the obvious alternative to the Republican penalty system. The larger states now feel they have won recognition of their numerical support for the ticket, as indeed they have, slightly. The five pivotal states will have 671 votes, 29 per cent of the total. In 1960, they had 409 of 1,521 votes, 27 per cent. Incidentally, the Republican National Convention of 1964 gave the pivotal states 358 votes, also 27 per cent of the total. Losers are the middle-sized states. The five smallest states, each with three electoral votes, and the District of Columbia, kept 4 per cent of the vote, although increased from 68 to 99 votes. They will have 63 votes, 5 per cent of the total, at the Republican Convention.

The larger convention also permits the Democrats to reward more loyal party workers on state and county committees. Moreover, size does not seriously hamper the conduct of a convention's business. No recent national convention has been small enough to engage in policy debate and none is expected to do so. A large convention has the virtues of allowing more people to participate in demonstrations and other events and of creating a more impressive national spectacle.

SELECTING CONVENTION DELEGATES

Delegate selection is a complex procedure which varies with the laws of the several states. Two distinctions are of major importance: the types of delegates and the methods by which they are chosen.

TYPES OF DELEGATES

Two types of delegates are recognized by both parties: "district" delegates and "at large" delegates. District delegates cast the votes assigned a state because of the number of Representatives it has in Congress. A common practice is to distribute a state's district delegates equally among the Congressional districts and, if the convention system of selection is used, to have the delegates to the state convention from each Congressional district nominate persons to represent them at the National Convention. The state convention then ratifies the choices.

"At large" delegates are assigned a state because of the two electoral votes for its United States Senators and for any United States Representatives who are elected from the state as a whole. Bonus votes also are assigned at large. At large delegates commonly are chosen by state conventions as a whole or by the people in a statewide primary election.

The practice of distinguishing between district and at large delegates has led some state Democratic conventions to send full-vote district delegates and half-vote at large delegates to the Democratic National Convention. It also can result in divided delegations, but gives a substantial advantage to the candidate who has majority support in a majority of a state's Congressional districts. For example, in the Republican State Convention in the State of Washington in 1952, a sharp fight took place between delegates supporting the candidacy of Senator Robert A. Taft and delegates backing Dwight D. Eisenhower for the Republican nomination for President. Taft delegates were in a majority in two Congressional districts, and easily named four delegates to the national convention to represent those districts. Eisenhower delegates were dominant in four districts and similarly won eight delegates. The remaining 12 delegates (4 for the Senators, 2 for a Congressman at Large, and 6 bonus votes) were chosen at large. The Eisenhower delegates, being a majority of the convention as a whole, insisted upon a roll call vote for each at large delegate contest, and easily won them all. Eisenhower thereby won

20 of the state's 24 votes at the Republican National Convention.

METHODS OF CHOOSING DELEGATES

Three methods of choosing delegates are provided. Twenty-nine states permit state political party conventions to choose delegates to the national conventions. Eighteen prescribe or permit primary elections of some sort. Three allow the state central committees of the political parties to name the delegates.[6]

State conventions constitute an indirect method of delegate selection. Commonly the process begins with precinct caucuses held by the party leader of each such election unit in his own home. The precinct caucuses select delegates to county conventions which in turn name delegates to state conventions.

Running for selection as a national-convention delegate at a state convention often is purely a personal matter. The average delegate spends several hundred dollars of his own money and gives a week or more of his own time to serve. If there is no contest for the presidential nomination, would-be delegates solicit votes among personal friends in their party. Rarely do they promise any sort of action on platform issues or organizational questions which may arise. If there is a fight over convention delegates, as the Republicans had in 1952 and the Democrats in several states in 1960, slates of delegates may be assembled to campaign for votes by pledging support for their favorite candidate.

Presidential preference primaries take several forms. The most common permits each candidate for nomination to put forward a slate of candidates for delegate. Some states even permit slates of unpledged delegates. The voters in the primary then choose among the slates. The entire delegation can thus be won by whichever candidate wins the largest number of votes for his slate of delegates. Because California, the second largest state, uses this system, its presidential preference primary in June can be a crucial step to the presidency.

Several states permit a variation on the slate of candidates. Wisconsin, for example, provides for the separate election of dis-

---

[6] Richard D. Hupman and Eiler C. Ravnholt, *Nomination and Election of the President and Vice President of the United States* (Washington: Government Printing Office, 1964), pp. 43-168.

PRESIDENTIAL ELECTION CALENDAR, 1964

Presidential Preference Primary Elections

New Hampshire	March	10
Wisconsin	April	7
Illinois	April	14
New Jersey	April	21
Massachusetts	April	28
Pennsylvania	April	28
District of Columbia	May	5
Indiana	May	5
Ohio	May	5
Nebraska	May	12
West Virginia	May	12
Oregon	May	15
Maryland	May	19
Florida	May	26
California	June	2
South Dakota	June	2

National Conventions

Republican National Convention—San Francisco, California	July	13
Democratic National Convention—Atlantic City, New Jersey	August	24
Presidential Election	November	3

trict and at large delegates. A divided delegation can result, as was the case in 1960 when Humphrey won four districts and Kennedy carried six and the at large delegates. Other states permit individual candidates for delegate to indicate candidate preference after their names.

Some states, like New York, elect the delegates in a primary, but do not provide for the designation of candidate preference. Because delegate positions are temporary and unpaid, and because attendance at the convention is at the delegate's personal expense, those running for delegate do not advertise their candidacy and thus are never known to the general electorate. Experience has proved that such nondesignation primaries are easily controlled by the regular party organizations.

CORRALLING DELEGATE VOTES

Nomination for President is gained by a majority vote of the delegates at a national convention. The convention ballots as often as is necessary to determine the winner (103 times at the 1924

Democratic convention!). Victory in such a system goes to the candidate who can assemble a majority first.

This is the simple principle upon which John F. Kennedy won the Democratic nomination in 1960 and Dwight D. Eisenhower the Republican nomination in 1952. But the road to that victory is both difficult and complicated as well as very expensive.

The rules of success are: First, see that your friends are elected delegates wherever you can. Second, where you can't control delegate selection, support a neutral leader who can, then work to win his support. Third, fight for delegates openly only where you have to, but avoid picking a fight when you're sure to lose.

The struggle for delegates starts early in election year. Each state sets a different time for the selection of delegates and may permit each party to choose them at different times.

Once the selection time table is set, each candidate goes after the votes in an orderly sequence. Victory in an early-chosen delegation can snowball into success in states where the outcome is in doubt.

THE DEMOCRATS IN 1960

The status of each candidate determines his tactics in winning delegates. In 1960, Lyndon B. Johnson, Senate majority leader, realized that it would be useless for him to contest presidential primaries in northern states. He concentrated instead on marshalling the state organization-chosen delegates from the South and on picking up delegates from the Mountain and Pacific Coast states where he had many friends in Congress.

John F. Kennedy, on the other hand, needed to prove that he was a top notch vote getter. He had to overcome the belief that a Catholic could not be elected President. And he had to become well known. He started with the New Hampshire primary in March and, without serious opposition, swept it. Emboldened, he risked all by entering the Wisconsin primary against Senator Hubert Humphrey from neighboring Minnesota. A narrow victory there on April 5, apparently with the overwhelming help of Republican Catholics who could cross over in the open primary, earned a majority of Wisconsin delegates but obliged him to enter a third key primary, in West Virginia, where Catholics formed but 5 per cent of the voters. Vigorous, well-financed campaigning and a sweeping victory on May 10 established him as a leading vote getter and knocked Humphrey out of the race.[7] Opposed by no other serious presidential candidate, Kennedy also carried the Indiana, Nebraska, Maryland, and Oregon primaries, netting 134 votes. These, with his block of 103 convention votes from the other five New England states, put him well into the lead.

Two other opponents awaited Kennedy in the wings: Adlai E. Stevenson, the Democratic nominee in 1952 and 1956, still adored by the liberals of the party; and Senator Stuart Symington of Missouri, who commanded the very important support of former President Harry S. Truman. Stevenson did not wish to fight for the nomination. Hoping for a draft, he hung back until the very last day before convention balloting, while his supporters dissipated their efforts for want of a determined leader. Symington's hope lay wholly in a convention deadlock. If the Kennedy drive fell short of gaining a majority of the votes, he could step forward as a most acceptable second choice. With few committed delegates, he was in no position to attempt a major showing of strength on the first ballot.

Shaping the drive for delegate votes was still another important American political tradition: the "favorite-son" candidates. When the political leaders of a state deem it advantageous to hold their strength in reserve so that a good bargain can be made at the convention, the traditional step is to pledge their delegation to one of their own political leaders, usually the Governor or one of the United States Senators. California, with 81 votes, led the list of favorite-son states at Los Angeles, followed by New Jersey with 41; Minnesota, which Humphrey still held, with 31; Iowa, with 26; and Kansas with 21.

Occasionally some delegations actually come uncommitted to a national convention. In 1960 two did, Pennsylvania with 81 votes and Illinois with 69. Thus three of the five big pivotal state delegations were hanging in the balance as the Democratic National Convention of 1960 opened. The strategy of deadlock, which had been Symington's from the start, now became Stevenson's as well. And Stevenson was at this point by far the more serious contender, for he had nationwide support and ready-made

---

[7] An excellent description of the 1960 struggle for delegates appears in Theodore H. White, *The Making of the President* (New York: Atheneum House, 1961), Chapters 2-5.

international issues in the U-2 debacle and the subsequent collapse of the summit conference.

But the Kennedy forces had not been idle while the convention states were selecting delegates. Michigan, with 51 votes, was the domain of a thoroughly efficient, citizen-led reform Democratic organization which had to be wooed directly, not undermined. After a conference with Senator Kennedy in early June, Governor Williams announced his personal endorsement. The bulk of New York's 114 votes were won by a quiet county-to-county campaign for district delegates. A major inroad was made in the mountain states, which Johnson had hoped to carry, when Stewart L. Udall lined up all 17 of Arizona's votes for Kennedy.

By the time the Convention opened, Kennedy had 600 votes of the 761 he needed for nomination. A struggle, brief but spirited, ensued between the Kennedy and Stevenson managers for the remaining uncommitted states. Kennedy had the advantage. He was organized and running. Stevenson wouldn't initiate the challenge. First Illinois, then Pennsylvania, caucused and announced overwhelming support for Kennedy. Minnesota, released by Humphrey, divided. California, strong for Stevenson, divided also.

THE NATIONAL CONVENTIONS

National conventions of both parties follow a traditional pattern of behavior which long has dismayed commentators and critics who do not understand the essentials of American politics. A convention has but one central purpose: to select a candidate for president who can be elected. All else must be subordinated. Above all, the convention must avoid a grand debate on issues of the day which would surely divide and embitter the various elements of the party.

Thus events at a national convention are designed to unite the delegates and to subordinate their differences by centering on the nomination of the candidate for President and by giving each delegate something to do about it. Each state is invited by roll call to place a candidate in nomination. Delegates then seize the spotlight by a "great demonstration" for their favorite candidate when his name is placed before the convention. National attention comes a second time to each state when the roll is called to announce the votes for presidential nominee. Such rituals are not nonsense as so many have tried to make the American public believe. They serve a fundamental and important political purpose. They attract the attention of the voting public to the task of choosing a President. They dramatically introduce the party's presidential candidate to the nation. And they emotionally commit the rank-and-file party workers on the scene to fight for victory.

Nominating speeches are an artistic specialty. The presidential candidate often seeks a spokesman who hails from a different part of the nation or who represents another wing of his party. The speechmaker extolls the virtues of the candidate—his qualities as a leader, his understanding of human needs, his command of the issues of the day, his blameless private life, his capacity to unite the party and the nation, his vigor as a crusader for goodness and justice, for freedom and democracy—but carefully refrains from mentioning his name. That comes last and is the signal for the demonstration.

Skilled nominating speakers "telegraph" the coming signal so that the demonstration will virtually explode upon the convention. A master of the art is Senator Everett Dirksen of Illinois, who closed his nomination of Senator Robert A. Taft at the Republican National Convention of 1952 by saying:

And so, my friends and fellow delegates, I present one whom I esteem as the amiable ambassador of our last best hope. I present one who is valiant for truth. I present a defender of the Republican faith. I present Mr. Republican, Mr. Integrity, Mr. American. I present Bob Taft.[8]

Pandemonium reigns. Delegates leap into the aisles, blowing horns, waving state signs, ringing bells, carrying balloons, wearing huge campaign buttons and colorful hats, throwing paper plates or confetti, lifting banners with slogans reading "Madly for Adlai" or "Go With Goldwater"—anything that will attract attention and show how enthusiastically they back their man. Around

[8] *Official Report of the Proceedings of the Twenty-fifth Republican National Convention Held in Chicago, Illinois, July 7, 8, 9, 10, and 11, 1952* (Washington: Republican National Committee, 1952), p. 353.

the convention floor they parade while the convention band or organ strikes up the candidate's theme song—"The Eyes of Texas Are upon You" for Lyndon B. Johnson, for example. Delegates lock arms, sing the theme song, chant "We want ——." This is the delegates' hour, their chance to impress the national television audience and perhaps to be picked out of the excited crowd by the folks back home.

THE DEMOCRATIC NATIONAL CONVENTION OF 1960

The Los Angeles convention followed the traditional procedures with gusto. On Tuesday, July 12, it heard the proposals of its platform committee and, after dissent on the civil rights plank was aired by southern delegates, shouted the program through.

Late Wednesday afternoon the nominating speeches began. Orville Freeman, Governor of Minnesota and one of Senator Humphrey's leading supporters, offered the name of John F. Kennedy in a good but routine speech. Johnson's and Symington's names were placed before the Convention. All received rousing demonstrations. Meanwhile the galleries were filling with Stevenson followers who had managed by hard work and excellent organization to obtain some 4,000 tickets of admission.[9]

Then rose Senator Eugene McCarthy of Minnesota, also a loyal Humphrey man, to make one of the greatest nominating speeches in American convention history—for Adlai E. Stevenson. Electrified, the crowd responded to his questions. Eloquently he pleaded for the leader who had brought the citizen-politician into his own, who twice had led a revitalized party.

As Stevenson's name was shouted out above the roar of the crowd, there erupted the greatest, most spontaneous, most wildly enthusiastic demonstration within the memory of anyone present. The galleries came alive with signs. Stamping and chanting "We want Stevenson," a solid wall of people marched around the galleries. A huge ball of petitions demanding his nomination was bounced from hand to hand above the delegates' heads across the convention floor. But on the floor many delegates stood at their seats, moved by the demonstration, but knowing that Stevenson could not be nominated.

[9] *Ibid.,* p. 198.

The roll call of the states followed promptly. As the tally advanced it became clear that Kennedy was, if anything, running slightly ahead of the more than 700 votes the afternoon papers had predicted. Tension mounted as the count grew. Thirteen votes short of nomination, the call reached Wyoming, the very last state. Wyoming's state chairman held 15 votes and dramatically cast them all for John F. Kennedy, "The next President of the United States."

THE REPUBLICAN NATIONAL CONVENTION OF 1960

By January, 1960, it was fairly obvious that Mr. Nixon would be the Republican presidential nominee. Indeed, after the Resolutions Committee fight (mentioned in Chapter IV) the nomination procedure itself was anticlimatic.

There were no hectic confrontations before state delegations as occurred in Los Angeles; there was no last minute "wheeling and dealing" as is the case when a hard-fought race for the nomination is in progress. There was instead a series of well-ordered nomination and seconding speeches for Vice President Nixon; the nomination and seconding of Senator Barry Goldwater; Senator Goldwater's withdrawal; and then the roll call. Even though Goldwater had officially withdrawn, ten Louisiana votes stuck with him as the roll was called; Nixon received 1331. Then the Convention voted to make the nomination unanimous for Nixon.

There was a slight protest over the choice of the vice-presidential nominee but, as in the controversy over the platform revision, effective action by several key leaders ultimately smoothed the way for Nixon's personal choice, Henry Cabot Lodge.

THE SEARCH FOR DELEGATES IN 1964

THE DEMOCRATIC ASSURANCE

In 1964 the search for delegates has been reversed from the 1960 pattern. President Lyndon B. Johnson, by moving swiftly upon his accession to office to confirm his support for the Kennedy legislative program and by insisting upon frugality in federal administration, virtually precluded organized revolt by northern liberal Democrats and solidified conservative southern support behind him. Attention to economic development in the West, particularly of natural resources, insured loyalty from that quarter. Thus the President could avoid the preference primary elections confident that he would be the only serious Democratic candidate and that he could depend upon the delegates selected both in the primaries and at Democratic state conventions to support his quest for a first full term in office.

THE REPUBLICAN CONTEST

The situation at the Republican National Convention in 1964 will be quite unlike that of 1960. Indeed, the fight for delegate support had begun in earnest almost as soon as it became officially known that Nixon had lost the presidential race to John F. Kennedy.

Governor Rockefeller appeared at the National Committee only days after the election was over. Some of Senator Goldwater's backers, cognizant of the beckoning opportunity, began to plan their campaign even before President-elect Kennedy took office.

The contingencies of political life altered the situation drastically between November, 1960, and July, 1964. For the first two years Rockefeller had clearly been the front runner for the nomination. Then, after the Governor's divorce and remarriage, Goldwater had appeared to surge into the lead. With Kennedy's assassination, talk of a compromise candidate was heard more and more frequently. Senator Thruston A. Morton was advanced by some as the logical choice to fill the compromise role; so were Henry Cabot Lodge, Governor George Romney of Michigan, and Governor William Scranton of Pennsylvania. And Richard Nixon, though hurt badly in the estimation of some by his 1962 gubernatorial defeat in California, was the clear choice of Republican voters at the grass roots in January, 1964, as he had been in January of 1960.[10] After some statements denying interest, Nixon agreed that he would serve again as his Party's nominee if called upon to do so.

And so, with the beginning of the new year of 1964, the strange campaign began. By the end of January two candidates had announced—Goldwater and Rockefeller. Scranton, Nixon, Romney, and Morton seemed available but reluctant.

[10] The Harris poll showed Richard Nixon leading on January 21, 1964.

John A. Wells, the director of Rockefeller's national campaign, saw the race as a two-man affair. Wells based his prediction on recent history which, he felt, showed that in two-man fights for the nomination, one of the two announced candidates emerged victorious—not an unannounced candidate.[11]

Andrew Tully, nationally syndicated news columnist, saw the matter in an entirely different light when he commented a day later:

Republican officials who know what they are talking about now say flatly the race for the Presidential nomination has narrowed down to the two leading noncandidates—Richard Nixon and Pennsylvania's Governor William Scranton.

"Forget about Rockefeller and Goldwater," said a man who has been in every GOP campaign since the 1940's. "Neither of them has a chance to take it, no matter what happens in the primaries. Rockefeller's divorce and remarriage cooked him, and Barry is too right-wing for this day and age. The party couldn't take a chance on either of them."[12]

To some analysts the race was, indeed, shaping up as another 1920 contest, when the Republican front runners were General Leonard Wood and Governor Frank O. Lowden of Illinois. Each was unacceptable to the wing of the Republican Party supporting the other and, ultimately, both were eliminated in favor of a compromise candidate, Warren G. Harding of Ohio.

But while announced candidates assessed and reassessed their preconvention strategy and while unannounced candidates continued to announce their "reluctant availability," a rash of favorite-son candidates appeared across the land.

Wisconsin, Ohio, and Pennsylvania had been eliminated from the primary lists through this device. Wisconsin's 30 votes were apparently going to Congressman John Byrnes; Ohio's 58 delegates were to be pledged to Governor James A. Rhodes; Pennsylvania's 64 votes were going to Governor William W. Scranton. Added to these 200 votes were the 48 votes which Michigan,

[11] "Rockefeller Aide Sees Two-Man Race," *New York Times,* Sunday, January 19, 1964, p. 57.

[12] Andrew Tully, Bell-McClure Syndicate, *Delaware* (Ohio) *Gazette,* January 20, 1964, p. 4.

without a primary, would give to Governor George Romney; Kentucky's 24 votes, likely to go to Senator Morton; Colorado's 18 votes, pledged to Senator Gordon Allott; and Minnesota's 28 votes, likely to go to former Congressman Walter H. Judd of that state.

The 318 uncommitted votes in these states alone outnumbered the 299 votes controlled by states in which primaries influencing delegate votes were likely to be held (New Hampshire, Maryland, District of Columbia, West Virginia, Florida, Indiana, Illinois, South Dakota, Oregon and California).

Until President Kennedy's assassination, Goldwater planners were hoping that the Senator would rout Governor Rockefeller in the March 10 New Hampshire primary and thereby clinch a first-ballot victory at the convention. The reevaluation forced by Kennedy's death yielded the decision that Goldwater might now have to enter a number of primaries, opposed or unopposed, to demonstrate his strength. The Rockefeller leaders, meanwhile, were choosing their battlegrounds; New Hampshire on March 10, Oregon on May 15, and the big California contest on June 2. The possibility existed that they would enter the lists in Illinois, on April 14, as well.

In January, Rockefeller and Goldwater organizations began to take shape in the key states having primary elections. The contests promised excitement and possibly some surprises. But the fact remained that with the near record number of favorite-son candidates, with the southern bloc committed largely to Goldwater, and with New York's 92 votes safely in the hands of Rockefeller regardless of what happened in the primary contests, it was unlikely that either Rockefeller or Goldwater would concede before Convention time.

There was another reason why neither Goldwater nor Rockefeller was likely to pull out of the race before the time when the actual balloting could demonstrate that either or both did not have the necessary support to win. That reason was that as long as they brought substantial support to the Convention they would have a claim to a major voice in the drafting of the platform. This, in itself, was an important matter to these two men who had disagreed violently over the content of the 1960 platform. On January 21, 1964, while campaigning in New Hampshire, Senator

Goldwater underscored his basic opposition to the 1960 document by disavowing it. Rockefeller at the same time continued to hold it high as a model of Republican principles and as a plan for progress and a blueprint for a better America.

Meanwhile the "reluctant" candidates waited in the wings. Richard Nixon had shown a surprising strength among the voters in early 1964 national samplings of public opinion. Henry Cabot Lodge had found support both in mock Republican conventions on college campuses and in the New Hampshire primaries on March 10, where he took about 35 per cent of the votes and first place even though he was not on the ballot. The strength of Governor William Scranton, too, was clearly on the rise as winter turned into spring and as political interest increased throughout the nation. High-level strategy meetings in early March, which involved Governor Scranton and former National Republican Chairman Leonard Hall, among others, gave strong evidence that Scranton, indeed, might lead the third force which could ultimately capture the nomination in July.

Chapter IV

Drafting the Platform

WHAT PLATFORMS ARE

National party platforms are illustrations, *par excellence,* of the basic characteristic of compromise which underlies the American two-party system. Every four years the two major parties attempt to find and to state a series of official positions which will unite as many as possible of the disparate interests which are uneasily allied to the party or have some members who appear to be active or potential supporters.

The writing of the national platforms becomes, in one sense, the first stage in the legitimization of certain positions advanced by various groups in society. These groups do not expect specific policy pledges from the political parties in the platform document; they do hope, however, that the party leaders will, through the platform, indicate that their special objectives are also in the public interest. Through such recognition political leaders serve notice upon the nation as a whole that certain policy proposals deserve serious consideration by elected officials.

Party platforms, then, are guidelines, not pledges of action. They are, moreover, guidelines which are set down by only a small segment of the membership of a political party, a segment which, incidentally, is not necessarily representative of the inarticulate attitudes of the millions of nominal Democrats or Republicans back in Everytown, U.S.A., or even representative of the delegates to the conventions.

Party platforms, of course, are only one aspect in the development of national party policy. More important, perhaps, are the policy pronouncements by the candidates for the presidency, vice presidency, and Congress during the campaign and the party action taken at the national levels of officialdom following the election.

If we cannot look to the national party platforms for definitive party positions on all major campaign issues, neither can we state that platforms are of no importance. Significant contrasts do appear in these documents which indicate important differences between the parties in direction, emphasis, and approach.

Most platforms have contained certain basic items: eulogies of the party's record, some general declarations denouncing the opposition and favoring democracy and Americanism, reference to some current crucial nonparty issues, and a limited number of definite pledges.

The preliminary drafting of the platform ordinarily is initiated long before the National Convention's Resolutions Committee meets. If the party's likely nominee is the incumbent president, the White House staff itself usually writes the platform and very few changes are expected at the hands of the Resolutions Committee. The Democratic platforms were drafted thus, basically, in 1936, 1940, 1944, and in 1956 and it will likely be created in the same way in 1964 if President Johnson is the Democratic candidate.

When a party is not so fortunate as to have a sitting President as its candidate, it usually expands its effort to obtain the thinking of various segments of the party and of the community at large regarding platform content.

This expansion can be accomplished in several ways. The Democrats in 1960 staged a series of regional public hearings so that all interested parties could make their views known. Or party leaders may request the public at large to communicate opinions regarding the platform by letter or telegram, as was done by the Republicans in 1960. Pre-convention Platform Committee hearings are also ordinarily held just prior to the formal convening of the National Convention. Sometimes these are *pro forma* meetings with only a few hours devoted to the process. On other occasions, the preconvention platform hearings have lasted as long as a week, as was the case with the Republicans in 1960.

Even when extensive preconvention public platform hearings are held, however, the platform itself ordinarily has been hammered out in rough outline long before the Resolutions Committee first convenes. The Democrats in 1960, for example, turned the task of drafting the platform over to four skilled writers in Washington weeks before the Los Angeles convention.

It should be noted that the platform written by the Resolutions Committee is not always accepted. Notable floor debates on the content of the platform marked the Democratic conventions of 1920, 1924, 1928, and 1948. At times, dissenters have proved that the positions espoused by the Resolutions Committee did not reflect the thinking of the majority of the convention. In 1948, for example, a liberal faction in the Democratic Party succeeded in gaining a majority of the delegate support to adopt a civil rights plank over the vigorous objections of the so-called Dixiecrat group.

WRITING THE REPUBLICAN PLATFORM, 1960

Unlike a number of his predecessors, Republican Chairman Thruston B. Morton took a very great interest in the preparations for the platform phase of the 1960 Republican National Convention. Early in 1960, in line with the desires of President Eisenhower and other White House leaders, Morton selected Charles A. Percy to be temporary chairman of the Resolutions Committee.

Percy, a young Chicago industrialist, was best known to Republicans as the chairman of a special long-range study committee on Republican program and progress which had met throughout 1959. His study group, which included Republican leaders from widely varied vocational backgrounds and ideological positions, ultimately published a report entitled *Decisions for a Better America*. Ostensibly, Percy had the friendship and support of a large number of the nation's top Republicans. Yet when his selection was made known there was marked dissatisfaction with Percy's appointment on the part of several high-ranking House and Senate members. To satisfy these Republicans on Capitol Hill, Chairman Morton appointed Congressman Melvin Laird of Wisconsin to assist Percy with the Resolutions (Platform) Committee work.

Each state selects its two-member delegation to the Platform Committee. Chairman Morton, however, in consultation with Percy and Laird, carefully picked the chairmen of eight platform subcommittees. More than past Party national chairmen, Senator Morton took a deep personal interest in the background and the quality of the men and women who were to determine the basic nature of the 1960 Republican campaign document.

THE PUBLIC SUGGESTIONS

As Chairman of the Resolutions Committee, Percy approached the problem of public involvement in a different way from his Democratic counterpart, Chester Bowles. Bowles had held a number of regional public hearings on platform content. Percy, in contrast, issued a release on January 19, 1960, inviting the American people to take part in the development of the Republican Platform through two devices. He stated, in part, "We urge and will welcome suggestions from individuals and national and regional groups. We want to consider a wide range of opinion from every segment of American life."

He asked individuals to write to him indicating their personal views and he promised that the eight subcommittees of the Resolutions Committee would give every opportunity for individual and group hearings in Chicago.

The number of letters, telegrams, and telephone calls which came to Chairman Percy was indeed impressive. They came from individuals from every walk of life and represented all shades of political opinion. Some were written in Chinese. Some were extremely lengthy and costly telegrams. Still others were written by cranks and came in most imaginative shapes and on an endless variety of writing materials.

Meanwhile, in order to assess the kind of platform which the members of the Resolutions Committee desired, Chairman Percy had mailed to each of them a mimeographed letter requesting information from them on this matter. It was an interesting letter for it suggested, among other things, that the Resolutions Committee members choose between: (a) a long, a brief, or something-in-between platform; (b) a platform with a central theme or one with a catalog of items; (c) a platform which promised many things to interest groups or one which would serve the general interest of the nation.

Forty-two of the eighty-four who responded to Mr. Percy's questionnaire wanted a brief platform whereas forty-two wanted something in between. Seventy-three wanted a central theme; four wanted a catalog. Seventy-eight wanted a platform basically addressing itself to the general interest of the nation, whereas two wanted a platform with promises to interest groups and two wanted to involve both. The theory that a multitude of special interests may constitute the general interest seems to have been overlooked by most of Percy's respondents.

THE DRAFTING PROCESS

The official program for the 1960 Republican Resolutions Committee began at 10 a.m. on July 19 with a coffee hour at the Sheraton-Blackstone Hotel in downtown Chicago. At 10:30 the temporary officers selected by Chairman Morton were officially installed as the permanent officers of the Resolutions Committee. (The Resolutions Committee is more popularly known as the Platform Committee.)

Addresses were given by Chairman Morton, Mr. Percy, Dr. Lee A. DuBridge, Dr. Lawrence Gould, and Secretary of the Treasury Anderson. After a brief lunch period, the full Committee heard from Governor Rockefeller, Admiral Radford, Representative John Byrnes of Wisconsin, Senator Barry Goldwater, and Clarence B. Randall.

After these opening speeches, the Committee reconvened at 5 p.m. to organize their subcommittee hearings for the following day. It is interesting to examine one or two of the subcommittee hearing schedules to see who, in fact, does appear before a typical National Party Platform at one of its preconvention hearings.

On Wednesday, July 20, the following individuals and groups appeared before the Foreign Policy Subcommittee: United Presbyterian Church, Friends Committee on National Legislation, American Association for the United Nations, Inc., League of Women Voters, National Committee on Captive Nations Week,

American Israel Public Affairs Committee, American Council for Judaism, Major General Julius Klein, American Legion, AMVETS, 1960 Campaign for Disarmament, Polish-American Congress, American Farm Bureau Federation, Republican State Committee in and for the District of Columbia, International Economic Policy Association, Inc., American-Latvian Association, the National Council for Jewish Women, Americans for Democratic Action, the American Friends of the Captive Nations, and Norman Raise, President of the Cedar Society.

On the same day, the following groups appeared before the Agricultural and Natural Resources Subcommittee: Keep America Beautiful, League of Women Voters, Investors League, Inc., Save the Dunes Council, National Rural Electric Cooperative Association, Water Pollution Control Advisory Board, National Association of Soil Conservation Districts, and the Utah Mining Association.

The hearings of these and the six other subcommittees went on from Wednesday morning through Friday afternoon. By Friday evening, July 22, the eight subcommittees had drafted what they felt were sound statements on which to base the National Republican campaign of 1960.

THE REVISION PROCESS

Back in Washington, however, Richard Nixon had just decided to take an action which would soon complicate the work of the Platform Committee.

For on this same Friday evening after the Platform Subcommittee Chairmen had retired, confident that the bulk of their tedious task was over, Richard Nixon met with Governor Nelson Rockefeller in New York to discuss changes in certain of the Subcommittee drafts.

When the Saturday-morning newspapers revealed the nature of the momentous midnight meeting in Governor Rockefeller's apartment, even the Vice President's Convention Advisory staff appeared stunned (Meade Alcorn, Len Hall, Ray Bliss, Mort Frayn, Lee Potter, Bob Finch, and others).

The true story of the events leading up to this amazing meeting of the Vice President and the Governor of New York and the personalities involved have remained a mystery to the newsmen and commentators who otherwise have written fairly accurate and complete accounts of the election of the President in 1960.

In any case, the Platform Committee was thrown into utter confusion by the events which had transpired the night before in New York City. The members of the Committee were angry and they were tired. They were resentful and some of them were on the verge of mutiny. From Senator Barry Goldwater's headquarters in Chicago came the following statement:

> Unprecedented last minute attempts to impose upon the Republican Platform Committee platform provisions from a point 1,000 miles away from the Convention has caused deep concern on the part of conscientious Republicans attending the Convention at Chicago.
>
> If a spokeman for the ultra-liberals is to be permitted to dictate the Republican Platform, it seems logical that this same spokesman should become an announced candidate for the presidency and thus be prepared to assume the responsibility for carrying out the ultra-liberal positions of his Platform.
>
> What are we doing to the men and women of good conscience who have labored on the Platform Committee in Chicago for more than a full week, if we now give in to this pressure and accept cut and dried Platform provisions. . . .
>
> I have great confidence in the integrity of the men and women on the Platform Committee. I am encouraged by statements made to me by members of the Platform Committee during the noon recess today. Several members of the Committee for whom I have the highest regard have assured me that the Platform Committee can well write the provisions of the Republican Platform and will refuse to accept this last minute pressure technique.

Had it not been for Chairman Morton's straight-from-the-shoulder talk to the Platform Committee on Saturday morning, it is likely that at least two men might have walked out of the Resolutions Committee and taken their entire state delegations back home with them. Following Chairman Morton's effective plea for party unity, and for a facing-up to the situation at hand, the Subcommittees (particularly those on Defense and Civil Rights and Immigration) went back into executive session in an attempt to rewrite the provisions of their plans in accordance with the wishes of the Vice President and Governor Rockefeller.

All during Saturday and Sunday the Platform Committee was in turmoil. Introduced into the grim atmosphere were comic situations created by a shortage of meeting space. The housing arrangements for the hearings had been made only through Saturday, at which time it was assumed that the Platform would have been written and the work of the Platform Committee would have been done. Consequently, many of the needed meeting rooms and other facilities had been scheduled for weddings and parties and dances. On one occasion, a wedding party was almost shocked into sobriety when harassed Subcommittee members marched into their former meeting room and demanded the quarters now occupied by gay and slightly inebriated celebrants.

What some reporters called the "total chaos of Saturday and Sunday" was, in a sense, made official when the Platform Committee formally voted by a two-to-one majority to stand by the Platform which had been drafted and approved on Friday evening. This was on Sunday, July 24.

While the Platform Committee members argued and threatened on the second floor, quite different activities were taking place on the seventh floor of the Sheraton-Blackstone. Here, in the luxurious set of suites which had been assigned for the final drafting of the Platform, representatives of the various ideological wings of the Party gathered to attempt to work out a solution to their dilemma.

Here, for example, were such leaders as Gabriel Hauge, former economic adviser to the President; Bob Merriam, representing the President; George Grassmuck, in attendance as a spokesman for the Vice President; Emmett Hughes, an emissary of Governor Rockefeller. The conflicts were real and at times appeared irreconcilable during that trying Sunday.

When it appeared that the Defense Subcommittee, partially through the urging of Eisenhower's man, Bob Merriam, would stand fast on defense, and the Civil Rights Subcommittee was unlikely to alter its statement on civil rights, the local Nixon team announced a decision of its own to go to the full Platform Committee on Monday regarding both civil rights and defense. If need be, the Vice President promised a floor fight at the side of Rockefeller before the entire convention on Tuesday.

When the Platform Committee reassembled for a Sunday-night session, irate and weary members threatened to revolt. Tempers flared. It was fortunate that the steady hand of Congressman Laird was on the gavel. Mr. Percy, undoubtedly a skilled leader with boards of trustees and business concerns, was not prepared nor politically experienced enough to handle the excited members of the Platform Committee.

The pressures which were brought to bear on certain members of the Platform Committee during the Sunday and Monday sessions came from the highest possible sources in American government and party life.

During those last few agonizing hours of the Platform Committee's work one could feel the tension in the air. Deeply held convictions—both liberal and conservative—were straining to be free of the bonds of party unity.

But as a result of the stubborn insistence on the part of the Vice President, the Platform Committee was left no choice. With bitterness in the hearts of many members, the Committee, after the Sunday marathon session, now voted by another two-to-one majority to reverse its previous decision and to accept the rewritten planks on civil rights and defense. Governor Rockefeller and Vice President Nixon had won their battle.

The Vice President, hurrying out to Chicago days earlier than planned, had followed Senator Morton's appeal for unity and patience by a personal visit with small groups of recalcitrant members of the Platform Committee and by presenting, with deep conviction, his personal justification for the altered Platform planks. He insisted that the rewriting of certain segments of the Platform was not only a moral requirement from his standpoint, but a political necessity if he were to win the 1960 campaign. Thus one cannot overemphasize the Vice President's own role in the writing of the strong civil-rights and defense planks which ultimately became part of the 1960 Platform.

But there were other key personalities who operated effectively behind the scenes to help resolve the Platform Committee fight and to restore unity out of irate diversity and order out of chaos. Among them, Ohio State Chairman Ray Bliss must be ranked extremely high; so too must Dr. Gabriel Hauge. The constructive roles played by these men, known but to few people, were indeed crucial.

It is interesting to note as one reviews the writing of the Republican Platform in 1960 the extent to which academic leaders were used in the drafting process. Of the 28 men and women who worked closely with the Republican Platform Committee, over half were academicians by training or profession. Such names as Dave Abshire, Bob Forsythe, Bob Goldwin, Steve Hess, Carl Hess, Karl Lamb, Bill MacComber, Floyd McCaffree, Bill Prendergast, and Guy Waterman suggest the extent of utilization of academic people who, though perhaps holding other positions during the summer of 1960, were actually trained for and had instructional experience in American academic institutions.

DRAFTING THE REPUBLICAN PLATFORM, 1964

Although the fight for the presidential nomination will undoubtedly overshadow the drafting of the Platform at the Republican Convention of 1964, it is likely that the ideological disagreements which differentiate the major Republican presidential hopefuls will again make the deliberations of the Resolutions Committee exciting and important.

Should Governor Rockefeller win the nomination it is unlikely that he would accept a platform which does not reflect his views on such controversial planks as civil rights and medical care for the aged. If the nominee is Senator Goldwater, it can be expected that he, too, would insist on a platform which conforms with his ideological positions on a variety of issues.

Statements by representatives from both the liberal and conservative wings of the Republican Party during the preconvention period indicate that there will be concerted efforts to write into the platform specific planks which coincide with the pronouncements of the leading contenders for the presidential nomination.

Thus the task of the 1964 Resolutions Committee and of its chairman will again be an arduous one. Because of his experience and his ability to handle such difficult assignments, Congressman Melvin R. Laird of Wisconsin has been selected as Chairman of the 1964 Resolutions Committee.

It has been suggested that Laird will approach the job of drafting a platform in a different manner from the 1960 Chairman, Charles Percy. It is unlikely, for example, that the Committee under Laird's leadership will be divided into Subcommittees. The more usual pattern of a preconvention draft and full Committee hearings at the Convention will probably be resumed.

Whatever his approach, Laird will face the quadrennial problem of producing a document that accomplishes the basic purposes of a national platform, the development and reinforcement of broad public support for his party, while still presenting the American people with a set of guidelines which differ significantly from those of the opposition party.

Actually, as political leaders and scholars alike have pointed out, platforms in recent years have met both these criteria. Taking the 1948 platforms as examples, Republicans and Democrats differed on the Taft-Hartley Act, foreign aid, tax reduction, and the general question of national versus state powers. In 1952, 1956, and 1960 the parties again wrote national platforms which presented the American people with significant policy or guideline choices on such matters as civil rights, national defense, education, foreign aid and, again, the general question of states versus the national government.

Whatever one may say, however, concerning the ideological framework of and difference between national party platforms, the overriding fact is that political power and not policymaking is the major stake at a national convention. The nature of both party platforms will clearly reflect that reality in 1964 as in years gone by.

WRITING THE DEMOCRATIC PLATFORM, 1960

The Democratic national platform of 1960, entitled "The Rights of Man," was designed to portray the Democratic Party as a union of liberals. Paul M. Butler, then Chairman of the Democratic National Committee, believed firmly in the theory that political parties are united by political philosophy. Accordingly, he deliberately set about to convey that image to the nation through his Party's platform. Charges by former President Harry S. Truman that the 1960 Convention was "rigged" were widely circulated but generally misunderstood. As Paul Butler testified to the Convention, there was no rigging in favor of any candidate, nor could there have been. The rigging, if such it can be called, was purely ideological. It was an attempt to make sure that the platform would state the issues of the day as liberals saw them and would propose solutions to the issues which liberals would approve.

Liberals were given charge of the Committee on Resolutions and Platform by the appointment of Representative Chester Bowles of Connecticut and Philip Perlman of Maryland as co-chairmen. Drafts of possible planks for the platform were prepared before the Convention opened by subject-matter specialists who were drawn almost entirely from the liberal wing of the Party. A draft of the platform itself was prepared at national Party headquarters by a hand-picked team of liberals who paid slight heed to previous national platforms and made no use at all of state and county platforms adopted in 1960. The drafting team depended for content material primarily upon pamphlets which had been prepared by the Democratic Advisory Council, a liberal-wing group; upon the draft planks submitted by the liberal subject-matter specialists; upon the summaries of ten pre-convention platform hearings which were held in the late spring of 1960; and upon their own knowledge of the goals of liberal members of Congress.

THE ADVISORY COUNCIL

The Democratic Advisory Council was a major source of ideas for the platform. When it was formed in 1956, Speaker of the House of Representatives Sam Rayburn and Senate Majority Leader Lyndon B. Johnson had declined membership. Significantly, however, the 1956 presidential and vice-presidential candidates, Governor Adlai E. Stevenson and Senator Estes Kefauver, had accepted membership. They later were joined by Senators John F. Kennedy and Hubert Humphrey. Beginning in 1957, the Council had published 13 pamphlets on foreign affairs, on domestic problems, and on defense.

Ideas and materials for the Advisory Council pamphlets came from many sources. For example, in preparing a pamphlet on natural resources for 1960 publication, the Advisory Council's subcommittee on natural resources made an especially elaborate effort to gather widespread contributions. In the fall of 1959 a series of "position papers," each covering in detail one major phase of resource conservation and development, such as energy, water, lands, forests, and recreation, was prepared by experts in those fields. The position papers were used as source material in the preparation of a platform on resources adopted by the Western States Democratic Conference in Albuquerque, New Mexico, February 6, 1960. The Conference platform and the position papers were then used as the starting point for a new pamphlet by the Advisory Council which sought to make a coherent, parallel statement of needs, problems, and objectives within a single framework. This effort formed the foundation from which the "long-form" platform plank on natural resources was drawn. The final product was published in mid-October, 1960, as a campaign pamphlet, "Resources for the People" and appeared to be an elaboration of the platform plank on conservation. In fact, the platform plank was a summary of the pamphlet.

THE PRECONVENTION PLATFORM HEARINGS

A second major source of platform material was the preconvention platform hearings, which began April 28, 1960, at Philadelphia. Nine more were sponsored by the Democratic National Committee in rapid succession: May 6 at Minneapolis, May 12 at Detroit, May 27 at Denver, May 31 at St. Louis, June 3 at Salt Lake City, June 17 in Los Angeles, June 21 in New York City, June 24 in Seattle, and June 27 in Miami.

At each, attention was focused on one major field of interest, but local people were welcomed to speak on any subject they wished during one of the three hearing sessions. Thus foreign policy was highlighted at Philadelphia, farm problems at Minneapolis, natural resources at Denver, education at Salt Lake City, and urban and suburban problems at St. Louis. Hearings ran morning, afternoon, and evening and were deluged with requests to testify. Many persons had to be content with submitting written statements for the record.

Each preconvention hearing was conducted by a panel of four

or five distinguished Democrats which usually included a governor and a United States senator. But, because there was no way to be sure that panelists would also be members of the Resolutions and Platform Committee at the National Convention, a special staff man was employed to summarize the findings of each hearing and prepare the materials for presentation to the Platform Committee.

THE SPECIALISTS ON LANGUAGE AND SUBJECT MATTER

The large volume and variety of ideas, suggestions, statements, and proposals which emerged from these two processes posed a dilemma for the Party's leaders: How could they satisfy most of the legitimate desires expressed and yet keep the platform of reasonable length as a campaign document? Indeed, the need to present the platform to the Convention and, through television, to the nation, made length an urgent consideration. Experience in 1952 and 1956 showed that the reading of a long platform bored the Convention and rapidly reduced the viewing audience. Chairman Butler, with the concurrence of Congressman Bowles and Mr. Perlman, decided to illustrate the platform with three short movies covering foreign affairs, domestic affairs, and civil rights. With the making of this concession to audience attention, Mr. Bowles appears to have been the man who decided that the platform to be read to the Convention should not exceed 3,000 words.

A 3,000-word platform, however, could not begin to express the objectives which the varied component groups within the Democratic Party would surely expect, particularly on domestic matters. It soon became clear that a second, and much longer, version would somehow have to be provided. Accordingly, efforts were undertaken to draft two platforms—a "short form" and a "long form"—with the long form presumably to be presented to the Convention in written form and debated and adopted without being read verbatim from the rostrum.

Drafting of the two versions was undertaken in mid-June. Staff specialists with Congress, with the National Committee, and with the interest groups which identify themselves principally with the Democratic Party undertook to prepare preliminary drafts of both a short-form and a long-form platform. Many of these people had helped with Advisory Council pamphlets, written background position papers on these subjects, or had prepared statements for the preplatform hearings. Most of them were conversant with the pressing controversies in their areas of specialization and could be depended upon to put into the proposed platform language calculated to cover the field yet avoid unnecessary antagonisms.

To prepare a final, integrated, smooth-flowing product, a special four-man drafting crew was brought into National Committee headquarters. One was Mr. Bowles' administrative assistant; two were administrative assistants to prominent liberal Senators; one was a member of the Harvard University faculty of law. All had long experience in political affairs.

Chairman Bowles himself proceeded to prepare an integrated draft of the 3000-word short-form platform. Reflecting his concerns and his New England residence, it concentrated almost entirely upon foreign policy, civil rights, and pressing social and economic problems of urban areas. Final preparation of the long form was left to the drafting team.

Two of the administrative assistants on the drafting team quickly perceived the gross imbalance which would result if other areas of domestic policy were not covered, such as agricultural policy, education, labor, natural resources, public power, and veterans affairs. Without time to consult adequately with the subject-matter specialists who had prepared the draft versions, they re-wrote most of what had been given them to provide a single coherent style. Occasionally consultation was taken with the specialists, but more often they grumbled that they were not permitted to be of assistance.

THE FINAL VERSION

The result was a serious imbalance in the platform which is apparent in its final version, despite rather extensive revisions following the hearings by the full Resolutions Committee at Los Angeles. Domestic policy, always the area requiring the most delicate phrasing and most specific statements, was treated hastily and in some aspects inadequately. For example, natural resources and labor policy, two of the most complicated and explosive areas of controversy, were handled so inadequately in the short form and were covered so weakly in the long form that it became necessary to have specialists make rather extensive revisions of the drafts at the last minute in Los Angeles.

The Committee on Resolutions and Platform assembled in the Grand Ballroom of the Biltmore Hotel in Los Angeles on Tuesday, July 5. There, in plenary session, until Friday afternoon, it heard testimony from individuals and groups wishing to have their views included in the platform. No subcommittees on special subject-matter areas were set up and no separate subject-matter hearings were held.

At the end of the week, a 19-man drafting subcommittee was appointed from among the Committee members to work over the week-end. Once behind closed doors, the drafting committee was handed both the short-form and the long-form drafts. Chairman Bowles indicated that the long-form material would be in the nature of an appendix to the short form which was really to be the platform. A quick review of content, however, promptly disclosed the urgent need to have both as parts of the platform. Discussion resulted in which Chairman Bowles agreed to treat both forms equally as parts of the platform.

Debate in the drafting subcommittee centered on the strong civil-rights plank. Occasionally other gaps were uncovered, for instance the need for a plank on women's rights. By and large, however, the work of the four-man liberal drafting crew stood unchallenged. The Resolutions Committee's hearings in Los Angeles had contributed nothing of significance to the preparation of the platform.

Through long hours of the week-end, the drafting crew then undertook to combine the two forms so that the short form would appear in the final version as boldface introductions to the more detailed long-form provisions, which were to be printed in regular type.

Security was tight. Only five or six professional staff people from the drafting crew, the preplatform-hearings staff, and the Advisory Council staff appear to have joined the drafting subcommittee. Nationally known lobbyists hovered about the committee rooms but could get only assurances like, "You'll have nothing to worry about." Even an attempt by a nationally prominent Democrat to smuggle a copy of the platform to the *New York Times* was thwarted by an alert staff member.

Tuesday night, July 12, the Resolutions Committee brought out an "integrated" document. Lack of time had precluded extensive revision of the short-form draft, but the commitments to present the three short movies had compelled its use. Printed copies of the entire document were passed out to the delegates. Mr. Bowles then simply read the boldface portions of the Committee's report to the Convention, stopping three times for the short film interludes. The entire platform was adopted by approval of the motion to accept the Committee's report.

Only on the vigorous civil-rights plank was there formal, organized dissent. Delegates from nine Southern states presented a minority report which pleaded their cause in impassioned language. Yet it was in no sense an alternative platform proposal and was predictably shouted down.

Thus the complete 1960 Democratic platform was a fairly typical major-party platform. It indicated the direction in which the Democratic Party hoped to go without making specific promises to reach the destination. It reflected the objectives of the groups having significant power within the Party. And, by "glittering generalities," it also reflected the issues upon which the Party was so divided that no firm position could be taken. Yet, over-all, it was a platform with a strong liberal tone.

On the other hand, the version of the platform which was presented to the nation over television was not a typical major-party platform. The short-form passages and the movies were designed to portray a "responsible" party united by liberal principles; particularly concerned about foreign affairs, civil rights, and urban problems; proud of its past; and prepared to act cohesively in the future.

WRITING THE DEMOCRATIC PLATFORM, 1964

The 1964 Democratic national platform will most surely be a typical major-party platform in its content. The coalition of groups and sectional interests which have been dominant in the Democratic Party since the presidency of Franklin D. Roosevelt are dominant still. Organized labor; large urban party organizations; minority groups, especially the Negroes and the Jews; conservationists; liberal advocates of more federal action in social welfare and education; many of the old rural populist elements; and the new industrial interests of the South—all still can gain more from standing together than from defecting to the Republicans. All those who look to change through governmental initiative will turn to the platform for an indication of the Democratic view of the importance of their cause.

In its drafting, the 1964 platform can be expected to follow the pattern of New Deal and Fair Deal days. President Lyndon B. Johnson and his key staff men in all likelihood will determine its basic content. Yet his slain predecessor has already set the claims of administrative accomplishment which can be raised and has shaped the issues which must be discussed. Moreover, President Johnson would not have it otherwise. Since gaining the confidence of his Party's liberals is his foremost political task, he will hail the Kennedy achievements proudly and will steadfastly pledge—as he did to Congress on Thanksgiving eve in 1963— to continue the job.

Yet the Democratic Party must have a Johnson platform. The new President moved at once to insure that feature through the only sure avenue open to him: an unprecedented record of legislative achievement which would place a distinctive Johnsonian mold on the platform's phrases.

In preparing a preconvention draft of the 1964 platform for use by the Platform Committee, the drafters must perforce get information chiefly from the executive agencies of the federal government and, importantly, from the committees and the leaders of the Congress. No Advisory Council exists as a separate source of citizen-member feelings for the Party.

The pattern of preconvention hearings, used so effectively in 1960, was a Butlerism which President Johnson and Chairman Bailey may not choose to follow. Its value in arousing interest and in getting popular expressions of opinion cannot be denied, however, and its utility may yet commend it to the Party leadership.

The Committee on Resolutions of the 1964 Convention may be

expected to follow the traditional pattern of plenary hearings the week before the Convention and in the work of its drafting subcommittee to respond sympathetically to the suggestions provided by the President.

Yet whatever the procedure of draftsmanship and whatever the need to serve adroitly the many varied interests which comprise the majority coalition called the Democratic Party, the broad outlines of the 1964 program are sure to be liberal in domestic matters and committed to international leadership in foreign affairs.

Chapter V

Organizing the Campaigns

There can be only one boss in a political campaign. Democratic and Republican leaders alike have learned this rule the hard way.

When an incumbent President seeks reelection, the White House runs the campaign. The President puts the task into the hands of a trusted lieutenant who has all the powers of the office to back him up. The National Committee of the President's party is either turned over to the campaign manager, who becomes its chairman, or it obeys his orders. Thus did the Republicans win reelection in 1956 and the Democrats in 1936, 1940, 1944, and 1948.

A challenger faces tougher going. He must be prepared to take over his own National Committee lock, stock, and barrel or else face never-ending problems of coordination, duplication, and rivalry, to say nothing of unnecessary expense.

The organizational problem for a challenger is caused by a simple fact of political life: National Committees are neither geared nor staffed to handle a presidential campaign. They are set up to provide year-round services to state and county central committees. They grind out political propaganda; they stimulate auxiliary groups for youth, women, and special minorities; they do political research; they provide tips to improve local political organization; they assist in fund raising; and they do other related tasks.

During presidential campaigns, other talents are needed. Speeches must be written, campaign appearances must be advanced, separate "citizens" organizations must be established for the candidate, and money must be raised in large quantities. Moreover, the candidate needs the undivided loyalty of his staff; and the National Committee staffs, like federal civil servants, have remained neutral in the struggle for the nomination.

PATTERNS OF CAMPAIGN STRUCTURE

A nominee for President dares not depend upon the old National Committee staff to handle his campaign. He must either leave the old staff intact to serve him as best it can while he depends upon his own separate and personal organization (the "divided" system); or else he must construct a new "unified" National Committee staff from his own team and fit the old people in wherever they can be used. Ordinarily it is impractical to fire the old staff outright when all good men must be called to the aid of their party.

The "divided" system enables the candidate to throw his campaign into high gear quickly and economically. He can depend upon his own preconvention organization and he knows how to use it. Division of responsibility leaves him free to call upon the National Committee as opportunity arises without having to disrupt his own team. If the National Committee is headed by a chairman over whom he has little control or influence, especially if the chairman is a member of Congress (as recent Republican chairmen have been), the candidate is very likely indeed to find the divided system better than a unified operation which he might have difficulty commanding.

The divided system is fraught with perils, however. Inevitably the National Committee and its staff become aware of their secondary role in the campaign. As plans are made and actions are taken by the candidate's team without their advice, they conclude that they are being "ignored" or that the candidate is "refusing to work with the regular organization." In what they regard as self-defense, they may shift their efforts to their regular clientele or even divert their help to congressional contests. If they try to aid the presidential campaign anyway, they may dissipate much of their energy enlarging their own regular activities, duplicate work of the candidate's team, or inadvertently upset some hard-won gain. Worst of all, they are likely to fritter away badly needed campaign funds on projects which never receive a priority rating from the candidate.

The "unified" system has superior virtues and fewer problems. The party speaks only with the candidate's voice. National effort is concentrated upon winning the presidency. The strengths of the regular organization are added to those of the campaign team and thus the campaign efforts are legitimized in the eyes of the regular organizations at state and county levels. Finance can be centralized and spending limited to high priority tasks in the campaign.

If the candidate and his manager act decisively to establish and maintain their leadership, the problems of the unified system can be confined to individual reactions of the old-time staff of the National Committee. Each old staff member holds his job because he enjoys the special support of some key party figure. If a key old staff man is unceremoniously relegated to a subordinate role in the new regime, influential sources may quickly raise great pressure to reconsider the decision. Internal jockeying for position, bickering, and even foot dragging can emerge unless the new leadership makes assignments to the old hands with firmness and equity and makes sure that each does what is expected.

Few challengers have had the organization or the will to set up a unified campaign. Franklin D. Roosevelt was equal to the occasion in 1932. With James A. Farley as his manager, Roosevelt cleaned out the old Democratic National Committee personnel and installed his own high command. Farley ran a unified, centralized campaign which swept the Democrats into power for a twenty-year stay.

The ratification of the Twenty-Second Amendment, however, appears to have narrowed the choices in campaign organization for a candidate who seeks to succeed a two-term President of his own party. Somehow, he must take over the party organization and run it without offending the President, who unavoidably retains the power to control the party and who may also retain the desire as well. Both candidates who have attempted succession—Stevenson and Nixon—have lost. Neither was able to solve the basic problems of integrating his own organization with that of the incumbent President.

THE "UNIFIED" DEMOCRATIC ORGANIZATION OF 1960

In 1960, Senator John F. Kennedy had the easier organizational task. He had no incumbent President as a rival to his leadership and the outgoing chairman of the Democratic National Committee no longer commanded a substantial following of his own.

On Saturday, July 16, 1960, after the convention had nominated Kennedy, Paul M. Butler, Chairman of the Democratic National Committee since December, 1954, left the National Committee meeting in the Biltmore Hotel in Los Angeles a repudiated man. Never again was he to be consulted about the affairs of the Democratic Party.

In six years of devoted and energetic leadership, Paul Butler had managed to alienate nearly every segment of the Democratic Party. Taking seriously the recommendations of the Committee on Political Parties of the American Political Science Association in its 1950 report, "Toward a More Responsible Two-Party System," he conscientiously had tried to centralize his party and to unite it ideologically. In the process he outraged Southern leaders by inviting them to leave the party. He offered rivalry to Congressional leadership by making policy pronouncements himself, even though throughout his tenure his party controlled the Congress, and by appointing an Advisory Council which was spurned by Senate Majority Leader Lyndon Johnson and by House Speaker Sam Rayburn. He accused big-city organization leaders of joining with "segregationists" to oust him. He offended Congressional leaders by prodding them to act more swiftly on Democratic programs. He alienated state organizations by trying to finance the National Committee independently and by sending "regional representatives" into their midst to shape their actions. Finally, he estranged his last stronghold, the liberals, by opining in an unguarded moment in the spring of 1960 that Senator Kennedy would win the nomination over Senator Humphrey.

With such a tailor-made opportunity to take over the National Committee, John F. Kennedy should have had clear sailing to use the 1932 unified system of Franklin Roosevelt. But, for reasons of high policy, he made a preliminary decision that contained the seeds of organizational trouble.

John Kennedy's preconvention campaign manager was his brother Robert. They agreed that to name him national chairman would be a political blunder of the first magnitude. To "balance" the leadership, a Protestant Westerner seemed ideal. Senator Henry M. Jackson of Washington, who had supported Kennedy's drive for the nomination and campaigned openly to be his running mate, was a logical choice. Thus the East, the South, and the West were served.

While still in Los Angeles, the Kennedy team reviewed with Jackson the experience of previous Democratic candidates. Organization of the two most recent campaigns had been unsatisfactory. In 1952, although Stephen Mitchell was made national chairman, Governor Stevenson ran his campaign from Springfield. Liaison with the National Committee in Washington and with the White House was inadequate. In 1956, in an attempt to correct this weakness, Mr. Stevenson ran his campaign from Washington, D.C., under the leadership of James A. Finnegan, but Mr. Butler remained as national chairman. Physical proximity helped coordination, but divided responsibility continued the weaknesses of 1952.

Without hesitation, the Kennedys turned to the 1932 unified campaign system of James A. Farley as the key to success. The National Committee would be reorganized to serve the campaign. There would be one central staff, divided on functional lines.

But Jackson was chairman and Robert Kennedy was campaign manager. If the campaign really were to be unified and organizational discord avoided, one or the other had to be boss.

The organization did operate as a unified system and the boss was Robert Kennedy. Henry Jackson went on the road to give campaign speeches and left his lieutenants in Washington to handle the routine National Committee functions of acquiring space, purchasing supplies and materials, employing temporary personnel, and organizing such auxiliary services as telephones, mail, duplicating, and materials distribution. Robert Kennedy took over the National Committee's headquarters and adapted the existing staff to his campaign needs.

Such an arrangement was necessary, wise, and probably inevitable. The Kennedys brought a going campaign organization with them. Jackson had no team beyond his own office staff. Unfortunately, clear-cut organizational procedures to formalize the arrangement were never specifically adopted and promulgated.

For a time, two views were held of the structure of the campaign organization. The Jackson forces thought of the National Committee as operating in five parts: the regular Committee staff under Jackson was to continue essential services to the state and local committees and to congressional candidates while bending every effort to aid the presidential campaign. Robert Kennedy, using the preconvention Kennedy team, was to direct the presidential campaign proper. Senator Lyndon Johnson and his lieutenants, using their preconvention organization, were to run the vice-presidential campaign in coordination with the others. Matthew H. McCloskey, the Committee treasurer, was to raise and disburse the money. Mrs. Margaret Price, newly elected vice chairman of the Committee, was to direct women's affairs.

The Kennedy team, on the other hand, appears to have viewed the organization functionally, as a family affair. Fundamentally, it also had five parts:

First, Senator John F. Kennedy made the speeches and did the barnstorming. Four important campaign units reported directly to him without accounting to other officers of the National Committee or to the family team: (a) the Kennedy research team represented by Theodore Sorensen on the campaign plane and managed by Myer Feldman at committee headquarters; (b) the Kennedy speech-writing team under Archibald Cox; (c) the Kennedy press team headed by Pierre Salinger; and (d) the media department under Leonard Reinsch, which was responsible primarily for negotiating with Nixon headquarters concerning the television debates.

Second, Robert F. Kennedy served as campaign manager for the presidential campaign and had general supervision over all other phases of the work of the National Committee and its auxiliaries. Control was accomplished through "campaign coordinators" from the preconvention Kennedy staff, who were made responsible for the over-all direction of major parts of the National Committee. Three units appear to have been assigned as the immediate responsibility of the campaign manager: (a) the Organization Division, headed by Lawrence O'Brien, which stimulated efforts by regular state and local Democratic organizations and maintained a general check on the work of all divisions of the National Committee except those reporting directly to Senator Kennedy; (b) the Scheduling Office, which also reported directly to Senator Kennedy through Kenneth O'Donnell on the candidate's plane; and (c) the Publicity Division, which was entrusted to Roger Tubby as campaign coordinator.

Third, R. Sargent Shriver, Senator Kennedy's brother-in-law, formed various special-interest groups for Kennedy-Johnson. Shriver's job essentially was to create such units for the campaign. The specialized committees of the Democratic Advisory Council offered a nucleus from which to begin, so Mr. Shriver originally located himself in the chambers of the Council and drew heavily upon its staff for names and advice. Once the several divisions were under way, separate quarters were provided for them.

Fourth, Stephen Smith, also a brother-in-law of Senator Kennedy, was asked to raise money. He did so principally as treasurer for the Citizens for Kennedy-Johnson. Because of the $3 million spending limit imposed on national committees by the Hatch Act, his role became vital about the middle of October when the Democratic National Committee reached its spending limit and all income and expenditures had to be processed by Citizens for Kennedy-Johnson.

Fifth, Byron White, an old friend, headed the separate Citizens for Kennedy-Johnson to corral persons who wished to work exclusively for the national ticket. The Citizens organization coordinated its efforts closely with the Democratic National Committee and especially cooperated with Sargent Shriver's special-interest units. Some such units were housed with "Citizens" and often put out material for "Citizens."

The candidate's sisters appeared at women's meetings and, after Mrs. Kennedy (expecting a second child) could no longer accompany the Senator on tour, went with their brother as hostesses.

Neither the Kennedy nor the Jackson system was ever formalized. Indeed, informality in organization was deliberately retained and was defended on the theory that to structure the campaign organization would be to introduce "red tape" which would restrict flexibility, hamstring prompt decision making, and prevent quick action. In practice, after much trial and effort, both theories of organization were meshed together after a fashion.

Each division of the National Committee, whether long established or created for the campaign, was virtually turned loose to do all it could to win the election. Coordination among units was called for only when a joint enterprise was required. Big expenses were to be cleared with the Organization Division—Lawrence O'Brien, or his lieutenants Ralph Dungan or Dick Donohue—and each unit was supposed to have a budget within which it was expected to live. Policy statements were to be cleared with the Senator Kennedy's personal research staff headed by Myer Feldman. Coordination with the Johnson team was handled by William Welsh, a former research director of the National Committee.

Such an arrangement suited the well-established and close-knit Kennedy family campaign organization. For the newly created special-interest adjuncts, such as Farmers for Kennedy-Johnson, Viva Kennedy, or Business and Professional Men and Women for Kennedy and Johnson, such provisions were not inadequate. They had no on-going function to perform and could concentrate on a few well-selected mailings.

For the old National Committee staff, accustomed to minute control by the chairman over every step of the work, the new arrangement was bewildering. Where were they to report? What sorts of guidance could they expect? By trial and error they discovered that they were free to follow whichever program they deemed best. For approval of funds and policy statements they cleared with O'Brien and Feldman respectively. For personnel, equipment, supplies, and services they notified John Salter or Dan Martin in Jackson's office. They ended up reporting both to Robert Kennedy and to Henry Jackson. But many old staff people felt they were by-passing the chairman and that this by-passing was unwise.

Major shifts in staff assignments and location were made early in August. Left intact were the treasurer's functions, both fund raising and accounting. Similarly treated were the Women's Division, the Young Democrats, the Speakers' Bureau, the Voters' Service Bureau, and the "headquarters" services such as duplicating, telephones, and mail room. All were useful and created no conflict with the main thrust of the campaign.

On the other hand, the old Department of Political Organization and the Advisory Council were abolished and their personnel temporarily put to other and much less important campaign work.

As the campaign unfolded and the National Committee payroll swelled from 100 to nearly 500 paid employees, who were aided by untold numbers of volunteers, it became plain that the ordinary tools of administrative management were to be used primarily as emergency devices. Staff meetings were held when needed by those division chiefs who faced a problem. Some division chiefs, especially those concerned with policy statements and publicity for them, got together regularly for breakfast meetings on their own initiative.

Although a central clearing station for volunteer help was in operation, each unit was left to hire and fire paid personnel independently. As a result, one incompetent girl was hired and fired by six different divisions of the Committee.

As might be expected, performances of the divisions varied widely. The Community Relations Division, which concentrated on the religious issue, achieved remarkable success by distributing widely Senator Kennedy's well-received address to Protestant ministers at Houston. The Nationalities Division made deep inroads into the Polish vote by effective use of Prince Stanislaw Radziwill, a brother-in-law of Mrs. Kennedy. By contrast, the Veterans' Division program, run for all practical purposes by one weak secretary, was a near debacle. Having accumulated a list of veterans, which turned out to be well laced with Republicans, "Veterans for Kennedy-Johnson" mailed each veteran an invitation to volunteer as a worker in the Kennedy cause. Each respondent was sent a pamphlet and referred to his *state* Citizens for Kennedy-Johnson chairman, who usually was located in a distant city. The state chairman, however, was never notified of the existence of the volunteer! Worse, the burden of this "activity" proved so great that no other mail was handled. In January, 1961, a large box full of unanswered letters to Senator Kennedy from veterans around the nation turned up in the Division's files!

The imposition of budget controls was attempted on behalf of Chairman Jackson by William Perkins, but with only limited effect. Individual division heads were able to secure approval for spending projects variously from Treasurer McCloskey, Stephen Smith, Robert Kennedy, or his lieutenants; and some units, such as Labor's Committee for Kennedy and Johnson, Business and Professional Men and Women for Kennedy-Johnson, and Citizens for Kennedy-Johnson, had their own treasuries. One resulting minor crisis created some amusement. An end-of-campaign car caravan by the Young Democrats was scheduled, canceled the night before its departure, then re-authorized the following morning, all by different people able to make fiscal decisions.

Thus did the Kennedys take over the Democratic National Committee and confine the problems of the adjustment to the two most vulnerable of the old units. Fortunately, long hours, devotion, and real talent marked the efforts of most campaign operations. The success gained many have come, in part, through unified campaign organization, concentration on essentials, tight organization of key units, and flexible administration of auxiliary activities.

THE DEMOCRATIC ORGANIZATION IN 1964

The organization of President Johnson's campaign in 1964 presents a unique political problem. His unexpected accession to the presidency less than a year before the next presidential election and only nine months before the nominating convention precluded his moving to take over the executive branch and the National Committee with his own people, as most new Presidents would. Needing the Kennedy men in 1964 to help carry the North and East as they needed Johnson and his men in 1960 to help carry the South, President Johnson promptly asked the entire Kennedy team to stay, in the Cabinet, on the White House staff, and at the National Committee.

His request accomplished two other vital political objectives:

it signified the sincerity of his embrace of the Kennedy domestic program and it put on his team the only organization presently equipped to lead a revolt against him within the Democratic Party.

As the incumbent President, Johnson unquestionably will run the campaign from the White House. The National Committee will be expected to do his bidding and to serve him as he needs. Yet all the makings of a dual campaign organization are on the scene.

Between January, 1961, and November, 1963, the Democratic National Committee was converted into a thoroughgoing Kennedy organization. Its Chairman is John Bailey of Connecticut, who gathered in the New England delegates for Kennedy before the 1960 Convention. Treasurer Richard Maguire headed the Washington Scheduling Office for the Kennedy campaign. Other Kennedy men hold virtually all the important Committee posts.

At the White House, however, President Johnson has been assembling his own team to work alongside the Kennedy men whom he has asked to continue. Together the new, mixed, White House crew is thoroughly capable of mounting a sizzling Johnson campaign.

However, the Hatch Act, political realities, and organizational logic virtually require that still another center of organization be set up, even though it will surely be controlled from the White House: a Citizens Committee for Johnson and his running mate which will be commissioned to round up independent voters and will be legally entitled to spend $3 million on the presidential campaign.

The principal organizational problem will be for the White House team to define the roles of the Democratic National Committee and the Citizens Committee so that their various skills can be used best and with minimum clash and duplication. This will be no easy task, for the Citizens organization will probably be led and manned by Johnson men. Organizational rivalry with the Democratic National Committee can be avoided only by strong leadership from the White House itself.

Policy positions obviously will be shaped at the White House. All speech writing, press relations, and negotiations with the opposing candidate will necessarily be handled there. The presentation of the candidate must be in his own hands. With the staffing to accomplish this mission already at hand, no other arrangement will even receive consideration.

Scheduling also is a White House task. The Secret Service cannot legally have it otherwise. Political advance men might usefully be supplied by the National Committee if someone like Kenneth O'Donnell on the White House staff has firm control over the operation.

The raising and disbursement of campaign funds can profitably be divided between the National and Citizens committees. Because the entire spending limit of both committees will be needed and because both will be tapping different sources of funds, clearcut assignments should be possible.

Three big areas of activity, however, contain the seeds of trouble: organization, auxiliary groups, and propaganda. Organization through the regular state central committees is the natural province of the National Committee. But the opportunity to attract independents and Republicans will certainly generate a demand for parallel Citizens organizations in each state. Inevitably, state and local rivals within the Democratic Party will turn up in the separate organizations, depending on their status within the regular Party structure. Jockeying for position, attention, and rewards will usually follow.

Attracting the auxiliary groups could effectively be assigned the Citizens organizations since they, too, are an effort to attract support on a nonparty basis. Women, young people, and other groups usually organized by the Party could better be left to National Committee efforts. Such a logical arrangement may prove difficult to inaugurate, however, because some National Committee people have status with Negro and other special groups and will expect to participate in the effort to win their votes. Transfers of such National Committee personnel to the Citizens Committee would be the simplest way to keep assignments clear-cut.

The preparation and dissemination of propaganda will have to be divided between the National Committee and the Citizens Committee, probably determined by the primary targets to which their efforts will be beamed. Logic would have the National Committee appeal to Party identifiers, the Citizens Committee to independents and special groups. Control and coordination will have to be lodged in the White House, probably with men like Myer Feldman and Ralph Dungan, who handled that assignment in 1960.

The natural campaign structure for an incumbent President is the unified one. Despite the politically awkward timing of the succession, there seem to be few organizational problems which careful definition of assignments and firm presidential leadership cannot cure. President Johnson can be expected to run a unified campaign.

THE DUAL NATURE OF THE REPUBLICAN ORGANIZATION OF 1960

The problems faced by the Republican Party in 1960 were quite different from those faced by the Democrats. For by January of the election year it was assumed by most Republican state and national leaders that Vice President Richard M. Nixon would surely be the presidential nominee. Although some of Nixon's lieutenants were strangely uncertain of the Republican nomination so freely predicted for their candidate, a number of them were optimistic enough to move into Washington to "set up shop" with the coming of the new year. Nixon's lieutenants had done their work well. In the fall of 1959 they had anticipated an extended conflict in several presidential-primary states and at the Convention as well. But through their skillful planning, and through careful engineering by sympathetic Republican organization leaders in key presidential-primary states, they had been highly successful in discouraging the anticipated Rockefeller candidacy.

EARLY NIXON ORGANIZATIONAL EFFORTS, JANUARY-JULY

Early in January, many of these same men came to Washington to establish the framework of the Vice President's campaign organization. The several offices which were established were dedicated essentially to the capture of the Republican presidential nomination for the Vice President; but they also foreshadowed the Vice President's personal campaign organization which was basically to direct the national Republican campaign after the National Convention. In the Washington Building, scarcely four blocks from the National Republican Headquarters, a team of writers, researchers, and subject-matter experts were already turning out work as 1960 began. As this staff expanded, another office housing a Dick Nixon Club was opened close by at the Shoreham Building for the purpose of raising money and developing "personal-follower-group" strength in all of the 50 states.

At the swank Sheraton Park Hotel, two miles out Connecticut Avenue, Leonard Hall, former Republican National Chairman, had also established his headquarters. It was assumed that because of his prominent role in the successful containment of the Rockefeller movement, his wide Party contacts, and his management of the 1956 Presidential campaign, he would help fashion the strategy of the Nixon campaign.

On Capitol Hill close friends and associates of the Vice President arrived from California. Bob Finch, young, aggressive, former Los Angeles County Republican Chairman; Stan McCaffrey, a former Vice President of the University of California; and Herb Klein, California newspaperman, came to supplement the forces working close to the Vice President in the Senate Office Building.

REPUBLICAN NATIONAL COMMITTEE CAMPAIGN PLANS, JANUARY–JULY

Over at the Republican National Committee during this period early in 1960, the development of this Nixon campaign organization was duly noted. It was obvious to many of the long-time staff members at the Committee that the Vice President was not likely to replace these trusted lieutenants with professional committee staff men once the nomination was secured. Nevertheless, while Nixon's campaign staff was building, plans were also being made at the National Committee for the waging of the campaign which would mark the centenary of Abraham Lincoln's candidacy.

The Chairman of the Republican National Committee, Senator Thruston B. Morton of Kentucky, had proved to be one of the ablest the Republican Party had ever called to its top position. Possessed with an unusual ability to mediate between the liberal and the conservative wings of the Party, Senator Morton also has a sparkling humor and speaking skill which soon catapulted him into great favor as one of the Party's most popular and most articulate spokesmen.

Senator Morton, speaking in February, 1959, in Wheeling, West Virginia, had publicly announced that he was committed to the candidacy of Richard Nixon. When he assumed the Party chairmanship, however, he indicated in unmistakable terms that he considered it his responsibility to see that the facilities of the National Committee staff were made available on equal terms to all potential candidates for the presidential nomination.

During the early months of 1960, the National Committee staff was, indeed, reminded on several occasions that their services were to be made available to all leading presidential aspirants. It is true, however, that the personal relationships that existed between National Committee staff members and the omnipresent Nixon aides made it quite natural for the Vice President's assistants to request and to receive more help than was tendered to the staff of any other potential candidate.

As the winter turned into spring, the liaison between many of the Nixon people and their counterparts in all divisions at the National Committee increased. Speculations arose anew that perhaps once the convention had nominated the Vice President a unified campaign organization might ensue.

In looking forward to the 1960 campaign, Chairman Morton continually asserted in a forty-nine-state speaking tour that the Republican Party was the minority party and that if it were to be successful in 1960 and thereafter, it must broaden its base. Consequently, several new programs were established and several old programs were strengthened.

If one had compared the organization chart used in the successful 1956 campaign with that projected for the 1960 campaign it would appear that there were to be relatively few personnel changes. In 1960, many of the top-echelon 1956 personalities were back at their posts or were in roughly parallel positions in the rapidly developing Nixon campaign headquarters.

Leonard Hall, for example, the National Chairman in 1956, was now actively assisting in the direction of Nixon's campaign strategy. Robert Carter served as Executive Assistant to Mr. Hall, a post he had occupied in 1956. Cliff Folger, the Republican National Finance Committee Chairman in 1956, was now functioning as the chief money raiser for the Vice President.

In the line divisions, a 1956 Public Relations Director, Lou Guylay, had been brought back by Chairman Morton to direct the National Committee public-relations program for the 1960 campaign. Albert B. "Ab" Hermann, considered to be one of the better "professional" staff men in Party politics, assumed control of the campaign division. A Southern Division, not existing in 1956, had been added under the direction of I. Lee Potter, the Republican State Chairman for Virginia. New programs had been instituted by the creation of the Business Men in Politics, Senior Republicans, and the Arts and Sciences Divisions.

During the period from January through July, old and new programs alike were far ahead of similar developments in 1956, according to some long-time staff members. In the businessmen's division, for example, a list of graduates of businessmen's public-affairs courses had been developed in the hope that many of these people might be successfully drawn into the coming campaign. Likewise, in the Senior Republicans Division, a program to inform senior citizens of the accomplishments of the Eisenhower administration was linked with an active solicitation of the support of these people for the election of the Republican presidential candidate in 1960. The Arts and Sciences Division was identifying Republican-oriented academicians on campuses across the land and was attempting to recruit them for precampaign and campaign tasks.

Similar efforts were being made in the Labor, Agriculture, Veterans, Minorities and Nationalities Divisions. The Young Republicans were busy preparing a number of their young men for campaign field-work assignments and the Women's Division staged a "campaign countdown" April 2 through April 5, which was designed to inform the leaders of women's Republican groups across the nation of the issues in the coming campaign and of successful campaign techniques.

So it was that as spring ended and summer came to Washington, the National Committee staff was functioning essentially in the same manner that it had under the leadership of Chairman Len Hall in 1956. The organization chart which had been developed for the 1960 campaign by National Committee personnel suggested that the over-all campaign strategy would be determined by a group including the Vice President, the National Chairman, the director of a citizens committee, a representative of the White House, the Senatorial Campaign Committee chairman, the chairman of the Congressional Campaign Committee, and the Vice Presidential candidate for 1960.

AFTER THE CONVENTION

There were many sound reasons for believing that the 1960 presidential campaign would be virtually a rerun of 1956. In the first place, many of the top Nixon staff members were formerly of the National Committee staff, including a former National Chairman, his chief assistant, and a number of former Division heads. Likewise, the close relationship which had developed between January and June among the various Nixon offices and clubs and the National Committee staff personnel suggested at the very least a close cooperation between the top Nixon campaign lieutenants and the regular National Committee staff.

But some seasoned hands at the National Committee had noted certain signs as early as May and June which indicated that the 1960 campaign might well differ markedly from the 1956 effort in terms of direction and management.

The Vice President had demonstrated an unwillingness to brook criticism of his own campaign strategy; he had refused to delegate responsibility, and some members of the ever-increasing Nixon staff were extremely young and politically inexperienced. As the Convention approached, there was growing concern at the Committee over the shape of things to come.

After the National Convention had come and gone, and the National Committee staff had returned to Washington, some of the more experienced, whose forebodings had preceded the Convention, were now even more deeply disturbed. A number of events, largely unnoticed by the casual observer during the Convention, had convinced these National Committee staff people that the campaign indeed might be a disappointing one.

Nevertheless, when the various Washington offices resumed operation in early August, there was still considerable hope, in most quarters, that a unified campaign organization might be developed and that victory in 1960 was within easy reach.

And then things began to happen. First the Vice President injured himself and lost valuable campaign time. Next came the decision to debate Kennedy and the demoralizing effect of the first joint television appearance. Division after Division at the National Committee found itself rebuffed by Nixon organization people when they offered their services and suggested programs. What was happening? What was going wrong?

It had now become obvious to all that the Republican National campaign of 1960, from an organizational standpoint, was to be based upon a dual effort. The Vice President and his staff were obviously trying to create a new Nixon image and a new image for the Republican Party. Mr. Nixon had insisted on a stronger civil-rights plank and a more vigorous approach to national defense because he believed firmly in these positions, and he believed that the Republican Party had to move ahead on these fronts. Now as the campaign proper got under way, it was his announced intention to woo votes which were not ordinarily cast for Republican candidates. He understood quite well that the Republican Party was a minority party. He felt his only chance for victory was to be found in the regular Republican vote plus the votes of millions of Americans who are quadrennially undecided as between the Republican or Democratic candidate.

And so he turned away from the leadership and the programs of the Republican National Committee because he felt that this leadership and these programs would be too partisan in orientation. Because he had great faith in those lieutenants who had done such a skillful job in obtaining the nomination for him, Nixon determined to lean heavily upon his own personal campaign organization and to use the Republican National Committee staff almost as an auxiliary to his own campaign.

Just as it was quite natural for candidate Nixon to make a "candidate" type decision as to the nature of his campaign organization, so it was quite natural for the members of the Republican National Committee staff to react adversely to such a decision. They were, by virtue of background and experience, opposed to a dual campaign organizational structure. For it was a firmly held conviction among these men that the Vice President could have found campaign management skills in abundance and much of the kind of program he needed at the National Committee itself.

PATTERNS OF OPERATION IN A DUAL ORGANIZATION

With the development of a dual campaign organization, the question always arises as to which programs are to be directed from which organization. In the Republican campaign of 1960, all divisions and programs considered basic to the success of the campaign were directed by the Vice President's own immediate staff.

In some campaign areas there was almost complete control of a given campaign effort from the Nixon headquarters, with the staff personnel from the National Committee physically relocating and becoming an integral part of the Nixon-Lodge campaign staff. One thus shifted, for example, was the top agriculture specialist at the National Committee—Mr. Rollis Nelson, a talented and trusted speech writer and expert in the politics of agriculture.

In other areas such as nationalities, the National Committee retained its own Division personnel but the leadership for the campaign effort was transferred to the Nixon-Lodge headquarters where a newly appointed leader managed the Division effort.

A third pattern in the dual organization structure developed where the National Committee staff was given direction of the campaign effort for both organizations. This pattern developed in the campaign for support of the academic community. For example, the executive director of the National Committee's Arts and Sciences Division was given the additional responsibility for directing the Nixon-Lodge Scholars Program.

In certain other areas where dual efforts existed, such as in Minorities, Labor, and the Senior Republicans, the programs and proposals of the National Committee staff were very often entirely overlooked. Postmortems of the election often pointed to the costly by-pass of the talents and experience available in some of these crucial fields. Labor and Minorities, for example, had no budget. Without any real demonstration of interest on the part of the Nixon-Lodge Headquarters, both divisions suffered from gross underutilization during the entire post-Convention campaign.

Another of the great weaknesses which is likely to develop when a dual organization is employed concerns delegation of authority and assignment. Inefficiency and duplication often result. Professor Neil Cotter[1] notes this dilemma in his example of the Republican organization's research efforts in the 1960 campaign.

. . . I find that a friend of mine who attempted to analyze in shorthand terms the allocation of responsibility for research in the Republican campaign effort for 1960 made the following note: "Grassmuck vs. Hamlin vs. Shepley vs. GOP." The reference is to the fact that George Grassmuck, a political scientist from the University of Michigan, was taken on by the Nixon campaign staff in a research capacity. Prior to George's joining the Nixon campaign group, John Hamlin, formerly an assistant to the President with an office in the Executive Office Building, had moved into a suite in the Sheraton-Park Hotel, where he proceeded to put together a file on Kennedy for the use of the Vice President. For a time, many people regarded Hamlin as the Nixon research man. When Professor Grassmuck came along, many people regarded Professor Grassmuck as having replaced Hamlin. Then along came Mr. James Shepley from the *Time-Life* organization. At this point many persons wondered who had replaced whom. Cordial as this trio's relations were with personnel on the Republican National Committee staff, there was always a question in the Committee as to whether the Research Division of the Republican National Committee was working with, for, or being worked against by the research staff of the Nixon campaign organization.

The illustration of the difficulty of coordination in the research field could be multiplied many times over as between the Nixon-Lodge campaign staff and the National Committee operation. There appeared to be very little coordination among state Nixon-Lodge headquarters and the national Nixon-Lodge office as well. As director of a campaign division at the National Committee,

[1] Cornelius P. Cotter, *Technical Specialists in the 1960 Republican Campaign,* unpublished paper delivered at the 1960 convention of the American Political Science Convention, St. Louis, Missouri, September 8, 1961, pp. 4 f.

Arthur Peterson attempted to coordinate his activities with those of the Nixon-Lodge national headquarters but seldom was able to meet with success. As director of one of the Divisions in the Nixon-Lodge operation, he attempted to develop coordination and communication between the state Nixon-Lodge headquarters and the national Nixon-Lodge office, but again his efforts met with extreme frustration.

The budget problems created by the dual campaign organization constitute one of the most unfortunate aspects of the entire campaign. Thus at the end of October in 1960, with election day imminent, the Republican Party found itself with a debt of $1,183,000. In January, 1961, the National Committee found itself with a post-election debt of staggering proportions. The figure exceeded $700,000.

Issues, candidates, financial support, and the party image are all well-known essentials to a successful political campaign. An analysis of the 1960 campaign reveals, however, that the element of campaign organization and management can also be crucial.

One can easily understand the difficulties of a candidate in quest of a new Party image. Vice President Nixon's decision to set up a dual campaign organization was probably made to facilitate the building of this new Party image. Some political leaders would insist, however, that the Republican candidate for the presidency would have been well advised to utilize Republican organizational support to a greater degree, perhaps through a unified campaign effort.

ORGANIZING THE REPUBLICAN CAMPAIGN, 1964

The organizational approach which the Republican Party will take in the presidential campaign of 1964 will depend upon several factors. One important consideration is the question of national party leadership. Congressman William Miller has indicated that he will resign the National Committee Chairmanship at the conclusion of the 1964 Convention.

A controversy has raged for some time over whether the Republican Party should continue its practice of selecting its National Committee Chairman from among its leaders in Congress. Strong support has developed for the appointment of a full-time professional organization chairman. In the latter connection, Ohio's State Chairman Ray C. Bliss has most often been mentioned as the logical choice. His reputation and influence have continued to grow with his repeated victories in Ohio and the development of the Republican State Chairmen's Advisory Committee which he heads.

If the Republican National Committee seeks and obtains a professional organizational chairman like Bliss, it is likely that the presidential campaign would be directed from the National Committee. In such a development the nominee's top staff people would probably be integrated into the over-all campaign program as set by the National Committee Chairman.

A unified campaign would also result if the presidential nominee simply took over the top National Committee staff positions following the Convention. This take-over would be accomplished either through the appointment of a National Chairman to serve as a figurehead for the nominee's own campaign director or by the new Chairman's actually directing the campaign from the vantage point of the National Committee. In such an event, permanent Committee staff personnel would be temporarily shifted in assignment to secondary roles insofar as strategy and tactics were involved.

If, on the other hand, the nominee chooses to separate his own personal organization from the National Committee and sees the Committee as essentially a coordinating and servicing organization, a dual campaign organization will result again in 1964.

Thus the organizational approach to the 1964 Republican presidential campaign turns on two questions: (1) Will the National Committee attempt to alter the image and operation of its staff through the selection of a highly respected, full-time professional organizational chairman? (2) Depending upon the answer to question 1, what will be the attitude of the presidential nominee toward a unified or a dual organizational campaign? Time alone will tell.

Chapter VI

Enlisting State and Local Support

THE PAROCHIAL FOCUS OF STATE AND LOCAL PARTY ORGANIZATIONS

The American political party system is decentralized in three key ways: (1) The two major parties are loosely knit associations composed of individuals and groups with widely divergent interests, backgrounds, and ideologies. (2) In the main these associations gain direction and thrust only during elections. (3) The power to make decisions concerning candidates, financial support, and such party policy as does exist is largely in the hands of state and local party leaders and elected public officials.

Presidential elections in American politics accordingly constitute a periodic and sometimes painful wrenching of the sinews and muscles of party organization. The conflict has grown as the party system has grown. For although a major goal of parties in America is to win elections, more particularly presidential elections, the state and local organizations are not basically oriented in the direction of national concerns. Their day-to-day problems quite naturally center in state and local politics; yet once every four years, they are expected to completely readjust their focus for a period of three to six months.

This decentralized party system is quadrennially forced to become, at least in part, a centralized party system with campaign plans, party propaganda, and issue accentuation dictated from the national level. To many career politicians, the change means an invasion of their province. Organizations geared to local, congressional, and state contests are asked to redirect their thinking, to tie into their staffs the amateurs from the so-called "presidential party," and to attempt to implement the most recent innovations in campaign organization and extension suggested by the campaign master minds in Washington. In some states, where circumstances appear to warrant it, the local organizations may even be expected to "stand by" while the "citizen" or "volunteer" organizations move in to direct the presidential campaign efforts with such assists as they request from the regular party organization.

From the perspective of the national party organization the conflict is seen in a different light. Programs which the National Committee has spent considerable time and money to initiate and develop are never tried; party propaganda which could have tremendous impact upon the outcome of the campaign is never completely distributed; the presidential and vice-presidential candidates' time is partially wasted on the wrong kinds of meetings. In short, the tools which might bring victory in November are not properly utilized.

After almost any national campaign a third interpretation of the problems of developing presidential support at the state and local levels is advanced by the leaders of the volunteer or citizens groups. These men and women are ordinarily relative amateurs in politics. They are, on the other hand, usually prominent people, selected to reflect the support the presidential aspirant has from certain important groups in the community. Accustomed to community deference, these leading businessmen, educators, agriculturists, labor leaders, doctors, and the like are frequently quite unhappy when they are forced to subordinate their judgment about running the campaign to that of some junior staff man attached to either the National Committee or the state organization. When the candidate loses, the local chairman of the Volunteers for X remembers his effort to present the "future president" at his alma mater, Public School No. 5, and feels that the professional party leaders were unknowing as well as ungrateful. He feels humiliated even if the candidate wins.

Out of this triangle of interests and approaches a presidential campaign must be fashioned at the state and local levels. During the four years between presidential elections the scant contact between the state or local party leaders and the National Committee staff reinforces the sense of remoteness caused by the keenly felt differences between state and national interests in practical and ideological concerns.

Open conflict between what has been called the "presidential party" and the state and local organizations appears early in the presidential year. As soon as the discussion of possible candidates begins, state leaders clearly perceive that their interests are at stake. They are naturally wary of nominees who might hurt their state ticket, or perhaps jeopardize the reelection of their delegation to Congress. For that reason, candidates who occupy the more extreme positions along the liberal-conservative continuum are bound to have ardent supporters and equally determined detractors. Many southern Republican leaders have made known their desire for Goldwater as the 1964 candidate because they believe he would substantially strengthen their state Republican organizations. Most New York Republicans, on the other hand, are convinced that a Goldwater nomination would hurt their state ticket considerably and would diminish significantly Senator Keating's chances for reelection.

Southern Democrats will undoubtedly use the same kind of argument against the selection of Senator Hubert Humphrey or Attorney General Robert Kennedy as President Johnson's running mate in 1964 while northern Democrats will insist that a well-known liberal is needed on the ticket to offset what some fear is a "conservative" Johnson image.

A second conflict arises between the presidential campaign managers and the state and local leaders in the area of campaign strategy and propaganda. Leaders in each state and in each locality have their own intelligence systems. The day when the morning "coffee break" constituted the public exposure of the organization politician has long since passed. In many state committees and in more than a few city headquarters, long before the campaign year begins, party chairmen and their staffs are busy reading and rereading reports of professional pollsters, scrutinizing key precinct election returns, and conferring with various community leaders in order to understand and prepare for the political climate of primaries, conventions, and campaigns.

Regardless of how sophisticated or how unsophisticated the means employed to detect current political opinion may be, the local and state leaders feel that they have a better understanding of their area than do the staff people from the National Committee or from the nominee's own inner circle. Thus controversy develops over such matters as what kind of speech the candidate should give; whether a whistle-stop train tour of the state would be better than a car caravan; whether the appearances in a central city should be under the auspices of the volunteers or of the regular organization; whether the local candidates should appear with the presidential nominee.

All of these questions involve the presidential campaign triangle mentioned above: the National Committee's interests and plans, the desires of state and local party headquarters, and the involvement of the ubiquitous volunteers. In anticipation of these very problems the National Committee, as the official headquarters for the "presidential party," continually attempts to develop programs which will facilitate a unity of approach and an understanding of the difficulties involved in a presidential campaign. To a lesser extent, and during a much shorter period, the national volunteer organizations also make a concerted effort to enlist and develop effective support at the grass roots. Let us examine some of the long-range Republican and Democratic National Committee training programs as well as those specifically developed and employed during the 1960 campaign. Attention also must be given to the corresponding activities undertaken by the citizens organizations during the 1960 presidential campaign.

REPUBLICAN NATIONAL COMMITTEE EFFORTS IN 1960

In January, 1959, after the decisive Republican defeat of 1958, Meade Alcorn, then Chairman of the Republican National Committee, looked forward to the 1960 election and strongly recommended that the National Committee channel an increased portion of its resources and a larger number of its staff in the direction of improving state and local organizations. Speaking to the members of the Republican National Committee in Des Moines on January 22, Alcorn stated:

A political party without precinct manpower is like a ship without a crew. It may stay afloat, but isn't going anywhere. . . . We need a drastic overhaul of our manpower situation.

Chairman Alcorn went on to suggest nine specific programs which, in his opinion, should be put into effect immediately in preparation for the 1960 campaign. Among these proposals were a *nation-wide recruiting program* to enlist two million additional precinct workers by September, 1960; the establishment of *Citizenship Service Committees* to obtain attractive party candidates; the formation of *To the People Committees* to hold public forums on issues and the need for political action; *Regional Training Conferences* to school the new recruits for the 1960 campaign; creation of *survey teams* to analyze county organizations; and the development of *apprentice programs* to train young Republicans in party leadership roles.

Some of these proposals were not new. In 1950, for example, the National Committee had sponsored one-day regional training conferences with the "faculty members" of these "political schools" (as they were then designated) drawn from the more experienced campaign directors in various state headquarters and in unusually successful congressional candidacies. The curriculum for these schools had included instruction in political tactics, organizational improvements, publicity techniques, and current issues.

A second Alcorn suggestion, the nation-wide recruitment drive, had been given an unusual twist in 1954 when just such an activity was organized under the title of Poll Takers of America. Devised by the National Committee's Women's Division, it sought both to gauge the reaction of the public to the first two years of the Eisenhower administration and concomitantly to add as many precinct workers to the party rolls as could be recruited from among the persons polled.

An important difference between these two National Committee efforts is worthy of note. The 1950 regional training conferences resulted from the joint efforts of the National Committee staff and the staffs of the Congressional and Senatorial Campaign Committees. The 1954 Poll Takers project, was, on the other hand, undertaken by only one division at the National Committee.

This latter approach was precisely what Alcorn wanted to avoid insofar as major organizational-improvement programs were concerned. Either all divisions should pull together on these priority programs or a separate Division of Political Organization should be created. The Democrats, indeed, had three years earlier formed a separate division devoted to political organization.

The Republican National Committee, however, decided to continue its policy of program development within the separate divisions of the Committee staff. Thus it was that during the 1960 presidential campaign the so-called training and liaison activities were carried on essentially through three divisions: (a) The Women's Division; (b) the Young Republicans; and (c) the Campaign Division.

It is interesting to note that in 1960 no section in the national headquarters was delegated the major responsibility of liaison with state organizations, in contrast to 1952 and 1956. Rather this task was apparently conceived as a basic concern of all of the headquarters divisions.

THE WOMEN'S DIVISION

The Women's Division attempted to help prepare state and local women Republican leaders for the coming campaign through two pre-convention programs in 1960. The first was a four-day conference called Campaign Countdown. The far-ranging agenda included sessions on National Security, Our Nation's Resources, Party Organization in Rural Areas, Party Organization in Urban Areas, Party Organization in the South, and other topics. It also included instruction in publicity techniques, operation of a speakers bureau, utilization of radio and television, fund raising, and winning of the farm, labor and nationality-group vote. Time was given to a general consideration of the major issues in the 1960 congressional and presidential elections.

The second Women's Division training activity was a Campaign Correspondence Course consisting of a series of monthly "chapters" which ultimately formed a textbook on practical politics. Geared to the developments of the 1960 campaign, these monthly assignments were designed to lead the student worker into an active and effective role in her precinct organization. The topics covered in the textbook were generally the same as those featured during the four-day April conference.

THE YOUNG REPUBLICANS

The Young Republicans have for ten years conducted a national conference of their own which, not so strangely, closely resembles the Women's Conference in scope and method. The standard topics of finance, publicity, issues, organization, and the like are thoroughly covered and, in recent years, these schools have emphasized the *training* function of Young Republican leadership. In 1960, for example, the YGOP national conference gave considerable attention to the Chamber of Commerce Action Course in Practical Politics as a model for training courses to be conducted by Young Republican leaders at the local-club level.

One very tangible effort to establish a link between the National Committee and state and local YGOP groups began with the brief schooling of twelve young men at the Committee in the rudiments of political organization and campaigning. They were then sent to various states to help coordinate state organization and individual club activities with the national YGOP campaign program for the national ticket.

THE CAMPAIGN DIVISION

The Campaign Division, under the direction of Albert B. "Ab" Hermann, developed for the 1960 campaign a "training package" designed to put at the disposal of the average county chairman and candidate for Congress or the state legislature the skill, experience and thinking of the best leadership in the Republican Party.

The approach was at once unique in its conception and sweeping in its scope. The training aids included materials on campaign organization methods and the use of campaign volunteers, a series of illustrative charts, and filmed presentations by the President, the Vice President, and leading Republican Congressmen. The "package" even made provisions for the inclusion of filmed presentations by incumbent state legislators and Congressmen (or candidates for these offices) from the constituency in which the films were being shown.

The entire project was titled the Republican Roundup and Refresher Workshop. In the words of the author of the "package," J. J. Weurthner:

. . . This . . . workshop can be a useful tool for the local GOP Chairman. It gives him the opportunity to bring together in one meeting his committee organization, women, volunteers, Young Republicans, finance people, graduates of business practical politics courses—anybody and everybody who wants to be a part of the campaign effort.

The Republican Roundup and Refresher Workshop was more involved, however, than a simple set of tailor-made films and the application of some group-work theories. For it involved the hiring of a field man or field woman to travel with these workshops and handle the arrangements for their presentation. The field men were hired through the state committees by the state chairmen to work only within one state.

The role of the field man in the management of the Republican Roundup and Refresher Workshop was twofold. He was to move from county to county, presenting the workshop sessions to as many Republican groups as he reasonably could. But he was also charged with the responsibility of developing a complete list of any graduates of practical-politics courses in each locality, and of helping the Republican organization in each community to develop ways and means by which these recent practical-politics-course graduates could be successfully drawn into the campaign plans for the November elections.

This latter responsibility had much to commend it as a potentially significant activity since a conservative estimate placed the number of practical-politics-course graduates in the United States at well over 200,000 by September of 1960. (These were graduates from courses sponsored by a wide variety of organizations such as the National Association of Manufacturers, the AFL-

CIO, the Ford Motor Company, chambers of commerce, and others.)

It was expected that personnel from the state organizations would work with these field men to make effective use of particularly promising recruits. From the standpoint of control and support, then, the Republican Roundup and Refresher Workshop was a state program, but the materials and the method were national in origin and, in a sense, national in orientation.

Less heralded than the national conferences and the packaged-deal training innovations were the relationships which developed between the functional sections of the Campaign Division and similar divisions at certain of the larger state headquarters. Since the majority of state headquarters just do not have the kind of budget to support functioning division personnel in the fields of labor, agriculture, nationalities, and the like, such liaison activities were limited.

A majority of Republican state headquarters do have at least one man functioning in the general area of public relations and publicity. In 1960 most state headquarters sent a representative to a week-long conference in Washington. There, these representatives were acquainted with the services of the National Committee and of the Congressional and Senatorial Committees, and were offered suggestions as to how best to utilize these services, particularly with reference to the presidential campaign.

The programs and procedures which have been briefly examined thus far were attempts to bridge the gap between the national and the state and local organizations. But they were not, for the most part, designed specifically for the presidential campaign.

Before the Nixon-Lodge campaign programs are considered, brief mention should be made of one event in which both National Committee and Nixon-Lodge organizations went to the grass roots looking for support under one banner. The occasion was "Pat for First Lady Week," October 3-8, 1960.

Four high-level women leaders (Mrs. Clare B. Williams, Assistant Chairman of the Republican National Committee; Mrs. Peter Gibson, President of the National Federation of Republican Women; Mrs. Carol Arth, National Director of Women's Activities, Volunteers for Nixon-Lodge; and Mrs. David G. Fernald, Co-Chairman, Young Republican National Federation) issued joint statements setting forth the role of their individual groups in the week's activities.

Mrs. Williams suggested the regular Republican State Vice Chairman and each County Vice Chairman initiate a vigorous effort in "Pat's Precincts," with a "Pat's Parade" to kick off the whole affair. Mrs. Gibson stressed the need to intensify the Neighbors for Nixon meetings during "Pat Week." Mrs. Arth urged a concentration of coffee caucuses and shopping-center programs during "Pat Week." Mrs. Fernald announced the expediting of "Projects for Pat" during the October 3-8 period. This effort to unite all womenpower for Nixon behind one drive apparently was quite successful and was one of very few such united efforts during the entire campaign.

ENLISTING SUPPORT AT THE GRASS ROOTS— VOLUNTEERS FOR NIXON-LODGE, 1960

Shortly after nominees Nixon and Lodge had returned to Washington, their official citizens organization was named. It became the National Volunteers for Nixon-Lodge. The Chairman of the organization was Charles S. Rhyne of Washington, D.C., a former president of the American Bar Association. Rhyne's major field of interest is international law. He has been for some time a leader in the World Peace Through Law program. Although the new Chairman planned to devote full time to his Nixon-Lodge duties, he did turn over the administrative management to a young New York businessman, Peter M. Flanigan. Assisting Flanigan was E. H. "Ned" Harding, a New York public-relations man.

Several members of the Vice President's campaign staff were put to work on a chairman's manual; others were sent into the field to organize.

By September 15 Chairman Rhyne announced that forty-one states had been organized. In some, the organization was mostly paper. In others, paid professionals took charge and began to develop extensive operations.

Meanwhile the Volunteers for Nixon-Lodge *Chairman's Manual* had been completed and issued. The purpose of organizing state and local Nixon-Lodge Clubs and committees, in the words of the *Manual,* was:

. . . To mobilize broad Nixon support for effective action . . . While the Nixon candidacy will, of course, be supported by the Republican organization, many of your neighbors will prefer to work solely for the election of Dick Nixon and to carry on their activity through an independent organization. Your club is that independent organization.

The staff office for the Volunteers in Washington under Flanigan's direction supplied the local clubs with "launching kits" (including research and promotion materials) and with special-interest items (such as feature films on the Vice President). It also attempted to furnish a measure of coordination with other Volunteer activities in the immediate area and gave to each club a direct contact with the Nixon Campaign Headquarters.

The *Chairman's Manual* explicitly instructed the local clubs ". . . never to attempt to replace nor compete with the Republican Party in your state or community."

Although the regular Party organization will gear its efforts to the election of candidates at all levels, the presidential race . . . which is our *single objective* . . . still is of *primary importance* to the overall Republican campaign.

This makes it inevitable, and essential, that we work together harmoniously and effectively.

In its desire to elect Richard Nixon, the Party recognizes the vital importance of broadening the effort beyond Party lines. And this is where the Nixon Volunteers and your Club come in.

Our job is to enlist, stimulate and activate Independents and Democrats, as well as Republicans, in the Nixon campaign. The Republican Party, of course, will focus its main attention toward turning out the Republican vote.

Moving independently and forcefully toward the same objective, Nixon Volunteers and the Republican Party together can develop the mighty momentum necessary for victory in November.

Your role, then, is to supplement and broaden the Republican effort, cooperating with the Party, but working independently and autonomously.

The Manual had much to say about how to handle public relations, suggested a wide variety of campaign activities (including coffee caucuses, first-voters parties, television and radio parties, smokers, library parties, fair booths, parades, and rallies).

Headquarters specifications and finance came in for substantial treatment as well. The *Manual* made very clear that every Nixon club operated on an autonomous and self-sustaining basis and that the local clubs had no direct financial obligation to the national campaign organization.

A still more direct approach was made by the Volunteers organization to individuals who evinced some interest in the Nixon candidacy. It was called Operation SNAP (Support Nixon at the Polls). SNAP packs, consisting of buttons, literature, sign-up postcards, and a request for financial support, were mailed to all persons who responded to various mass mailings (doctors, lawyers, professors, and other categories). The recipients of the SNAP packs were assumed not to be members of Nixon clubs and hence were given suggestions similar to those for club members, involving the recruitment of at least six friends for Nixon, mailing postcards, holding parties, writing "letters to the editor," distributing campaign literature, canvassing, and getting out the vote on election day.

It is difficult to assess the effect of the Volunteers organization. Undoubtedly the impact varied from state to state. In Ohio, where the Volunteers were successfully integrated into the total campaign effort under the direction of Republican State Chairman Ray C. Bliss, support for the Vice President and Ambassador Lodge was unquestionably broadened without organizational conflict or duplication. And the overwhelming Nixon victory in Ohio strongly supported Chairman Bliss's views about tying "citizens" organizations into the total campaign strategy designed by the regular Party organization in a given state.

But there are very few men in American political life with Bliss's skill at resolving conflict and with his understanding of effective campaign organization. In some states, where Volunteers organizations insisted on a status completely separate from the regular Party, there may well have been merit in their case.

REPUBLICAN EFFORTS AT THE GRASS ROOTS, 1964

One of the major effects of the 1960 defeat was to direct the attention of Republican leadership once again to the problems of state and local party organization. Attention was focused particularly on one area of chronic Republican weakness—the big cities in the industrialized and populous states of the Northeast—Detroit, Philadelphia, Newark, Boston, New York, Chicago, St. Louis, Pittsburgh, Cleveland, and Baltimore. The margins by which Kennedy carried the states of New York, Pennsylvania, Michigan, Illinois, Minnesota, Missouri, Maryland, and New Jersey were provided by one large city in each state. In the 13 cities of more than 300,000 inhabitants located in these eight states, Kennedy amassed a plurality of 2,400,000 votes.

This figure was a surprise to some Republicans, for the most striking aspect of the 1956 presidential election was the erosion of the Democratic Party in these same cities. Eisenhower had carried 10 of the 20 largest northeastern cities and received more than 40 per cent of the vote in all but two—Detroit and St. Louis. His success led political analyst Samuel Lubell, writing in 1957, to conclude that the Democratic majorities in the cities had been slashed so drastically the Republicans must be rated as favorites to win the White House in 1960.

The break through in 1956 was not followed by the organizational effort which might have solidified some of these gains. Except for Nelson Rockefeller's strong showing in New York City, the 1958 elections indicated the Republican beachhead established in these cities in 1956 had been lost.

Because of the sizable losses in the big cities for the Republicans, analysts freely stated that it was here that the presidential election of 1960 was indeed won for Kennedy and lost for Nixon. Senator Thruston B. Morton, well aware of the 1960 voting statistics, appointed a Committee on Big City Politics to study the problem. State Party Chairman Ray C. Bliss of Ohio was appointed its chairman.

The studies of the Bliss Committee brought to light the fact that is manifest during presidential election years—that in most states there is basically no organization at the grass roots worthy of the name. It found, for example, that in only 8 of 27 of our largest cities are all precincts manned by Republican Party workers. From this survey came a series of recommendations by special subcommittees on Party Organization and Candidate Recruitment; Labor, Business, Professional and Independent Groups; Nationalities and Minorities; Public Relations; Use of Surveys and Educational Methods.

The subcommittee reports are thorough and realistic, yet imaginative. If the suggestions they make can be implemented the Republican position in the big cities will surely be strengthened for the 1964 elections. But who will follow through? What counts in politics is the production rather than the pontification.

Following the issuance of the Bliss report, some regular Republican state and local organizations made every effort they could afford to implement its suggestions. In some areas, extra-Party organizations which had formed even before the committee had studied the big-city problem appeared determined to move with or without the official Party blessing.

In Illinois, for example, the Republican Citizens League was formed in 1961 to build a broader and stronger grass-roots organization. The initial emphasis was upon recruitment and training of a force of workers in the Chicago metropolitan area. The League stated from the outset that its purpose was to do the jobs which the formal Party organization had not successfully performed—to provide workers where the Party organization had none, to take care of the difficult areas in which representatives of the Republican Party are captives of the Democratic machine, to establish contact with voters who are untouched by or unresponsive to the organization. The League has established a harmonious relationship with the formal Party hierarchy and has several high-ranking Party leaders on its governing board.

The Republican Alliance, a similar group established in Philadelphia early in 1961, also undertook basic organizational activity. It was independent of the Republican city organization, and, unlike its Chicago counterpart, it did not initially enjoy cordial relations with regular Party leaders in Philadelphia.

These extra-Party organization groups can perhaps improve Party strength at the precinct level and perhaps are needed in special circumstances. But they are ordinarily short-lived and quite limited in scope. A more promising development that has occurred since 1962 may have great long-range significance for the improvement of American political parties at the state and local levels.

In December, 1962, Republican National Committee Chairman William Miller appointed Ohio Republican State Chairman Ray C. Bliss to head a Republican State Chairmen's Advisory Committee. The purpose of this group (which included all Republican State Chairmen) was to generally advise the National Committee on developments within the various states and to direct the thinking of the National Committee to the perennial problems of state and local Party organization. Under the leadership of Bliss, this association of State Chairmen has met quarterly to examine various programs carefully and share interpretations as to the reasons for individual successes and failures.

The significant innovation here is that the actual "line officers" involved in campaign direction and organizational improvement are talking with one another rather than being talked at by a staff man who may not be exposed, regularly, to their day-to-day problems.

In January, 1964, 46 of the 51 (the District of Columbia is included) State Chairmen or their executive directors attended a three-day workshop. The "esprit de corps" of this particular association was, at that time, extremely high and there was a universal feeling that finally a realistic starting point had been found from which to build more responsible and more responsive state and local Party organizations, not only for the 1964 presidential election but for many years to come.

THE DEMOCRATIC PATTERN IN 1960

The takeover of Democratic Party organization by the Kennedy family team in 1960 improved relations with state and local

Party organizations during the campaign. The Kennedy team replaced a National Committee regime which had alienated many state and local Party organizations. It depended heavily upon the regular Party machinery, to the great satisfaction of the regular organization leaders. It was able to coordinate state Citizens committees gracefully through its close family-liaison system. It had an experienced working organization which inspired confidence and commanded loyalty and hence provided effective leadership.

Yet the takeover was accomplished at a heavy price in long-run political organization at the state and local levels. The Division of Political Organization of the National Committee, carefully built up over a five-year period through the strenuous efforts of the Advisory Committee on Political Organization—led by Neil Staebler, Michigan's gifted state chairman—was wiped out overnight in early August. Its director, Deputy Chairman Drexel Sprecher, was relieved of authority and relegated to a minor role directing Educators for Kennedy-Johnson. Its assistant director, Arthur Chapin, was assigned work in the registration drive. Its regional representatives were assigned to duty for a few weeks with the Kennedy coordinators in the states where they lived, then discharged.

Had the Division of Political Organization been merely a tool for centralization of the Democratic Party in the hands of Chairman Butler, as his detractors seem to have portrayed it to the Kennedy team, wholesale reorganization might have been justified as an essential step in the assumption of power. But the Division of Political Organization had been engaged primarily in a comprehensive program to train precinct workers, county organization people, and state Party leaders. Calling upon the talents of several of the nation's outstanding adult educators, the program had applied the latest group-work techniques to teach practical political skills, to develop leadership ability, and to stimulate cohesive local group action. Although no official count was ever assembled, an estimated 25,000 persons were trained by the new techniques over a four-year period. Many would have been available to man the precincts in an orderly way in the 1960 campaign, but none of them was used unless, in the words of the former assistant director, they walked in and volunteered for duty.

The story of the Division of Political Organization is worth repeating, briefly, because it illustrates what can be done to upgrade a political party composed of citizen-volunteers and it underscores the importance of looking before acting when newly assuming administrative power. For, despite the need to place a Kennedy man in command of Democratic political organization, there was no compelling necessity to jettison the training program in order to conduct the campaign. The two were complementary, not conflicting. The training program could as easily have been shelved for the duration and its organizers turned to harvesting its fruits under the guidance of the new men in power.

The Committee on Political Parties of the American Political Science Association in its 1950 report, "Toward A More Responsible Two-Party System," had recommended the strengthening of internal party democracy and organization. Enamored of the "party responsibility" theory underlying the report, Chairman Butler took the advice of the political scientists and in 1955 established an Advisory Committee on Political Organization. Fortunately, he selected as chairman of the Committee Neil Staebler, state leader of the Party's most effective citizen organization.

Mr. Staebler, who believes in applying group-work techniques to encourage political discussion, stimulated his committee to explore at considerable length the organizational problems and needs facing the Democratic Party. The experienced men and women who participated wisely proposed measures which took advantage of Party decentralization and diversity, and avoided steps designed to centralize Democratic Party organization.

The first step, in 1957, was to create a Division of Political Organization in the National Committee, headed by a Deputy Chairman. Next, a system of regional representatives was established to assist the Deputy Chairman for Political Organization and to provide full-time field work with state and county central committees. Six regions were delineated: Northeastern, Southern, Central, Northwestern, Southwestern, and Western. In addition, Arthur Chapin of New Jersey was appointed Assistant to the Deputy Chairman to give special attention to minority groups.

Six regional meetings, held around the country in September, 1957, to introduce the new system of regional representatives, generated the conviction that the training of party workers was an urgent organizational need. The Division of Political Organization thereupon undertook four very promising ventures in leadership training: the Precinct Worker Training program, the County Leader Workshop program, the Leadership Conference program for state leaders, and the "You Decide" or Neighborhood Discussion program. Adult educators were called in to prepare materials and to suggest techniques for meetings.

The Precinct-Worker Training Program. Precinct needs were met first. The adult educators promptly prepared an instructor's manual which outlined an eight-hour precinct workers' course divided into two instructional sessions of three hours each and a two-hour field exercise. Modern group-work techniques were encouraged in the training sessions, which used films, buzz sessions, panels, questions and discussion, role playing, field work and reports thereon, and listening groups. Formal lecturing was held to a minimum. A precinct worker's Handbook also was prepared to serve as a textbook for each trainee.

The first step in implementation was to train instructors capable of presenting the precinct program. Beginning in November, 1957, fifty-six instructors' courses were held in 36 states, with the bulk of the sessions coming in the first year of the program. Approximately 1,500 instructors were graduated. Hundreds of precinct-worker training courses were given by the graduates, but no record exists of how many. Some 30,000 precinct handbooks were sent out, most of them for use in training courses.

The County-Leader Workshop Program. In August, 1959, a program to train county leaders was inaugurated. A county leader's handbook had been previously prepared to serve as a textbook for the course. A carefully prepared manual for workshop leaders was issued September 15, 1959. Again a six-hour course using group-work techniques was programed to cover topics such as "Problem Analysis," "How to Conduct Effective Meetings," "How to Get Good Press," "How to Finance Your Party,"

"Candidate Recruitment," and "Campaign Planning." The program, operating on a do-it-yourself basis, went over well.

The Leadership-Conference Program. Beginning in the summer of 1959 and continuing through the spring of 1960, state Party leaders in each of five different regions were invited to a three-day conference at a central city. No training manual was used and no textbook prepared. Instead, three people experienced in adult leadership were sent to conduct each conference. Basic group-work techniques were followed. Each party leader was given a looseleaf notebook with index tabs for the major topics so that he could jot down the ideas he wanted to keep. Discussions centered on "The Many Duties of a Party Leader," "How to Get People into Politics," "What Makes an Organization Effective?" "Understanding People—the Leader's Job," "How to Share Leadership," "Improving Party Relations," and "Simple Steps in Solving Political Problems." State leaders themselves played the roles in problem scenes which showed how one might deal with a labor organization or how to placate a dissident party faction.

The "You Decide" Program. At the 1960 National Convention a new neighborhood discussion program was launched. Seven elaborate "flip charts," designed to stimulate discussion, were prepared and more were planned. Accompanying each flip chart was material to enable any interested Party member to lead a discussion of the facts and problems raised. Emphasis was placed upon participation in small groups rather than speechmaking by a discussion leader. Adult educators again were called in to help prepare materials and to help train those who volunteered as discussion leaders.

Although some scoffed at these efforts and others even argued that they were a waste of money, no one could actually claim offense. The outcome of the 1958 election, the success of the 1958 and 1959 Dollars for Democrats Drives, and the creation of sparkling new volunteer political organizations in many states which long had been Republican strongholds soon muffled the doubters.

THE CAMPAIGN FOR STATE AND LOCAL SUPPORT

Three direct efforts were mounted by the Kennedy managers

to insure state and local organizational support. Regular Democratic organizations were stimulated through the Democratic National Committee by State Coordinators selected from preconvention Kennedy supporters. Independents, pro-Kennedy Republicans, and anti-organization Democrats were rounded up by Citizens for Kennedy-Johnson. Nonvoters were made eligible to participate by a slam-bang Voter Registration Drive in cooperation with state and local Party organizations.

Heading up the system of State Coordinators at the Democratic National Committee was Lawrence O'Brien, who reported immediately to Robert Kennedy. O'Brien conducted much of his work through two lieutenants, Ralph Dungan and Richard Donohue, who provided central staff services to the State Coordinators and received information from them about the progress of the campaign. State Coordinators dealt not only with state central committees but also directly with county central committees, when appropriate.

Dungan and Donohue sought as much political intelligence as possible. From their gleanings, they advised upon campaign scheduling, policy emphasis, and special-group appeals. In general, Donohue kept track of the North and East, Dungan the South, Upper Middle West, and Far West. However, they worked closely together, as a team, and each knew much of the situation in all states. In the West, particularly, where Kennedy lacked a strong base and close political advisers, they both kept touch with developments.

In the last few weeks of the campaign, the scheduling and speech writing teams depended heavily on the intelligence reports of the O'Brien operation to establish where the candidate should go, how much time he should spend, and what he should emphasize in his speeches. O'Brien himself joined the tour group one day a week to make an oral report on how the campaign was faring in each state and to check personally on the information he was receiving. The information and the organization team's analysis of it proved to be reassuringly accurate.

Citizens for Kennedy-Johnson.   Citizens for Kennedy-Johnson was thoroughly independent of the Democratic National Committee. Quartered across Washington, D.C., in the preconvention Kennedy headquarters in the Esso building, it had its own funds, its own organizational structure, and its own program.

Three main assignments fell to Citizens for Kennedy-Johnson. They provided an independent organization for people who wanted to help elect Kennedy President but who couldn't or wouldn't work with a regular local Democratic organization. They raised funds and, after mid-October, paid the campaign bills.[1] They established several special auxiliary committees to woo the votes of veterans, young people, senior citizens, businessmen, and nationality groups.[2]

Byron L. "Whizzer" White of Colorado, Rhodes Scholar, All-American football player, and a close friend of John F. Kennedy, served as National Chairman of the Citizens organization. His principal lieutenant for general organization work was Fred Dutton of California.

White personally reported to Robert Kennedy and for all practical purposes operated as a sixth male member of the Kennedy family team. Occasionally, Dutton provided needed liaison. Throughout the campaign, coordination with the Kennedys was kept informal and depended upon very frequent telephone and face-to-face contacts. However, the Citizens Committee maintained no contact with the office of Chairman Henry M. Jackson of the Democratic National Committee and felt no obligation to do so.

White promptly set up an organization parallel to the Democratic National Committee in all states except in the South, where the Citizens activities were handled through the regular Democratic organizations. A state chairman was appointed and usually a woman cochairman. County chairmen were designated in urban and semiurban counties, but no attempt was made to organize Citizens committees in most small rural counties. Some states organized thoroughly, anyway. In California, a Citizens Committee for Kennedy-Johnson was established in every county.

Special emphasis was given to women's roles in the campaign, for White and Dutton felt that women in general needed greater recognition in politics and wanted to identify with Senator Ken-

---

[1] See Chapter X, Financing the Campaigns, for details.
[2] See Chapter VII, Attracting Special-Interest Groups, for details.

nedy. Many women were appointed local chairmen. Special events for women were featured. News stories were prepared aimed at the women's pages in the newspapers. A particular effort was made to enlist women from middle-income families who were likely to have had a good education and to be able to spare time from household chores to help win the election. Assignments were even divided to create additional spots for women volunteers.

Taking a leaf from Larry O'Brien's book, White selected coordinators for each region to stimulate the state Citizens committees and to provide political intelligence. He also set up a press section and a speakers' bureau to service his state organizations.

State Citizens' chairmen were urged to work closely with the regular Party organizations and were asked to accept the plans of the Democratic state chairmen. Unfortunately, such pleas were sometimes ignored. Effective and energetic state chairmen, as in California and Michigan, welcomed the Citizens organizations as useful extensions of their influence. Where a Democratic organization was divided, even crumbling, as in New York, the Citizens Committee had to carry the principal burden of campaign organization. In some states, especially if the state chairman were weak or inexperienced, rivalry developed.

Although White and his men conscientiously sought real independents to fill their ranks, a great many Citizens leaders turned out to be well known Democrats. In Philadelphia, for example, the Citizens Chairman was Mayor Dilworth! The weaker the regular Democratic organization or leadership and the stronger and more effective the Citizens effort, the greater the opportunity became for clashes between them. In some places volunteer Citizens leaders turned out to be leaders of rival Democratic factions who used the new Kennedy organizations to rally their followers, raise funds, and stage a revival of their power. The rise of such problems of local rivalry was, however, regarded as the price of having a Citizens movement. Despite its impact on the health of some local Democratic organizations, Robert Kennedy viewed the effort as an over-all gain, for he was anxious to get as many campaign activities going as possible.

Smaller than the Democratic National Committee, more cohesive, and single-purpose, Citizens for Kennedy-Johnson was able to launch telephoning campaigns, prepare and distribute pamphlets, get out news releases, and supply films directly to state committees with much greater expectation of their being placed in the hands of local units and actually being used than could the National Committee.

The Voter Registration Drive. A separate, but closely related emergency activity involving the state and local Party organizations was the Voter Registration Drive, led by United States Representative Frank Thompson of New Jersey. Organization was informal and lines of authority fluid. Thompson did not believe in organizational charts and staff meetings, so had neither. Housed with Citizens for Kennedy-Johnson, the Drive's leaders maintained close personal liaison with White and Dutton, but reported directly to Robert Kennedy. Late in the campaign, the Registration Drive's staff merged with Citizens to get the newly registered voters to the polls.

The Registration Drive started with a rush and kept its momentum. Congressman Thompson was appointed Drive leader on July 21 and was given until October 5 to get the job done. Immediately he assembled a talented and experienced crew to assist him. Roy Reuther, brother of the President of the United Automobile Workers and its political-action leader, became Deputy Chairman. Thus organized labor's vast capacity to reach the working people was put at Thompson's command. A week later he was joined by Bob Burkhart, Executive Secretary of the New Jersey Democratic Party; Mrs. Katie Louchheim, former Vice Chairman of the Democratic National Committee; and Arthur Chapin, also of New Jersey, who had long experience in the political organization of Negroes. Gerhardt Falcey of New Jersey also came aboard to train canvassers, Scott Powers to assist Burkhart, and Chuck Roach to direct publicity.

Turning immediately to state organization, Thompson appointed drive chairmen in all states except poll-tax states where registration was already closed. By July 29, with chairmen in nearly all states and local chairmen in the major metropolitan areas, he was able to hold a meeting in Washington attended by representatives of 20 states and 35 cities. There he explained the problem, provided basic information, and told what he wanted.

The problem was simple. Forty million Americans, eligible to vote, had not bothered to register. Public-opinion polls repeatedly had demonstrated that the bulk of these nonvoters were poor, ill-educated, and uninterested. But the Kennedys reasoned, and the polls confirmed, that the vast majority of them would vote Democratic if they could be brought to the voting booths. Thompson set a goal of ten million new registrations by October 5.

Beginning August 1, Thompson set out for a series of regional registration meetings. The first, in Philadelphia, brought in Drive chairmen from Delaware, Maryland, New Jersey, Pennsylvania, and West Virginia. The program was reviewed in detail and the need for haste emphasized. Boston was next; then Thomson went on across the nation, returning to New York City on August 9 for the final meeting.

Next, on August 19, to prove the merit of the registration effort, Thompson launched a pilot project in Baltimore, Maryland. Forty college students and recent college graduates were recruited. Top specialists were brought in from Washington to train them. Agreement was reached with local Democratic leaders to concentrate on 60 key precincts which were known to have a large potential Democratic registration. Canvassers were told to register Democrats, not to bother with Republicans. The results were sensational. In one day 2,600 people were registered in the Drive, all but 39 of them as Democrats!

Training teams promptly fanned out to use the technique and to equip others to train canvassers. Kansas City, St. Louis, Syracuse, Utica, Rochester, New York City, and other centers heard the word.

Funding was minimal for so crucial an effort, an estimated $500,000. The Registration team raised $35,000, got an additional $100,000 from the Democratic National Committee. Local funds were made available where needed. For example, in New York, Syracuse supplied $5,000. Fortunately, the American Heritage Foundation and the National Advertising Council engaged in a very extensive advertising campaign to promote voter registration. Much of the cost of a mass-media appeal was thus shifted from the Democratic Registration committee.

By the day registration books closed in the last state, Thompson's estimates showed 9,750,000 more Americans registered to vote than ever before. How many the Democratic effort added could never be determined. But in so close an election, the Voter Registration Drive, like several other factors, could easily have made the difference.

JOHNSON'S RELATIONS WITH DEMOCRATIC STATE ORGANIZATIONS IN 1964

An incumbent President has an enormous advantage in dealing with the state and local organizations of his own political party. Although he needs them to register the voters and get out the vote, they need him even more to give them personal status and to help carry their state and local candidates to victory.

The reasons are quite obvious. First, the President of the United States is by far the greatest news maker in the world. Wherever he goes, all eyes follow. When he appears outside the nation's capital, his coming is invariably the most important local news. Schools close, business is adjourned, and whole communities turn out to hear him speak and even to see him pass by. If he calls attention to a candidate for Congress, or to a candidate for statewide office, or especially to a candidate for a lesser office, he focuses public attention and confers status on that man or woman as nothing else can do. No amount of paid television time, no volume of pamphlets handed out from door to door, can lift an unknown local candidate into the spotlight as can a few words of special praise from the President of the United States, spoken in his own home town.

Second, if the President is a popular figure, as the early polls in 1964 indicated President Johnson is, he is viewed by his party's leaders as "strengthening the ticket." His name and reputation will bring extra voters to the polls. While voting in his party's column, the voters tend to pull the lever on the voting machine or mark the ballot for all his party's candidates. A product of the American long-ballot system, this bonus to the state and local candidates is known as the coattail effect. The lesser candidates are said to "ride the President's coattails" to victory. The greatest example of the coattail effect in modern times was the landslide victory of Franklin D. Roosevelt in 1932, which carried into office virtually every Democrat on the ticket at every level.

If President Johnson's coattails continue to look very long indeed as 1964 advances, he can be expected to deal primarily with the regular Democratic state and local organizations. He can with easy grace respond to their demands, voiced at the Democratic National Committee meeting in early January, 1964, that no separate Citizens organizations be set up at the state and local level as in 1960. The state organizations will need him, as he needs them, and by and large they can be depended upon to give unswerving loyalty to his cause.

On the other hand, the need still exists to attract independents and Republicans to the Johnson banner. A skillful compromise therefore appears possible. A national Citizens for Johnson Committee, which carefully avoids establishing state and local units, could be set up to handle a share of the national campaign expenses and to provide a tent for special backers of the President. State and local activity to attract independents and Republicans could then be left to units of special-interest groups such as Farmers or Businessmen for Johnson, provided the leaders of such units were suggested systematically by the local Democratic leaders and did not become open rivals for Democratic Party power. Since local-level special-interest activity on behalf of an incumbent President rarely operates as a threat to an established regular political organization, such a compromise can be looked for in 1964.

Chapter VII

Attracting the Special-Interest Groups

The United States has been populated by immigrants. Its 190 million inhabitants have come from nearly every nation in the world. As a symbol of welcome to the "huddled masses yearning to breathe free," Liberty's statue stands in New York Harbor.

PATTERNS OF GROUP POLITICAL GEOGRAPHY

Successive waves of immigration, the concentration of various groups of immigrants in different localities, the ways the newcomers have made a living, and the varied reasons for their coming have greatly shaped American politics. No brief portrait can adequately describe their complexity.

The majority pattern of American politics was set by the first, largest, and longest continuing wave of immigrants, the white Protestants from England and Scotland. Still a near-majority of the population, they gave the United States the English language, the English common law, the English traditions of politics and government, and a new concept of their own: the separation of church and state. They drafted the Constitution and basic laws and they have provided most of the nation's leaders. Their reasons for coming and their convictions about the basic organiza-

119

tion and purpose of government have set the perimeter of political debate throughout American history.

The original British immigration had two basic motives: to obtain religious freedom and to improve individual economic opportunities. Thus the New England and Middle Atlantic States, even colonial New York, were peopled by religious dissenters— Congregationalists in New England, Dutch Reform in New York, Quakers in Pennsylvania, Roman Catholics in Maryland. In the South, where Episcopalians predominated in the lowland areas, the Scotch-Irish brought the Presbyterian faith to the Piedmont and the highlands. Later came the Baptists and Methodists, who now are dominant there.

Religion has always been important in American politics. The nation is deeply committed to the separation of church and state and to the Protestant concept that every person has the inalienable right to worship or not to worship as he pleases. Religion, then, is a private matter in the United States. More than one-third of the population belongs to no church at all. Thus no religious group has had either the numerical strength or the moral basis to seek special support from the government and Americans have come to regard the existence of many different and completely private religious groups as a characteristic of freedom and democracy.

Next on the scene were the Negro slaves, virtually all imported from Africa before the War of Independence. Kept in bondage until the Civil War of 1861-1865, this group of some 19 millions has proved the most difficult to assimilate. Concentrated heavily in the South until the 1940's and still largely centered there, the Negroes have acquired the English language and the Protestant faith (largely Baptist and Methodist) of their former owners, but have been confined chiefly to minor roles both economically and socially. Inheriting a matriarchal society from their two hundred years of slavery, dwelling apart and, in some states, receiving their schooling apart from white society, the Negro community has developed its own social standards and strong in-group feelings which are having significant political impact.

The third major wave of immigrants was the northern Europeans, chiefly Germans, Swedes, Norwegians, and Danes, and mostly of Lutheran faith. Triggered by the failure of the liberal

German revolt of 1848 and by faltering economic opportunity in the north country, the immigration had two important features: it came before the American Civil War and it settled in the rich farming country of the upper Middle West, chiefly in Illinois, Wisconsin, Iowa, Minnesota, and North and South Dakota. At the same time, the potato famine and political and religious strife in Ireland induced still another wave of movement: the Irish Catholics, who flocked in great numbers to the mill towns of New England and to New York until that city had more Irish than Dublin.

Just before and after the Civil War another and minor wave of immigration came from the Orient when Chinese and Japanese laborers were induced to work in the construction of the transcontinental railroads. Never a significant number on the mainland, they did become the most numerous group in Hawaii.

The last great wave of immigrants was from southern and eastern Europe and came principally in the last decades of the nineteenth and the early years of the twentieth century, before the First World War. Since that time, immigration has been strictly controlled on a national-origins quota basis. Led by Italians, this wave also brought in large numbers of Poles, and some Greeks, Russians, and people from the smaller Balkan states. Attracted by the opportunities in industrial development, these people flocked to the cities of the East and to the mining and steel towns of the Appalachian highlands and the Great Lakes: Pittsburgh, Scranton, Cleveland, Toledo, Detroit, Gary, and Chicago. Few ventured to the Far West and virtually none to the South.

The Far West, as a result, was in the main peopled by eastern Americans, many looking for new land and better economic opportunity, although the Mormons settled Utah in search of religious freedom. A mixture of the eastern settlement pattern, its northern states were settled largely from New England and the upper Middle West, its southern tier from the South.

The politics of the incoming peoples were greatly influenced by the economic opportunities they found and by the domestic issues of the times. Opposed to slavery and favoring the principle of the Homestead Act, the northern European farming immigrants were strongly pro-Union during the Civil War and as a result became overwhelmingly Republican in politics. On the other hand, the Irish immigrants, working in the mills and homes of the dominant English group in the northeast, found themselves unwelcome in the party of Lincoln and rallied around the Democratic banner as the Knights of St. Tammany. The southern European immigrants, also working for wages in the cities and also Catholic, therefore found common cause easier to make with their Irish brethren than with the northern European farmers. With the formation of labor unions in the 1890's and the early decades of the twentieth century, these Democratic groups became a major component of the labor movement.

The Civil War, however, also divided the original English stock. The North, defending the Union, became overwhelmingly Republican. The South sought refuge in the Democratic Party, which it was to dominate for two generations. Postwar alliance between the southern white leaders, virtually all Protestants, and the northern big-city immigrant forces, mostly Catholic, was not long in coming. Alliance clearly was to their mutual advantage for they had a common opponent and a common interest in changing the pattern of political power.

The Republican alliance of the Protestant British and the northern Europeans in the northern states was a solid one, however, and controlled national politics for nearly 70 years. Its demise was heralded in the early 1900's when the farmers of the upper Middle Western and Plains states began to find that their interests—in controlling business monopolies, in the development of natural resources, and in the regulation of railroads and utilities—were in conflict with the interests of their eastern Republican colleagues, who were dominated by manufacturing and trading interests. First the farmers organized, particularly in the Farmers Union, to protect the small farmer and to provide cooperative marketing and buying. Turning to politics, they became Populists, Progressives, Farmer-Laborites, some of them even Socialists. After a generation of groping, many of their sons joined the Democrats in 1932 to establish the New Deal and remake that Party into the present-day majority.

Shifting with them were the Negroes. After the Civil War,

those few Negroes who voted generally were Republican, for Lincoln had freed the slaves. But the party of Lincoln seemed to do little more in their behalf and appeared to some to espouse the cause of the employer and business more than the aspirations of the workingmen. Accordingly, many defected. Franklin Roosevelt's New Deal captured the Negro people en masse. Today, only the Jews are more strongly Democratic.[1]

The New Deal also captured the bulk of the labor movement, which originally had been heavily Republican, when the rise of the industrial-union movement brought new leaders and millions of new union members in steel, automobiles, electrical appliances, textiles, rubber goods, and other mass-production industries. Thus the new majority coalition of the 1930's was a union of big-city immigrant groups, organized labor, the traditional leaders of the South, Negroes, small farmers of the upper Middle West, and western conservationists.

History, then, made the two parties what they are and dictated the patterns of appeals which the two candidates would make in 1960. John F. Kennedy, the grandson of an Irish immigrant, symbolized in a very special way the aspirations of all the more recent immigrant groups which had become the backbone of the working class. Yet he knew enough not to emphasize his religion. Kennedy himself had been raised in the main-stem American schools and understood the concept of separation of church and state. He also understood very well that within his Party only the Irish, Italian, and Polish groups in large numbers shared his religious faith. The northern Europeans, the white voters in the South, the Negroes, and the ideological liberals from the northern British stock were overwhelmingly Protestant and were a substantial majority in his own Party. And he could not overlook the very influential Jewish community. Kennedy, then, needed the support of a very heterogeneous collection of minority groups which he somehow had to weld together behind him.

Richard M. Nixon, on the other hand, was operating from the relatively homogeneous base of Protestant British and northern European stock which comprises a near majority of the popu-

[1] Angus Campbell and others, *The American Voter* (New York: John Wiley & Sons, Inc., 1960), pp. 159-160.

lation. Composed of the majority of business and professional men and including a good proportion of the farm owners, his Party represented the bulk of those families which had found America a place of economic reward and who wished to keep it so. His basic problem was to keep these conservatives behind him while converting to his cause enough of those who wanted change to enable him to win the presidency. The obvious source of new strength for him was the dominant Protestant British stock of the South, which theoretically should have common ideological cause with their brethren in the North. But in 1960, such realignment was foreclosed by the economic aftermath of the Civil War, still felt in the South; by considerations of Party advantage; and by the desire of Southern Congressmen to keep the advantages of seniority. Yet, in part because he shared the religious faith of the South and of many of the disadvantaged groups, Nixon very nearly won anyway.

THE KENNEDY FAMILY APPEAL FOR SPECIAL-GROUP SUPPORT

John F. Kennedy used his family to great advantage in 1960 in appealing to the many economic, social, and nationality groups in the United States. The candidate himself attracted a large number of Catholic voters who ordinarily support Republican candidates, but who saw in Kennedy a symbol of themselves and an opportunity to vindicate their faith.[2] Polish Prince Stanislaw Radziwill, husband of Mrs. Kennedy's sister, campaigned among the Polish-Americans. R. Sargent Shriver, husband of Senator Kennedy's sister, organized and managed the operation of a wide range of special-interest groups for Kennedy and Johnson.

Upon taking control, while still at the Democratic National Convention, the Kennedys discovered that the Democratic National Committee had a Civil Rights Division, largely on paper. The Committee had no units to attract special economic groups or to

---

[2] Philip E. Converse and associates found that 4.3 per cent more Catholics voted for Kennedy than a Democratic candidate normally can expect. See Philip E. Converse and others, "Stability and Change in 1960: A Reinstating Election," *The American Political Science Review*, LV (June, 1961), 269-280.

make special appeals on issues. Sargent Shriver promptly was commissioned to establish as many such groups as might be useful. Some beginnings were made in Los Angeles. Once in Washington, Shriver used the contacts which had been built up by the Democratic Advisory Council to create at least a dozen such groups.

Organizationally, the special units fell into three categories: divisions of the Democratic National Committee, independent citizen organizations which raised their own funds and technically were independent of the Committee, and divisions of Citizens for Kennedy-Johnson. In practice, all kept in touch with Sargent Shriver and all but two or three cleared their expenses through Ralph Dungan or Richard Donohue in Lawrence O'Brien's office at the National Committee.

THE NATIONALITIES DIVISION

The Nationalities Division developed by far the most complex machinery, partly because of the variety of appeals it tried to make and partly to adjust to a sister organization, the Nationalities Division of Citizens for Kennedy-Johnson. Fortunately, the latter organization was set up principally to use the services of John T. R. Godlewski, who had headed the Polish Section of the Republican National Committee in 1956 and who preferred to operate through a Citizens committee. It concentrated almost entirely upon winning the Polish-American vote.

The Nationalities Division proper had four major sections— the German, Italian, Polish, and Spanish—and set up 26 special committees to make appeals, for example, to the Greek, Croatian, Czech, Slovak, Hungarian, Lithuanian, Chinese, Syrian-Lebanese, Armenian, Romanian, Bulgarian, American Indian, and Jewish vote.

Operating principally from a national headquarters in New York, it focused on six objectives in the key states of California, Illinois, Michigan, Minnesota, New Jersey, New York, Ohio, Pennsylvania, Texas, and Wisconsin: (1) voter registration of nationality groups; (2) personal actions by Senator Kennedy to demonstrate interest in nationality groups, consisting of a press conference with editors and publishers of foreign-language publications, a meeting in Hyannis Port with leaders of the principal nationality groups, and his appearance at a few large gatherings of nationality groups; (3) speaking engagements by leading Democrats before such groups; (4) radio tapes by Senator and Mrs. Kennedy; (5) press releases and statements to the foreign-language press and radio; (6) distribution of eight-page two-color illustrated folders in Spanish, Polish, Italian, and German. In addition, efforts were made to appoint state and local nationalities chairmen, to provide background materials on the availability of campaign materials, to supply sample speeches aimed at the interests of special nationality groups, and to get prominent leaders of nationality groups to endorse Mr. Kennedy. Some sections operated more widely than others—the German, for example, in 31 states.

Prince Radziwill proved to be especially popular. He spoke in virtually every major city having a concentration of citizens of Polish descent and appeared particularly with Polish-American Congressmen.

In addition to financial troubles, the Division occasionally ran into other problems. Its report on the Polish-American Congress Convention in Chicago, October 1, 1960, for example, records that just before Mr. Kennedy was to speak word was received that "a Polish priest from the Argentine intended to embarrass the Senator from the floor by shouting disapproval of the Yalta agreements. Immediately, five well-built delegates with large Kennedy buttons were posted surrounding this priest and looking at him while Senator Kennedy delivered his address. The psychological effect of this quelled any desire for spirited embarrassing shouts from the floor."

VIVA KENNEDY

An independent Spanish-language operation stimulated the formation of 200 local-level Viva Kennedy clubs in the 21 states which have concentrations of Spanish-speaking citizens. Its principal activities were registration drives, particularly successful in New York and California; distribution of literature, buttons, automobile bumper stickers, and banners in Spanish; recruiting of eight major platform speakers who were fluent in Spanish to address rallies; preparation of press releases for Spanish-language newspapers;

and the distribution of Spanish-language radio tapes.

Hampered by lack of funds and by a slip in the preparation of a campaign pamphlet between Carlos McCormick, its Washington leader, and Pedro A. Sanjuan, who led the New York effort, it nevertheless involved many Puerto Rican leaders who previously had taken no part in presidential campaigns.

BUSINESSMEN FOR KENNEDY

Businessmen for Kennedy were organized as two independent groups and a division of the National Committee. The key unit was the National Committee of Business and Professional Men and Women for Kennedy-Johnson. Working closely with it was the Businessmen for Kennedy Division of the Democratic National Committee and the Greater Washington Committee of Business and Professional Men and Women for Kennedy-Johnson. Technically, the businessmen's national committee headquartered in Chicago and was chaired by Governor Luther Hodges of North Carolina. Its Washington affairs were handled by Herbert Klotz, who served as the staff director for the entire program.

Unlike most of the committees, the businessmen's group was an important source of funds. At least $500,000 was collected by the national businessmen's committee, $34,800 by the Greater Washington group alone. In addition to covering its own expenses, the committee was able to pick up several large campaign bills, at least one for television time.

Its principal other activities were the formation of thirty-five state-wide committees, the preparation and dissemination of campaign literature aimed at business and professional people, and the preparation of economic and business statements for Senator Kennedy which were submitted to Myer Feldman for clearance.

LABOR'S COMMITTEE

Labor's Committee for the Election of Kennedy and Johnson made no attempt to form a mass citizens' movement. Its purpose instead was to stimulate the regular Committees on Political Education of the AFL-CIO and other labor units to get out the vote in the campaign. Organized late, on September 20, it was composed of 60 top labor leaders and was led by George M. Harrison, Grand President of the Brotherhood of Railway Clerks. Co-Vice-Chairmen were Arthur Goldberg, then counsel for the AFL-CIO and the United Steel Workers, and Joseph D. Keenan, Secretary of the International Brotherhood of Electrical Workers. Its list included most of the famous leaders of the labor movement, among them Walter Reuther of the automobile workers, James B. Carey of the electrical workers, and David J. McDonald of the steel workers. A special women's division was headed by Esther Peterson.

Operating on a labor-supplied budget of $45,000, most of which dribbled in after the campaign was over, Labor's Committee distributed two million pieces of literature; circulated prints of a film, "Kennedy Speaks to Labor"; pressed a national "Get Out the Vote" campaign complete with prizes for communities and districts making the best increase over 1956; channeled requests for automobile bumper strips, pictures, and signs to the Democratic National Committee; prepared 1,500 copies of a long-playing record of political songs, "Ballads for Ballots"; and placed "Don't Miss the Bus" car cards in street cars and buses in 18 of the nation's largest industrial centers.

FARMERS FOR KENNEDY-JOHNSON

Farmers for Kennedy-Johnson set up units in as many states as possible and used an elaborate system of regional directors to coordinate activities and to provide special advice in particular commodity areas. The state and local organizations stimulated farm rallies for Kennedy, participated in local arrangements for his visits, and encouraged turnouts of local citizens. Local groups also inserted paid advertising in weekly newspapers, distributed Farmers for Kennedy-Johnson literature, supplied speakers before local groups, raised funds, and talked up Kennedy for President—a very important technique in rural areas.

A series of printed and mimeographed pamphlets and statements on many farm problems was prepared and mailed to a rather extensive list of farmers and persons interested in agriculture. The central staff also handled heavy correspondence on farm problems which flowed into the National Committee and prepared farm speeches and statements for Senator Kennedy, for clearance through Myer Feldman.

Organizationally, "Farmers" operated as a Division of the Democratic National Committee. It was stimulated by Sargent Shriver and cleared budget requests through Ralph Dungan and Richard Donohue. Its ten-man Executive Committee was headed by Claude Wickard, former Secretary of Agriculture. A nine-man professional staff operated the Washington office.

SENIOR CITIZENS FOR KENNEDY

Senior Citizens for Kennedy was designed to rally the supporters of Medicare to the Kennedy bandwagon. Its chairman was Representative Aime J. Forand, sponsor of the bill to provide medical care for the aged through the Social Security system, and its staff director was Dr. Blue Carstenson, who now is Executive Director of the National Council of Senior Citizens, Inc., Medicare's chief lobbying organization.

The unit was proposed by Carstenson to Ralph Dungan, who cleared its establishment with Lawrence O'Brien. Thus Senior Citizens operated as a branch of the Democratic National Committee, although it maintained liaison with Citizens for Kennedy-Johnson through Fred Dutton and portrayed itself publicly as a nonpartisan citizen effort. Its $30,000 budget, provided by the Democratic National Committee, permitted the hiring of two professional and clerical people and the dissemination of four main pieces of literature.

State organizations of Senior Citizens for Kennedy were formed in forty states and special efforts were made in five more. Many local clubs were formed so that 490 state and local chairmen served during the campaign and more than 35,000 senior citizens joined local Kennedy clubs.

Senior Citizens turned up one special asset: many of its members had time to give to the campaign. Carstenson was able to recruit full-time volunteers of top quality in Washington, including a retired Congressman. State and local committees had similar experiences where Senior Citizen Club members proved available to man Democratic Party campaign headquarters during daytime hours, stuff envelopes, do telephoning, and render other services.

An estimated 17,500 retired citizens contributed volunteer services at all levels during the campaign.

To convert the older voters, who traditionally tend to vote Republican, more than 3,500,000 pieces of literature were distributed, of which 700,000 went in direct mailings to them. Drop-in centers were established. Eighty-one Social Security rallies attracted 64,000 senior citizens. Congressman Forand made 22 radio and television appearances. These efforts, plus paid advertising in three states, especially California, led Carstenson to estimate that 5 million older Americans heard their message.

CIVIL RIGHTS DIVISION

A Civil Rights Division to capture 80 per cent of the Negro vote was set up under the personal direction of Sargent Shriver. Organizationally a division of the Democratic National Committee, it quickly ran into personality problems as several of its leaders jockeyed for position. The effective leader was Harris Wofford, who served as Campaign Coordinator for Civil Rights. His key supporter was Louis Martin, editor of the *Chicago Defender,* a major Negro newspaper, who handled press and public relations.

Although an attempt was made to establish a field organization, and state coordinators were appointed in 33 states, both Wofford and Martin acknowledged that it was ineffective. The main achievements were in publicity and propaganda, where an effort was made to identify Kennedy with Negro aspirations.

Two main themes were beamed to Negro voters: First, the anti-Catholic attacks on Senator Kennedy were stemming from the same sources as anti-Negro attacks. Second, Kennedy was in the Roosevelt tradition.

To identify Kennedy with Negroes, the Division distributed more than two million pamphlets showing the Senator surrounded by prominent Negroes and reporting his voting record and his concern for civil rights. A key event in this effort was the National Conference on Constitutional Rights, held in New York on October 11 and 12. Senator Kennedy delivered a principal address to 400 community leaders from 42 states, which was given wide distribution.

The second, much more dramatic, and possibly far more influential effort to show Kennedy's identification with Negro goals was Wofford's idea that Senator Kennedy call Mrs. Martin Luther King when, just ten days before the election, the Reverend Mr. King was sentenced to four months' hard labor in the Reidsville (Georgia) State Penitentiary for participation in a "sit-in" demonstration in a department-store restaurant in Atlanta. This call and Robert Kennedy's follow-up call to presiding Judge Mitchell appear to have helped bring about Reverend King's prompt release and are viewed by Louis Martin as having "triggered a new wave of pro-Kennedy sentiment among Negroes." The Reverend Mr. King's father, a highly influential Negro leader in his own right, immediately switched his support to Kennedy. Lou Martin and the Civil Rights Division promptly followed with one million pieces of literature and personal telegrams to Party workers across the nation in the last week of the campaign. Theodore White points out that this one phone call may have tipped the scales in the election.[3]

COMMUNITY RELATIONS DIVISION

The Community Relations Division was assigned the touchy religious issue. In his West Virginia primary defeat of Senator Hubert Humphrey, John F. Kennedy had set the pattern he would use. He would state unequivocally that he was dedicated to the separation of church and state. He would reiterate the constitutional principle that no man should be denied high office because of his religious beliefs. And he would imply that a vote for Kennedy was a vote for tolerance.

Two more religiously tolerant men than Congregationalist Hubert Humphrey and Quaker Richard Nixon could hardly have been found as opponents. Yet both were by such strategy forced to accept religion as an issue and virtually compelled to endorse the Kennedy position.

Kennedy's key move in handling the "religious issue" was his

---

[3] See Theodore White, *The Making of the President* (New York: Atheneum House, 1961), pp. 385-387 for a detailed narrative of the incident and an analysis of its political significance.

statement to the Greater Houston Ministerial Association on Monday, September 12. In one crisp paragraph he stated his case, earnestly and sincerely:

I believe in an America where the separation of church and state is absolute—where no Catholic prelate would tell the President (should he be Catholic) how to act, and no Protestant minister would tell his parishioners for whom to vote—where no church or church school is granted any public funds or political preference—and where no man is denied public office merely because his religion differs from the President who might appoint him or the people who might elect him.[4]

Followed by an open question-and-answer period, the talk was well received. The Community Relations Division promptly, adroitly, and quietly proceeded to exploit the candidate's position to the full. Film clips and tape recordings of the talk were widely circulated to television and radio stations. Pamphlets reproducing the speech were printed in large quantities and widely distributed.

THE YOUTH EFFORT

Young Citizens for Kennedy-Johnson and Students for Kennedy-Johnson operated jointly as adjuncts of Citizens for Kennedy-Johnson but in close cooperation with the regular Young Democrats Division of the National Committee. Richard Murphy, permanent staff director for the Young Democrats, coordinated the entire youth effort.

A series of state-wide Kennedy car caravans during the last two weeks of the campaign was their unique contribution. A special national caravan from Washington, D.C., to New York was nearly canceled by confusion in the budget clearing process. Otherwise, the Young Democrats and their auxiliaries concentrated on supplying manpower for registration drives, county-fair booths, telephone committees, election-day activities, Dollars for Democrats drives, and the "You Decide" discussion program on college campuses. Some 700 campus clubs were established and 350 Kennedy-Johnson Teen Clubs.

THE WOMEN'S DIVISION

The Women's Division of the Democratic National Committee,

[4] U.S. Congress, Senate, *Freedom of Communications,* Vol. I (Washington: Government Printing Office, 1961), p. 208.

with a permanent staff in being, handled women's activities without the establishment of any special campaign units. Basically providing support and volunteers to assist main-line programs, their principal activities were holding a "Strategy for Victory" luncheon on October 29, supplying women speakers, aiding Dollars for Democrats, pushing the Voter Registration Drive, and organizing listening parties for the great debates. The scheduling of appearances of Kennedy family women and of Mrs. Lyndon Johnson was handled separately but in close cooperation with the Women's Division.

SMALLER SPECIAL-GROUP ACTIVITIES

Five other small groups played a minor role in attracting special-interest groups.

The Kennedy-Johnson Natural Resources Advisory Committee was a unique unit which operated out of the Congressional office of its Chairman, Representative Frank E. Smith of Mississippi. Confined to a $2,000 budget, it engaged primarily in the dissemination of a series of five pamphlets on natural resources, the last two of which were produced directly by the Kennedy Research Team. Most of the work was done by Congressman Smith himself, using his own office personnel as volunteers.

Educators for Kennedy-Johnson was set up principally to counteract the efforts of Arthur Peterson, the Republican National Committee Faculty Fellow, who had amassed a sizable list of college professors who were willing to aid the Republicans. Limited to a $1,200 budget, it developed a list of 15,000 Democratic educators to whom it sent one mailing containing campaign literature and a plea for funds.

The Urban Affairs Division sought the support of city officials, principally by promoting an Urban Affairs Conference in Pittsburgh on October 10, 1960. Working closely with an allied group, Mayors for Kennedy-Johnson, it prepared a special kit of mimeographed leaflets on urban issues, handled correspondence on urban questions, and promoted telephone campaigns to get out the vote in public-housing areas. Uniquely, it worked very closely with the office of Democratic National Committee Chairman Henry M. Jackson.

Special Projects, under Michigan State Chairman Neil Staebler, filled requests from Congressional, state, and local candidates for personal endorsements from Senator Kennedy, pictures with Senator Kennedy, and information on campaign issues. Requests for material not already in printed form were referred to the Research Division of the Democratic National Committee. In addition, Staebler pushed his "You Decide" discussion program. Some 2,000 flip charts were sold, principally on problems of Senior Citizens and Farmers. Others on Civil Rights, Opportunities for Youth, Peace, Education, and Housing received lesser emphasis.

Veterans for Kennedy-Johnson mailed invitations to veterans to work for Mr. Kennedy but had no system to use volunteers. Also assigned correspondence from veterans, it failed to answer their letters. Off to a bad start, it changed leadership in midcampaign, but never was effective.

JOHNSON GROUP APPEALS IN 1964

For the 1964 campaign, some committees for special-interest groups will again have to be established by the Democratic candidates. Only the Young Democrats and the Women's Division and the Civil Rights unit have been carried over and these on a minimum basis.

Special efforts to win support from Negro, farm, labor, business, and conservation groups are likely to generate special divisions or separate citizens' groups. Although early polls in 1964 showed Johnson's strength as formidable in all walks of life, his ability as a vote getter in the urban industrial states of the North and East, in the Republican heartland of the upper Middle West, and in the Far West was still unproved. Special committees which would permit prominent Negroes to support Johnson without simultaneously appearing to support traditional southern Democratic leaders clearly are essential. Similar citizens committees of business, professional, and farm leaders obviously would be useful.

With the Cabinet to support the campaign effort, however, separate committees in many areas may prove unnecessary. The mailing of materials prepared by the Cabinet officers to appeal to special groups and the scheduling of speaking assignments by Administration leaders could be handled directly by the National Committee.

Many of these decisions should be made by early summer, 1964, but some may come after the close of the National Convention. In any event, improvisation, in the usual fashion, appears likely to be common.

THE 1960 REPUBLICAN EFFORTS TO REACH SPECIAL GROUPS

From 1860 to 1932 the Republican Party was clearly the majority party in American politics. During this period, its Party leadership did not concern itself, in the main, with particular programs to woo the so-called special-interest groups. The Party base was broad; it could count on the support of a good portion of the farm population, the academic community, small business and large business, and even a sizable segment of the labor vote.

But with the coming of the Great Depression and the New Deal in the 1930's, the Republican Party lost its position of preponderance; it became the minority party. Although the presidential elections of 1952 and 1956 gave an unprecedented majority to the Republican national standard bearer, Dwight D. Eisenhower, congressional, state-house, and court-house election returns indicated that the Democratic Party was, at mid-century, still the stronger of the two major parties.

Republican Party leaders realized that attempts to enlist the support of voters in special groups must be improved and enlarged in areas where rudimentary programs existed and initiated where necessary.

The Republican National Committee's organization chart for the Eisenhower reelection campaign demonstrates the breadth of the appeals to special-interest groups which were extant at the committee in 1956. A Special Activities Board, under the direction of the Assistant to the Chairman, Miss Bertha S. Adkins, included a Minority Division, a Veteran's Division, an Ethnic Division, the Young Republicans, and the Women's Division. The Campaign Division, under Robert Humphries, sponsored programs in the fields of Agriculture, Nationalities, Labor, and Healing Arts.

By 1960 the National Committee had developed additional interest-group programs for Senior Republicans, the academic community, and business (particularly those who had received instruction in practical-politics courses in their home community).

The pattern for most of these special activities was identical. First came the identification phase, then the recruitment, the programing, and finally the attempt to involve members of these groups in productive campaign work. Some of the programs stressed assistance to congressional candidates in "marginal districts" as well as assistance to the national ticket. The assumption was made throughout all of these programs that the state and local organizations would benefit, too, from the broadening of the Party base.

Most of the special-interest divisions were year-round, continuous activities at the National Committee. In 1960 these were Agriculture, Labor, Nationalities, Minorities, Arts and Sciences, and Senior Republicans. The Veteran's Division, on the other hand, was resurrected only for the 1960 campaign. (It is true that the Women's Division is a kind of special-interest division also, but since it services such a large and broad constituency its role and approach is somewhat different from the smaller "auxiliaries" or special-interest groups mentioned above. The same thing applies to the Young Republicans and the National Federation of Republican Women's Clubs. Strictly speaking, these latter two organizations are not an integral part of the National Committee staff. They are separate from the Committee staff but are housed in the same offices.)

The report of the 1956 Republican National Committee's Labor Program illustrates the usual pattern of approach taken by the special-interest divisions. This report reveals that months before the actual initiation of the campaign, the Labor Division personnel had been occupied with the identification of Republican labor leaders and union members. Much to the surprise of some, they had found a considerable number actually active as Republican Party leaders.

Labor committees were then organized for the 1956 campaign on the county and city levels in twenty-five states. These labor committees ranged from 20 to 5,000 members. In some of the highly industrialized states as many as fifty such committees were formed. Other states had no local labor committees but did organize state-wide committees and, according to the report, a "minimum state labor campaign" to develop strength among laboring men and women for the National Republican ticket.

After identification and recruitment, the third step is program development. In this case, the major program consisted of meetings, banquets, and television and radio debates, the use of sound trucks, rank-and-file endorsements for the Republican ticket, all of which were organized and supported by the labor committees.

In addition, each of the special-interest groups ordinarily develops campaign materials stressing the candidates' concern and accomplishments in each of the special fields. Appropriate pictures of the candidates with prominent interest-group members are standard. It should be noted that to accomplish the recruitment phase of their general programs these divisions are often authorized to hire and pay a number of men for field organization and operations. Thus a special-interest group can be a very expensive campaign item for the National Committee during a presidential year.

As the 1960 campaign drew near, it appeared that the special-interest divisions at the National Committee would be asked to function as they had in 1956. But because the campaign was not directed from the National Committee the special-interest organizations in the Committee Headquarters tended to be overlooked or bypassed in the actual conduct of the campaign.

Although appeals to specialized groups were, indeed, framed by the Nixon-Lodge headquarters, the corresponding organizations at the National Committee were often not consulted and in some cases not used at all. The Farm group at the Republican National Committee appeared to be the only group, other than the Young Republicans, which was able to maintain a field staff in the 1960 presidential election. The National Committee was never able, adequately, to exploit the contacts which it has within the major labor organizations. The Minorities Division and the Labor Division were not allocated funds, and the persons responsible for maintaining contacts within these two groups were, as a consequence, literally hamstrung during most of the campaign.

Certainly this neglect was not the intent. It undoubtedly resulted from the organizational problems mentioned earlier in Chapter V. The costly effect of poor organization in this field is seen in a Convention incident. A good deal of effort had gone into preparation for a dinner honoring a large number of labor leaders and union-member delegates to the National Convention. The Vice President had been invited, along with other prominent Party leaders who would be in Chicago at that time. Some top Party leaders did appear. Governor Rockefeller, for example, came early and stayed late. The Vice President, however, was too busy with an overloaded convention schedule. He was unable to make even a brief appearance at this important labor dinner.

Over in the National Volunteers for Nixon-Lodge headquarters a different kind of approach had been decided upon—a direct-mail campaign. Consequently, mailing lists were purchased for a wide variety of interest groups and letters requesting support for the Nixon-Lodge campaign went to vast numbers of individuals within these groups.

Such letters of invitation, for example, were mailed to 232,000 doctors, 19,000 civic leaders, 100,000 scholars, 100,000 retired service officers, 200,000 veterans, 232,000 lawyers, and even to several thousand certified public accountants.

As affirmative responses were received, SNAP-packs (mentioned in Chapter VI) were mailed out to each respondent with the hope that the campaign material contained therein would be distributed and that the Nixon-Lodge treasury would benefit from contributions sent by the pack recipients. A report to Nixon-Lodge Volunteers division heads on the accumulative donations and the replies received from these various interest groups was issued daily by the Nixon-Lodge headquarters. Late in the campaign the Volunteers had tallied up roughly 18,000 replies from doctors, 1,500 from civic leaders, slightly fewer than 3,000 from scholars, a like number from retired service officers, over 5,000 from lawyers, and roughly 1,000 from the accountants.

This direct-mail approach, however, was not the only effort expended by the Nixon-Lodge Volunteers headquarters to develop support from various interest groups. The Volunteers also had organizers in the field to strengthen support among farmers and entered into some joint programing with National Committee personnel in the fields of Nationalities, Veterans, and Arts and Sciences.

It should be pointed out also that there were two distinct phases to the direct-mail campaign among special-interest groups. The direct person-to-person approach has been mentioned. The second aspect was an attempt to form state and local special-interest organizations throughout the country.

Thus the names of the nearly 3,000 academicians who had responded affirmatively to the direct mailing were supplied to state leaders of Scholars for Nixon-Lodge where such clubs existed. The clubs would then invite these interested persons to participate in their activities. A letter from the Southern California Scholars for Nixon and Lodge illustrates the kind of program these special-interest groups developed and how they used individuals suggested to them by the National Nixon-Lodge Volunteers headquarters. In some cases the corresponding National Committee Division supplied names as well.

A memo to one of the authors from E. H. "Ned" Harding illustrates the conceptualization of the utilization of interested scholars, doctors, veterans, and other categories by the Nixon-Lodge staff.

With our other committees we have been referring all those who want to participate in volunteer activities or to work on Mr. Nixon's behalf to the Volunteers chairman or to state representatives in their own state. Please don't hesitate to refer any of your people to organizational men in their state. Their job is to put all interested persons either in an advisory capacity at the state level or in a more active capacity in their local communities.

Where there were strong and extensive Nixon-Lodge state organizations and where respected and energetic leaders could be found to head up the various state Volunteers auxiliaries, the direct-mail approach proved effective. Unfortunately, such state organizations were the exception rather than the rule and the hurried attempt to recruit prominent leaders of special-interest groups was not always successful. What happened in too many states was that thousands of persons interested in assisting the campaign never were called upon to help.

This shortcoming points to a basic problem in the develop-

September 9, 1960

Dear Colleague:

Many scholars throughout the nation are uniting behind Richard
M. Nixon and Henry Cabot Lodge for the offices of President and
Vice-President of the United States. We hope that you are or
will become an active participant in this movement, without regard for your present or past political party preference.

We believe that the Nixon-Lodge team is particularly well-quali-
fied to serve our nation:

　　1. Their experience in international affairs best equips them
to deal with the wide-ranging aspects of American foreign
relations.

　　2. Their record of firmness in dealing with the threat of
Russian Communism is heartening and inspiring.

　　3. Their philosophy of individual freedom is in keeping
with our free academic tenets and sense of personal responsibility.

　　4. They are at home intellectually in an academic environ-
ment, and will be attentive to the view of scholars.

　　5. Their dedication to individual liberty is combined with
their high sense of social responsibility.

　　6. We can have confidence in these candidates because of
what they have done, because of what they are, and because
of the purposeful leadership we know they will provide.

If you share our confidence, we hope you will discuss this letter
with your colleagues, many of whom are receiving a copy, and with
the members of your family. As an important and respected member
of the community you are charged with a clear responsibility to
make known your judgements on this subject.

　　　　　　　　　　　　　　Yours sincerely,

　　　　Carl Q. Cristol　　　　　　　　　　George C. S. Benson

　　　　　　　　　　Co-Chairmen

A letter from Southern California Scholars for Nixon and Lodge. The margin carried a warning in solid capitals: "Please Remember: You can not
vote if you are not presently registered. The last date for registration is
September 15."

ment of political auxiliary groups. Ostensibly the purpose of the
groups is to broaden the base of party support. But more is required than simply identifying known Republicans among these
groups and then flooding them with literature.

If a doctor, lawyer, scholar, or labor leader goes so far as to commit himself to work for a candidate or a party, he then expects that opportunities will be offered him which will allow his energy and/or his talents to be used. Failure to offer them has been one of the major weaknesses in Republican auxiliary-group organization at the national level. The weakness, fortunately, is one that some state Republican Party leaders have noted. It can be expected that the serious reconsideration of the very premise upon which some of these programs have operated will lead to substantially different organizational approaches in 1964.

ATTRACTING SPECIAL-INTEREST GROUPS TO THE REPUBLICANS IN 1964

Unlike the Democratic National Committee, the Republicans have maintained at least token forces in most of their special-interest divisions since 1960. The work of the Agriculture, Labor, Minorities, and Arts and Sciences Divisions has gone on unabated and even though the Nationalities Division was not staffed continuously, volunteer and intermittent staffing has made possible a continuation of a program in that field.

The Women's Division, which, as we have seen, has been actively involved in a wide variety of political-action programs, is in 1964 particularly interested in recruitment of support from special-interest groups. A program called GROW (Grass Roots Organization of Women) is not designed to draw membership away from existing Party auxiliaries but to direct previously uncommitted women to such appropriate groups as do exist. The Women's Division program is divided into six special activities including: Women in Minority Groups; Women in Nationality Groups; Farm Women; Women in Education; Women in the Labor Force; and Women in Business and the Professions. The root problem remains, however. After identification and referral, *what* are these people going to do that will make them feel that they are really involved in worthwhile campaign efforts? This question remains the key to the successful development of auxiliary groups in national campaigns. It will require careful planning and local and state organizations which are prepared for the kind of influx of volunteers which auxiliary group activity produces.

And the local and state organizations have indeed been working on this very problem.

The Big City (Bliss) Report made particular mention of ways in which to improve the Republican position with respect to special-interest groups. These suggestions, along with recent conference sessions at the State Chairmen's Association, forecast organizational improvements involving effective utilization of volunteers from special-interest groups.

A Bliss subcommittee on Labor, Business, Professional, and Independent Groups, for example, recommended five general steps to be taken in those areas: (1) Develop realistic, regular communication with the action leaders of both labor and business groups. (2) On this foundation, build a responsible relationship with labor and business. (3) Provide immediate, meaningful assignments within the Party and its affiliates for volunteers from these groups. (4) Give recognition and express appreciation for support and interest. (5) Give strong Party leadership, and follow through with programing, staff, and budget.

The Subcommittee on Nationalities and Minorities stressed the importance of organizing metropolitan-area minorities and nationalities committees long before the advent of the actual presidential campaign; and the Subcommittee also stressed the need to make such activities permanent.

Pointing toward the 1964 campaign, the Nationalities and Minorities Subcommittee suggested specific means by which state and local organizations might improve their programs. Among these suggestions were:

1. A policy of recognizing the traditional observances of each ethnic group should be instituted through regular use of special messages from Republican VIPs.

2. A special *Speakers Bureau* of prominent national, Congressional, state and local Republican officials should be developed for key engagements at conventions, banquets, commemorative occasions, and regular meetings of language-culture organizations.

3. *The Foreign Language Press* must be contacted regularly to develop effective working relations with them. This activity could be coordinated with appearances and press releases to cover the activities of the above-mentioned Speakers Bureau.

4. *Foreign Language Radio Stations* in big cities offer similar opportunities for broad coverage. The large number of foreign language broadcasts found in major metropolitan areas provide the same relationship to their listeners that the press does to those who must use the foreign language press. Therefore this channel also must be used to the greatest possible extent.

5. Republican Party supporters should be encouraged to utilize these communication media in every possible way.

6. Party organizations should develop advertising budgets providing for regular periodic advertising in all foreign language communication media.

Finally, the Republican Workshops, strongly supported by Republicans of such diverse outlooks as Nelson Rockefeller and Barry Goldwater, will probably increase their role in 1964. These are groups of men and women who meet to learn Republican Party principles, purposes, and structure in series of discussion sessions conducted by a trained leader with a prepared outline. Increasingly strong, vocal, and effective since 1955, active in twenty states and rapidly increasing in membership, they have taken a sophisticated approach that has appealed especially to issue-oriented people deeply concerned over the functioning of the American two-party system. The Workshops cut across many of the groups already mentioned. In many states they are conducted jointly with Women's Republican Clubs; in others they operate as separate auxiliaries.

There is evidence that a "new look" is being given the traditional approach to special-interest groups in both parties. The deep concern over this problem on the part of such outstanding state leaders as Republican Ray C. Bliss of Ohio and Democrat Neil Staebler of Michigan has virtually assured a transformation in these programs. The basic difference between the new and the old will be (1) the establishment of *continuous* rather than *sporadic* activities in these fields; and (2) *realistic programs* in which special-interest volunteers can be fitted into the parties' over-all program both between and during election periods rather than *idealistic promises* of campaign utilization that never can be fulfilled.

Chapter VIII

Presenting the Candidate

 A candidate's image can make him or break him. If he can convince the people that he has both the personality and the political philosophy to understand their wishes, as Dwight D. Eisenhower and Franklin D. Roosevelt were able to do, he can be unbeatable. If, instead, he uncovers flaws in these qualities, he is headed for defeat.

THE STRATEGY OF IMAGE AND NAME FAMILIARITY

What is "image" anyway? Image has a special meaning to political professionals. It refers to the impressions a candidate leaves with the public about his personality and his philosophy of government.

Personality can be all important. The American people expect their Presidents to be paragons of virtue. First of all they must be warm, outgoing, "human." They must enjoy people and understand them. This touch or spark has marked all the recent Presidents.

Next, a candidate for President must be virtuous. One major mark of virtue is having a happy family life, with an adoring wife and children, and even grandchildren. Other marks of virtue are honesty, trustworthiness, and a record of having opposed "machine" politicians. The virtue of a candidate is suspect if he has stooped to mud slinging or has accepted large sums of money or other substantial gifts.

Third, a candidate must be "big enough for the job." He must, as some eastern politicians put it, have "heft." Fundamentally, being "big" means having experience, competence, wisdom, and understanding equal to the job. The candidate should have discharged some very important assignments with distinction. He should be alert, adroit, and sensible in his public speaking. Often their actions show men are "big" or "little." Little men act little by name-dropping, by parading their achievements before others, by being condescending to those whom they regard as beneath them, by obviously seeking honors and rewards beyond their merits. Big men behave like Abraham Lincoln—humble, modest, concerned and sympathetic with the problems of even the weakest of their fellow men.

A candidate's philosophy of government can also seal his fate. He must fit the times. If the times change, as they did for Herbert Hoover, and he does not change, as Hoover did not, defeat may follow.

Generally in American politics the moderate center has been the path to victory. Candidates of clearly liberal or conservative hue, like William Jennings Bryan and Alf Landon, have mounted interesting but disastrous campaigns. Yet, when the time is ripe, a candidate can take a bold position and lead the nation, as Lincoln did against secession and as Franklin D. Roosevelt did against depression.

Once a major candidate has created a firm public image of his political philosophy, as Senator Barry Goldwater and Governor Nelson Rockefeller had done by the spring of 1964, he usually is stuck with it. If the times fit his image, he may receive the call. If they don't, he is more than likely to see the nomination pass him by.

"Name familiarity" is professional jargon used to describe the extent to which the general public knows even a candidate's name, let alone anything he stands for. It rests on the simple logic that a voter has to know a candidate's name before he can decide to vote for him.

Name familiarity is acquired by repetition. The more often a voter sees or hears a candidate's name, the more likely he is to remember it. The more he remembers the candidate's name, the more likely he is to remember other things about the candidate and, hopefully, the more likely he is to vote for him.

The psychological importance of repetition in making a name familiar to large numbers of people and the psychological importance of such familiarity with a name as a condition for an individual's identifying with it in some way have been well demonstrated by brand-name advertising. Nationally advertised products will be purchased, even at a higher price, by people who sincerely believe these products are better than unadvertised alternatives of higher quality.

The lessons of repetition in brand-name advertising have been given practical application by professional politicians. For the price of one 30-minute telecast which may attract but a limited viewing audience, a candidate can flash his name on the screen many times for many days in 20-second spot announcements which the viewing audience will be far more likely to see. In 1960, both presidential candidates used numerous spot announcements and avoided using formal 30-minute studio programs to present their names and views.

ADVERTISING AND THE USE OF THE MASS MEDIA

No presidential candidate can meet all the people. He must depend upon advertising and the mass media to carry his name and his image to most of his fellow citizens.

Presidential candidates use the mass media to establish a public image in two main ways. They appear on television and radio and they make news and buy advertising space in the press.

In 1960, the Republican National Committee employed Campaign Associates and the Democratic National Committee retained Guild, Bascom, and Bonfigli to handle national advertising for the presidential campaign. Both firms handled most of the time and space buying for their clients. Each party paid nearly a quarter of all its campaign expenditures to its advertising agency. The Republican National Committee paid out $2,269,578 while the Democratic National Committee spent $2,413,227.[1]

[1] Herbert E. Alexander, *Financing the 1960 Election* (Princeton, N.J.: Citizens' Research Foundation, 1962), p. 31.

Nevertheless, advertising agencies do not run national presidential campaigns. Some agencies do, however, suggest advertising programs which become a basic part of presidential campaigns.

In 1952, for example, Rosser Reeves, a representative of a small New York advertising firm, strongly recommended a television campaign for General Eisenhower featuring maximum penetration through the use of numerous short spot announcements. The General himself was to appear in each announcement.

Three basic arguments were advanced for such an innovation. The cost would be low per thousand homes reached. Spots, unlike full-length programs, would reach people not already for a candidate. Spots would allow concentrated efforts in the relatively few critical states which could not be counted in either candidate's column.

Reeves, a volunteer, got agreement on his plan from Walter Williams, the national chairman of Citizens for Eisenhower, and from John Hay Whitney, the chief fund raiser for the Eisenhower organization. Ultimately, fifty spot announcements of twenty seconds each were prepared and approximately $1,500,000 was spent on their presentation. The contents of the spots were statements of concern and general promises, each of which helped reinforce the favorable image of experience, kindliness, and sincerity which Eisenhower enjoyed as a result of his World War II command positions.

Today, New York advertising agencies continue to remind political leaders who are interested of the fact that television can play a crucial role in any major election. Speaking to the Republican National Committee in January, 1962, Carroll Newton, vice president of Batten, Barton, Durstine and Osborn, said:

It is estimated that 9 out of 10 homes in the United States will have television this fall, and that the average one of the homes will have a set tuned in with someone looking at it more than 5 hours every average day.

During the evening hours 6 out of 10 families are watching, with about 1.7 adults at the TV set at any given moment.

Assume there are three television stations in the city in which you reside, and assume that your candidate is on television at a particular minute between 8 and 9 in the evening on each of these stations. In that one television appearance, your candidate has shown himself—practically in the flesh—to more than half of the potential voters in his constituency.

And people seen on television are living, breathing, alive individuals to the viewers, even though the candidates themselves find that hard to believe as they look at that unwinking eye of the TV camera.

Television represents the sole opportunity of presenting a flesh-and-blood candidate to *all* the voters who will or will not elect him.

While it is not true that TV is the deciding factor in all elections, it *is* true that TV *can* make the difference in a close election.

In the first week of October, 1956, a national sample of 2,400 eligible voters was asked where they learned most about the campaign. The survey showed that TV was the most important source of information by a rather wide margin—49 per cent vs. 38 per cent for newspapers.

On the farm—it was TV by a substantial margin. 56 per cent of the farmers said they learned most about the campaign from TV. A significant breakdown was made by income groups. This indicated that as incomes decrease people rely more heavily on TV—and it is in lower income areas where the Republican party has traditionally had greater difficulty in attracting voters. Television was the major source of campaign information to 58 per cent of the people with average incomes.

At the time this study was made 37.7 million U.S. families had TV sets. It is estimated that more than 49 million families will have TV sets in October, 1962, and the importance of TV will be about 25% greater than these figures show.

These surveys strongly suggest that you cannot afford to allow your candidate to be seen at his best less often than his opponent.

The fact that television does exert a tremendous influence over voter choice may not be questioned by many in 1964. But should it? Consider Washington, with his ill-fitting false teeth and smallpox scars; Lincoln, with his heavy features and warts; or Jefferson, often described as having "shifty eyes"—would they do well in a modern television-centered campaign? Was John Kennedy's handsome young face more important in his victory than his articulation of views on crucial issues? Or did Nixon's appearance on television detract from the content of his expositions?

Answers differ. But some reporters have recorded the fact that interviews with voters in the crucial Wisconsin and West Virginia primaries indicated a universally favorable reaction to John Kennedy's television appearances even if that reaction were grudging.

Certainly television does impose new demands and offers new opportunities to the individual politician. For the political party it means that it, too, has new responsibilities as well as opportunities.

Before the turn of the century, every effort was made to secure a candidate who was at ease in small groups of powerful political leaders and who also could be eloquently persuasive when facing a crowd of twelve to fifteen thousand people, many of whom would commit themselves following the speech or debate. In the 1960's, a party looks for a man who is at ease, articulate, and attractive when facing the television cameras and who likewise can spark the massive gatherings of a purely partisan nature. He must be an expositor as well as an orator.

Television is unquestionably extremely important in projecting the *symbolic* image of a candidate. Another kind of image, however, is of major concern to influential community leaders and hence to party strategists: the candidate's *instrumental* qualities. The symbolic image of a candidate is the voter's inference as to what kind of president the aspirant would make in general: his basic social and intellectual qualities. The instrumental image is the voters' inference as to what the candidate, as president, will do in certain substantive fields under various conditions.

The importance of the instrumental image has grown with the ever expanding number and variety of interest groups. While television exalts the factor of personality, the interest-group leader wants to know a candidate's views in a given area of political concern. The candidate must, then, from time to time eschew the capsule comment and the deliberate dodge and endeavor, instead, to spell out his over-all philosophy for a particular constituency. The occasion may come when the candidate speaks to the national convention of an interest group, or it may be made by the preparation and dissemination of policy statements. How the 1960 presidential candidates reacted, in general, to the problem of image projection, both symbolic and instrumental, will now be examined.

PRESENTING RICHARD NIXON IN 1960

As Richard M. Nixon prepared for the 1960 presidential campaign, his image was a matter of major concern. There were many favorable aspects. Among them were his impassioned rebuttal to Premier Khrushchev, in the famous Moscow "kitchen debate"; his unflinching courage in the face of a barrage of rocks, sticks, and human spit during his tour of Latin America; his intelligent handling of the affairs of state during President Eisenhower's illnesses; his stubborn insistence on following through on every lead given him in the famous Hiss case. Nixon's advisors felt that these aspects of his image should be reinforced.

But another side was negative. It reflected the strong reactions to some of the tactics Nixon employed during his first campaigns for the House and for the Senate, the charge of having used unfair accusations against opponents in both campaigns. He had been labeled by some as the "parlor McCarthy," and the label and the image stuck.

Nixon's biographers have pointed out that the complete story of his House and Senate campaigns is involved and two-sided. There was no denying, however, that Nixon's campaign tactics in those races had antagonized a sizable proportion of the so-called community-thought leaders across the nation—people Nixon wished to win over to his side. The problem, as characterized by a popular song, became one of "accentuating the positive and eliminating the negative." Several tactical steps were involved.

The first, taken long before the convention, was the issuance from the Volunteers for Nixon offices of a set of *Question and Answer Sheets* on the following topics: Civil Rights, Economic Policy and Philosophy, Africa, Social Welfare, Labor, Latin America, Education, National Defense and Security, International Communism, Agriculture, Economic Growth through Freedom, Why We Should Study Communism, National Resources, the Steel Strike Settlement, Politics, and some "off the record" comments. The tone of these succinct statements (five to twelve pages each) is scholarly and the political position—insofar as one can be inferred from such a variety of topics—is what might best be described as "moderate liberal" or what some have termed "liberal conservative."

These papers were released in a packet entitled "Become Better Acquainted with Richard Nixon." Their chief purpose was to impress thought leaders in particular with the Vice President's breadth and depth of vision and to reveal his concern over the major issues of the day and his reasonable position on them.

The second step was Nixon's choice of his running mate. Although the selection of the vice-presidential candidate is usually a matter of "balancing the ticket," geographically and ideologically, it was more than that for Nixon in 1960. His personal choice of Henry Cabot Lodge reflected how deeply he felt about conveying an image of ethical responsibility. For Nixon knew that community leaders saw in Lodge not only a respected internationalist but also the Republican on the 1950 Tydings Subcommittee investigating Senator McCarthy's charges of Communists in government who had filed a strong minority report critical both of Democratic laxness and of his Republican colleague's unfounded accusations. Thus the selection of Lodge can be interpreted as another action calculated to help improve Nixon's position with certain groups whose support was in question.

The third step was Nixon's decision to develop a dual campaign organization. Impressed with his need for a strong showing among the independents and the need to capture a sizable Democratic vote in addition to maintaining virtually all of the Republican support, the Vice President had determined to call his campaign signals from the Nixon-Lodge Volunteers Headquarters rather than from the National Committee (see Chapter V). He made this decision in part because he felt that many independents and many Democrats were anxious to work for his election but that most of these volunteers would refuse to work out of a regular Republican headquarters. Perhaps he felt that a campaign planned and administered by professional partisans would be less helpful to the creation of a strong image as a candidate of all the people than would a campaign planned and administered by relative amateurs representing independents and Democrats as well as his own party.

A fourth tactical step, aimed like the first at improving his instrumental image, was the issuance of a series of what were called *Position Papers* on the major issues of the day. The first of these was published on August 31, 1960, and the last about the middle of October. These policy statements were prepared essentially for the nation's thought leaders and, according to the field of interest, were dispatched promptly to interested respondents of the mass mailings to special-interest groups.

Although the ideological position taken in these papers represented the thinking of the Vice President, members of an impressive Policy Advisory Board went over the content of these statements with Nixon. The Board consisted in part of such academic notables as Henry Ahlgren, director of Wisconsin's Agricultural Extension School; John Burchard, dean of M.I.T.'s School of Humanities and Social Sciences; Arthur Burns, economist from Columbia; Paul Cherrington of the Harvard School of Business Administration; William Y. Elliot, professor of government at Harvard; Lon Fuller, Harvard Law School; John Hannah, president of Michigan State University; Joseph Kaplan, professor of Physics at the University of California, Los Angeles; Lawrence Kimpton, chancellor at the University of Chicago; Philip Thayer, dean of the School of Advanced Studies at Johns Hopkins University; and Millard Roberts, president of Parsons College. Industry and applied science contributed Marion Folsom, former president of Eastman Kodak; John Heller, director of the New England Institute of Medical Research; Charles Percy, president of Bell and Howell; David Sarnoff, board chairman of the Radio Corporation of America; Leonard Scheele, former U.S. Surgeon General; and Robert Sprague, president of Sprague Electric.[2]

[2] This list of advisors necessitates taking note of the perennial question about presidential politics: "Who were the speech writers?" Although several people in, around, and outside the Republican National Committee and the Nixon Campaign Headquarters wrote speeches, no complete speeches were ever written for the Vice President. He wrote his own.

That is not to deny that there were trusted lieutenants who did basic research and even turned a phrase or two. Some of the personalities assigned to this task in the 1960 campaign were well-known writers; others were not. Charles Lichtenstein, a young Notre Dame political scientist, was said by some to have been the phrasemaker in the Nixon research inner circle. Dr. George Grassmuck, a University of Michigan international-relations expert, was director of research, with the assistance of James Shepley from the *Time-Life* organization and John Hamlin from the White House.

The papers issued were not as numerous as originally planned. The pamphlets which were produced covered The Meaning of Communism to Americans, National Purpose, Education, the Scientific Revolution, Housing, and Medical Research. The composition of the Policy Board itself and the scholarly approach to these topics gave additional proof that these were not only policy papers—they were papers designed to convince the recipients that the Republican candidate was thoughtful and well informed and that if he were to become President he would surely be advised by highly qualified leaders from American academic and business life.

Image-building considerations contributed to Nixon's decision to carry his campaign to each of the fifty states and fitted with his strong compulsion to present himself personally to as many people as possible. Perhaps this compulsion was also an important element in his decision to debate Senator Kennedy.

It is impossible, of course, to say that the above steps were taken wholly for the purpose of strengthening Nixon's instrumental image and chipping off the rough edges of his symbolic image. Similarly, the steps taken to reinforce his areas of strength were undoubtedly informational as well as image-centered.

The general campaign literature, as indeed does most campaign literature, clearly reflects image orientation. The most elaborate mailing piece, for example, was thirty-two pages on newsprint in the *Life-Look* type of magazine format. On the cover appeared a warm and friendly Nixon. Eisenhower's letter of endorsement and a picture of the two in serious conversation followed. Then came a pictorial history of Nixon's family, his boyhood, his service in the Navy, as a Member of the House of Representatives,

---

Dr. William Peterson, a New York University economist; Charles Kline, a New York political publicist; John Franklin Carter, a newspaperman; and Dr. John Hiller, a Rockefeller Foundation medical researcher, along with Lichtenstein, were the basic drafters of the "position papers" and of many of the press releases which emanated from the Nixon-Lodge brain trust.

At the National Committee, research assignments received from the Nixon-Lodge Headquarters were handled by Dr. William Prendergast, then newly appointed to the research directorship of the National Committee staff. Additional assistance was given by Oliver Gale, former assistant to the Secretary of Defense, who was formally assigned to the "answer desk" at the Committee but whose actual duties ranged far afield.

It must be iterated, however, that despite all of this talent, the speeches were finally fashioned by the candidate himslf.

as a Senator, and as the nation's most active Vice President. Thirteen of the remaining sixteen pages were devoted to Nixon's experiences in both domestic affairs and international relations. Finally, three pages were devoted to the Nixon-Lodge team and the campaign itself.

Republican and Nixon special-interest-group organizations geared their campaign propaganda to the Vice President's record and to his statements of position in their field. Basic explications which had been prepared for the *Questions and Answers* packet were woven into special August and September publications for veterans, farmers, laborers, new voters, senior citizens, academicians, Negroes, businessmen, scientists, and nationality groups. Film clips, too, which showed the Vice President debating Khrushchev, touring Latin America, or serving in Eisenhower's absence were made a part of longer motion-picture presentations for special-interest audiences. These efforts were essentially designed for instrumental-image purposes whereas the general materials were basically symbolic in nature.

Did Nixon succeed in his extensive efforts to "accentuate the positive and eliminate the negative?" It is true that he lost the election. Many would insist, however, that despite his organizational shortcomings, the basic conceptualization of image projection employed by the Vice President was appropriate to his needs and to the time. It must be remembered when looking back at 1960 and looking forward to 1964 that the methods employed by Nixon brought him within a hair's breadth of winning the presidency.

CREATING THE KENNEDY IMAGE IN 1960

John F. Kennedy faced two basic problems of public relations in 1960. He had served in relative obscurity in Congress and had to become known. His youthful appearance and lack of major political assignments created an impression of immaturity and inexperience which he had to overcome.

He had, on the other hand, some very great assets. Being relatively unknown, he was free to build a national image geared to the times. His voting record was moderately liberal and he could convincingly demand action on programs falling in the broad center of the political spectrum. He was bright and quick, able to speed read three times as fast as the average person, and could examine and absorb a huge volume of complex "position papers" to lend depth to his public statements. He was handsome, had a good sense of humor, and made a warm and, appealing figure on television and on the speaker's platform.

He also had a three-year-old daughter and a young and very attractive wife who was expecting their second child. History offered no clues on the use of these latter assets, however, for they are the assets of a young man and presidential candidates had never been this young. They could not barnstorm with him, however, and courtesy to his audiences soon required him to offer some explanation. Theodore White, who accompanied John Kennedy on his first western trip in September, has told the story of how he learned that his young family was a political asset:

> Out of his sense of privacy, Kennedy had omitted mentioning his wife or her pregnant condition in the early days of his campaign—and a tribute to the wife is rigidly required in American political orthodoxy. Then, one noon in the warm sun in the little park behind the gleaming color-splashed courthouse of Eugene, Oregon, he impulsively offered the courteous excuse that his wife was absent because she was "otherwise committed." A friendly ripple of laughter followed. The next morning, in northern California, he had changed it to "My wife has other responsibilities," and a warmer laugh followed. By afternoon the phrase had become a forthright "My wife is going to have a baby." In the San Joaquin valley the next day it was "My wife is going to have a boy in November." It had become a certified gag; and that afternoon in Los Angeles, it became a press-conference question that ended a tense interchange of questions on religion. "How do you know it's going to be a boy?" asked the questioner. "My wife told me," said Kennedy, and the conference ended with a laugh.[3]

Youth, then, was not his problem. Name familiarity he could gain with advertising, by barnstorming, and by debating the Vice President. His real needs were to establish that he was mature and experienced and that he was a moderate liberal who wanted action.

[3] Thodore H. White, *The Making of the President* (New York: Atheneum House, 1961), pp. 306-307.

Kennedy, of course, carried the main burden of image building himself. For support he established four major units of the National Committee: the Kennedy Research Team, under Myer Feldman; the Kennedy Speech Writers' Division, under Archibald Cox; the Research Division, under Robert Oshins; and the Publicity Division, under Roger Tubby and Samuel Brightman. The entire operation was managed by two key men from the Senator's Washington office: Theodore Sorensen, his principal policy adviser, who accompanied him on the airplane, and Feldman, who stayed in Washington to provide continuous supervision over all four divisions. Feldman personally approved every statement issued by the National Committee which bore the signature of John F. Kennedy.

Feldman also headed the Kennedy Research Team himself. To provide adequate help, he recruited five full-time, highly experienced men, each of whom had specialized in a different subject-matter field. The team's basic task was to do deep research for Senator Kennedy himself. Key issues, selected by the candidate, were explored in great detail and 200 fully developed briefing memoranda were prepared for speeches and for the television debates. The team especially drew upon an exhaustive series of position papers which experts outside the Committee had prepared in the late summer.

In the later stages of the campaign, Feldman's Research Team even drafted speeches for Senator Kennedy, which were then called over the phone to the touring staff. Requests from the campaign plane came at any hour of day or night. At three one morning, Feldman was called from the Texas-bound air caravan and asked to discover by eight o'clock whether there had been any Irishmen at the Battle of the Alamo! The answer: yes.

The Kennedy Research Team also drafted or consulted in the drafting of brochures, statements, and other special materials for any branch of the National Committee which asked for help. Close liaison was maintained with the Publicity Division.

Roger Tubby, appointed Campaign Coordinator for Publicity, divided assignments with Samuel C. Brightman, the pre-Kennedy Public Affairs director. Brightman carried forward the regular National Committee publicity program, while Tubby handled Kennedy speech releases, telephone requests, press conferences, and a series of rebuttal pamphlets entitled, "Correction, Please." In a special appeal to the serious reading public, Tubby also prepared many by-line articles by the Senator for national magazines and newspapers.

The Research Division of the Democratic National Committee, which continued under the direction of Robert Oshins, supplied information on national issues and on the records of Republican incumbents to candidates for Congress and to state and local committees. Feldman and Oshins thought of themselves as serving different clients with different types of materials and as supplementing and supporting the work done by the other whenever the need arose.

The Speech Writing Division was the outgrowth of a patient Kennedy effort to develop a pool of top-flight intellectual talent. Shortly after winning reelection to the Senate in 1958, Kennedy and Sorensen had approached friendly faculty members at Harvard, Kennedy's alma mater, for ideas and advice. A group of a dozen professors had been formed under the leadership of political scientist Earl Latham of Amherst. Eventually expanded to 30, it was officially mobilized to support the bid for the presidency in January, 1960, at a breakfast meeting at the Harvard club. At that time, Archibald Cox of the Harvard Law School faculty, a specialist in labor law, had taken command of the group and several new names were added. Expanding the group as the campaign unfolded, Cox drew upon many of the nation's most distinguished scholars from Harvard, Massachusetts Institute of Technology, Yale, Princeton, and elsewhere. Among them were John Kenneth Galbraith, Paul A. Samuelson, Seymour Harris, Arthur Schlesinger, Jr., Walt W. Rostow, Jerome B. Wiesner, Willard Cochrane, Paul A. Freund, Arthur A. Maass, James M. Burns, and Edward Katzenbach.

During the summer, Cox moved to Washington, D.C., and recruited a seven-man staff to prepare drafts of all the anticipated full-dress speeches—one evening speech each day and possibly one or two others. The men came from several sources. One was a writer for *Look* magazine who had written for Adlai Stevenson. One was a free-lance writer from New York who had done no

previous political writing. Another was an administrative assistant from Congress who had long experience in preparing campaign speeches.

Cox and his assistants got ideas on policy goals and preliminary drafts of speeches primarily from his pool of professors, but
also used a wide variety of other sources. Since many contributors were in the Boston area, the coordination of their work was
assigned to Abram Chayes of the Harvard Law School. Cox told
Chayes what he needed and Chayes tapped the sources of knowledge.

Cox also established a Writers' Bureau in New York modeled
after the Writers' Bureau which had been set up there in 1952 and
1956 for the Stevenson campaigns. Drawing upon professional
free-lance writers and regular staff writers for periodicals, the
group included many distinguished authors and editors.

It soon became plain that neither of Cox's efforts was useful.
No opportunities were afforded the candidate to speak to a specialized audience which would appreciate an address in depth on
a special problem of public policy. Instead, Kennedy was making essentially the same speech to several small audiences every
day. Different areas of policy could be emphasized as the opportunity warranted, and special local information could be used, but
the formal addresses Cox was preparing were having to be rewritten, culled, or discarded.

Kennedy also found that he could not use the sorts of phrases,
quips, and quotes which the Writers' Bureau had supplied so effectively to Stevenson. Their product simply didn't fit Kennedy's
extemporaneous speeches, his oratorical style, or the audiences
he was meeting.

In mid-October the Writers' Bureau was abandoned and the
Washington Speech Writing staff was sharply reduced. Some of the
men left to assist Adlai Stevenson, who was campaigning hard
for Kennedy. Others went on the road as advance speech writers
for Kennedy.

An advance speech writer would visit a city about three days
before Senator Kennedy was scheduled to speak. Working with the
advance man and local Democrats, he would pick up local color
and local issues which the Senator could work into his speech. Ma-

terial was prepared in a form which Sorensen and Richard Goodwin could quickly screen and feed to the Senator on the plane.
Rarely did an advance speech writer attempt to prepare a full
speech. Ideas also were supplied by the remaining Washington staff,
working through Myer Feldman.

Kennedy's speeches, then, concentrated on building his image
as a moderate liberal who wanted action. Repeatedly he voiced
the theme, "We need to get this country moving again." Repeatedly he labeled the Republicans as the party which prefers to
"sit down, sit still, and look back." Nearly every specific issue
was handled in this context.

At Fort Dodge, Iowa, to a farming and industrial audience he
said,

But, if you think we can do better, if you think we can move ahead,
if you think we can reverse the downward trend of agricultural prices,
if you think we can build a better educational system and more security for our older people, if you think we can build a better defense,
if you think that the United States should reestablish the atmosphere
which existed through Latin America in the 1930's of the good neighbor, if you think the power balance in the world is turning against us,
not with us, then I want you to join with us. I want you to move
with us. I want you to decide in 1960 that we say "Yes" to the next
decade, and not "No"; that we want to move ahead, not stand still.[4]

At New York University, in a speech devoted principally to
foreign policy, he declared:

I cannot believe that any young man or woman who looks to the
future can possibly decide to sit down and sit still and look back with
Mr. Nixon and the Republican Party which has always opposed
progress. . . .

Now, in 1960, the choice lies between the candidate who in this
most revolutionary time runs on the slogan "You've never had it so
good," versus the candidate and a party that runs on the slogan of
the "New Frontiers" of the future. (Applause.)

On that basis, I ask your help. (Applause.) I ask your support. . . .
How many of you will be willing to pick this country up and move
it forward and make it shine once again? (Applause.)[5]

[4] U.S. Congress, Senate, *Freedom of Communications,* Part I (Washington: Government Printing Office, 1961), p. 319.
[5] *Ibid.,* p. 778.

At South Bay Shopping Center in Redondo Beach, California, he sounded the theme again:

I believe it is a choice between a candidate and a party that is willing to break new ground, that is willing to move ahead, that is willing to take this country off dead center, and between a party, the Republican Party, that looks to the past.

Now, as long as we in this country stand still, as long as we do not take advantage of our opportunities, we fail ourselves, and we fail those who desire to be free. This is a deadly struggle in which we are engaged and we can't afford to be second best. We can't afford to be second best in outer space. We cannot afford to have 35 percent of our brightest boys and girls who graduate from high school never get to college. (Applause.)

We can't afford men and women in the State of California out of work, unable to find a job. We can't afford to have 16 million Americans over the age of 65 who live on an average social security check of less than $72 a month. (Applause.)[6]

Why did Kennedy concentrate his image building upon demanding action in the moderate center rather than upon creating a reputation of maturity and competence? The Senator's own oratorical style, and the nature of the campaign appearances seem to be part of the story. The basic reason, however, seems to be that the first of the Great Debates solved both the name familiarity and the maturity-competence problems for John F. Kennedy.

THE GREAT DEBATES

The four debates between Vice President Richard M. Nixon and Senator John F. Kennedy in the 1960 campaign are a major landmark in world history. No greater audience has ever witnessed the discussion of public policies.

The debates, however, proved more important to the candidates for image projection than for clarification of their stands on issues. Tactically, they were a godsend to John Kennedy. Needing name familiarity and an image of experience and maturity, he gained both overnight by a very favorable performance in the first debate.

[6] *Ibid.*, p. 847.

Why did Richard Nixon debate? When the debates had been proposed, some of Nixon's advisers had counselled strongly against such a venture. Why, they argued, should the better-known Vice President admit the less-known Senator to be his equal by accepting the debate? Moreover, there was always the possibility that if Nixon had a "bad night" and if the Democratic candidate were unusually effective, substantial ground would be lost. Others thought television debates with Kennedy offered a great opportunity to demonstrate the difference between the two candidates. Those who favored the debates were confident that Nixon would easily emerge as the people's choice after such an encounter.

Nixon apparently agreed with the advocates of the debates. Partly he believed that he stood to gain from the effort. He felt he needed to dispel the notion that he was overly cold and calculating, and he was confident that his knowledge of the Administration would enable him to outpoint Kennedy. Partly, however, he was caught in a train of circumstances which had been started in 1956 and by September, 1960, left him little room for choice.

A debate between the major-party candidates for President had previously been practically foreclosed by section 315 of the Federal Communications Act and the interpretations of that section made by the Federal Communications Commission. If free time were offered the Republican and Democratic candidates, equal time had to be offered the Socialist, Prohibitionist, and other minor-party candidates. No network was prepared to enter such a jungle.

In 1956, Adlai E. Stevenson had initiated the idea by challenging President Eisenhower to debate. The White House rejected the proposal in early September by a brief statement saying that a debate would not dignify the office of President. Instead, later in the campaign, President Eisenhower appeared on a paid television broadcast to answer questions from a selected group of citizens in the studio.

After the election, Democratic National Chairman Paul M. Butler, an idealistic political reformer, would not let the idea die. Working with Frank Stanton, President of the Columbia Broadcasting System, he persuaded the other networks to undertake a joint effort to repeal the equal-time requirements of section 315 for the presidential candidates. Congress picked up the idea and in

July, 1960, suspended section 315 for the presidential campaign of 1960 only.

Thus Nixon found himself facing not only a challenge from Kennedy but also great pressure from the television networks and the public to use the specially granted freedom. Once the debate opportunity was publicly announced by the television networks, it was not easy for the Nixon forces to turn it down. Numerous excuses could have been offered to justify a refusal to debate, but Kennedy could easily have turned any of them to his advantage. So the Vice President accepted the challenge.

Beginning early in September, arrangements for the debates were laboriously negotiated among representatives of the two candidates and the three television networks. Kennedy, anxious to meet the Vice President, generally let his chief negotiator, J. Leonard Reinsch, accept whatever arrangements seemed reasonable. Because the networks were anxious to put on the debates and were striving hard to be fair, Reinsch found himself in the favorable position of being able to accept most of the network proposals. Nixon's negotiator, Herbert Klein, offered many suggestions on procedure, format, and arrangements. On most requests from the Nixon representatives, Reinsch went along, guided by the Kennedy policy of not letting little things forestall the debates.

On the number of debates, however, Reinsch held out for five. Nixon's managers, confident their champion would score a knockout in the first round, bargained for one. By yielding on the fine points, and with the support of the networks which had offered the time, Reinsch managed to wangle four meetings: September 26 from Chicago; October 7 from Washington, D.C.; October 13 with Kennedy in New York and Nixon in Los Angeles; and October 21 from New York.

Pressed by the networks for a "good show," the candidates' representatives accepted a format which reduced the "debates" to hasty generalizations on a wide variety of subjects. The debates would last an hour each. The first would be limited to domestic policy, the second to foreign affairs. The third and fourth were less restricted. For the first and the last debates, each candidate was permitted an opening statement of 8 minutes. The rest of the time would be devoted to answering questions put by a panel of four distinguished newsmen. Direct answers to their questions were limited to 2½ minutes, rebuttal answers to 1½. No notes were to be used. A fifth newsman would serve as moderator, introduce the programs, and close them. All three networks would carry the programs live.

Thorniest problem in the negotiations proved to be the candidates' schedules. Only by enormous effort were travel plans juggled to bring them together on the same platform for three of the four debates. For the third debate the problems proved insurmountable and a split screen was arranged. Significantly, perhaps, many observers felt that the third debate was Mr. Nixon's best.

THE FIRST DEBATE

The opening debate cast the die. Those who heard it on radio reported that the two seemed nearly equal. Those who watched on television overwhelmingly chose Kennedy as the winner. Kennedy had achieved all he had hoped. Nixon had suffered what some of his counsellors had feared.

The contrast on the crucial first debate had many facets and several causes. Yet it was less in what they said than in how they looked that made the difference. Kennedy arrived for the telecast relaxed, well briefed, confident, and fresh from a nap. Nixon arrived tense, unbriefed, and tired; and as he alighted from his car he struck his recently injured knee a severe jolt.

Each candidate had prepared for the encounter in typical fashion. John Kennedy had summoned to Chicago the leaders of his Research Team, Ted Sorensen, Richard Goodwin, and Myer Feldman. Feldman had brought his campaign files from Washington. For a full day the four operated almost around the clock "like young men at college cramming for an exam."[7] The effort centered upon filling Kennedy's head with all the latest figures, percentages, trends, and comparisons which would enable him to demonstrate his mastery of any questions which might be asked. A brainstorming session uncovered most of the probable questions and swift raids on the files developed answers for them. By Monday afternoon the candidate and his youthful "brain trust" had the key ideas on fact cards and were able to let Kennedy have a good nap, next take a last review of the cards with them, his brother Robert, and pollster Louis Harris; and then eat a relaxed dinner.

[7] White, *op. cit.*, p. 341.

Richard Nixon spent the day alone. Dependent upon his own memory and materials he carried with him, he prepared his opening statement and tried by himself to anticipate the coming questions. Having been forced to interrupt his campaign in early September because of his knee injury, Nixon was tired. Heavy campaigning to make up for the lost time had visibly emaciated him. Only as he drove to the studio did he take time for a hasty consultation with his television adviser on arrangements for the program and what he might expect in the debate.

On the air, the two candidates were startlingly different. Theodore White caught the picture with remarkable sympathy and understanding:

. . . the contrast of the two faces was astounding. Normally and in private, Kennedy under tension flutters his hands—he adjusts his necktie, slaps his knee, strokes his face. Tonight he was calm and nerveless in appearance. The Vice-President, by contrast, was tense, almost frightened, at turns glowering and, occasionally, haggard-looking to the point of sickness.[8]

The debate itself provided another contrast. Centered on domestic policy, it offered Kennedy the opportunity to voice his "action now" theme and to emphasize the Democratic Party's record of liberal domestic programs. Nixon, centering upon answering his opponent instead of capturing the unseen audience, repeatedly agreed with Kennedy's goals, then disagreed with his methods and offered an alternative. Whatever its merits for formal debating, this technique was decried as "me-tooism" even by his liberal Republican supporters.

Remedial steps were promptly taken in the Nixon camp and the remaining three debates were scored by the supporters of each candidate as a victory for their man. In all four debates both candidates proved themselves remarkably adaptable to this new form of presidential campaigning. It appeared that each could discuss anything within the allotted time of 2½ minutes and could rebut with equal ease for 1½. Unfortunately, the questions by the newsmen were sometimes trivial, occasionally improper, and often complex enough to be unanswerable in the allotted time.

[8] *Ibid.,* p. 346.

IMPACT OF THE DEBATES

More people watched the debates than voted for President. Estimates of the viewing audience ranged from 85 million to 120 million. Kennedy polled 34,227,096; Nixon 34,107,646.

The debates also made a major change in the use of television in the campaign. Originally the Democratic National Committee had reserved eight 30-minute periods for major nationwide television broadcasts so that the candidate could speak to the nation on the major issues of the day as Adlai E. Stevenson had done in 1952 and 1956. When the Great Debates were scheduled, most of that time was canceled, except for election eve. Instead, Kennedy appearances in key cities around the nation were telecast over regional networks and paid for by the participating state Party organizations. Never did he offer a formal nationwide address on a major policy issue.

Did the debates help people make up their minds? Polls taken during and after the campaign indicated that enough people said they did to have altered the outcome of the election.

Did the debates help shape the course of public policy by informing the people, as so many scholars think political debate should? Some observers said no, such innovations in presidential politics are unrealistic and irrelevant—unrealistic because presidents do not engage in crucial decision-making in 2½-minute periods; irrelevant because skill in debate does not prove that a man will make a good president.

Some observers said yes, that the debates were spectacularly successful, though not without faults. The proponents of continued debates insisted that the portraits of the candidates given the voters were unusually accurate. Moreover, they said, the debates were never intended to be more than very useful additions to other evidence on the candidates' qualifications for the presidency.

Will the major candidates debate in 1964? It is unlikely. Congress would have to suspend section 315 of the Federal Communications Act again and it has not been asked to do so. President Johnson, although a respectable speaker, has given strong signs that he does not relish public question-and-answer periods. With the Eisenhower precedent of 1956 to use and with a heavy program of legislation for Congress to enact, he is not likely to divert Congressional time to the suspension of section 315. He thus can easily avoid having to face directly the question of whether to grant his opponent a common forum in which, like Kennedy in 1960, the opponent would become known and would be able to demonstrate his experience and maturity.

President Johnson may not even receive a challenge. Senator Goldwater has said that he feels the President should not be a party to a debate. He is still the nation's President, says the Senator, even though he is a candidate. His position as a world leader and the integrity of his administration must not be subjected to the harassment of television debates. Senator Goldwater sympathizes with any public figure caught before the live television camera with well informed interrogators pressing in from every side.

Governor Nelson A. Rockefeller, on the other hand, sees the advantage to the challenger in debate. Early in the year he offered to debate Senator Goldwater on the issues of the campaign. He would undoubtedly challenge the President to debate should he be the nominee.

If the television debates were to occur in 1964, what changes might be made? Some of the sharpest criticism of the 1960 debates centered on the questions framed by the newsmen. It has been suggested that questions proposed by the candidates themselves might be better directed to the real issues and that the candidates could be judged not only on the basis of their answers, but also on the basis of the questions they asked. Follow-up questions have also been suggested to permit the debaters to pursue a question of major importance to the nation. With care, these and other improvements could make one or more nation-wide television debates a lasting feature of presidential elections.

PRESENTING PRESIDENT JOHNSON IN 1964

President Lyndon B. Johnson enters the 1964 presidential campaign with enormous advantages over any prospective opponent. No name is better known or more often before the public. No President has entered the office with greater national experience in high elective office. Twenty-four years in Congress, eight as the extraordinarily successful Leader of the Democratic

Party in the Senate, and three years as Vice President afford him maturity and experience which no prospective opponent can match. A Protestant, and one who loyally supported a Catholic President, Johnson faces no religious issue.

In 1964, then, President Johnson's problem of image building is utterly different from Kennedy's problem in 1960. He has none of Kennedy's liabilities, but lacks at least one of his key assets.

Lyndon Johnson must build an image as a national leader rather than a sectional one. The hurdle is high, but not insurmountable, even though no Southern leader has won the presidency since the Civil War.[9]

The building of a national image for Johnson turns upon his demonstrating real concern for the problems of the industrial Northeast, the agricultural Midwest, and the developing Far West. John F. Kennedy already had action programs under way designed to establish such an image and had a special one—the Appalachian Regional Development program—to appeal to the South as well.

In his service as Majority Leader of the Senate, Johnson frequently had taken a national view. He had engineered passage of the Civil Rights bill in 1957 and had secured enactment of such major Western goals as the Upper Colorado River Storage project. Yet as the senior Senator from Texas, he could never neglect the interests of his own state and section.

As President, Johnson has declared his belief in the Kennedy goals and has retained key Kennedy personnel, but these are not enough to be convincing. One can too easily jettison both once safely elected to a four-year term. Proof of his sincerity can come in only one way—through a dazzling exhibition of his legendary skills as a leader of the Congress to obtain enactment of several of the key pieces of legislation which had been stalled during Kennedy's lifetime.

This exhibition Lyndon B. Johnson promptly set out to make. While the nation was still in mourning for John Kennedy, he man-

---

[9] The only other citizen of a Confederate State to hold the presidency, Andrew Johnson, was a Union Democrat from eastern Tennessee who was Lincoln's running-mate in 1864 and who served out Lincoln's term after he was assassinated.

aged to break the longest appropriations log jam in Congressional history. A major tax reduction to spur economic growth sailed through Congress in the first six weeks of the 1964 session. The Civil Rights bill, a crucial item in winning the industrial Northeast, boomed through the House of Representatives on February 11 and headed for a long showdown, but probable passage, in the Senate. A strong message for enactment of medical care for the aged as part of Social Security went to the Congress to become either a major achievement or a major campaign issue for Johnson. A war on poverty was declared and Sargent Shriver, President Kennedy's brother-in-law, was placed in charge. Legislation to implement it was promptly proposed.

At every opportunity Johnson repeated his dedication to the action programs of the liberal wing of his party. Nevertheless he also won the announced support of Senator Richard B. Russell of Georgia, long-time leader of the Southern bloc. On all programs but civil rights he would enjoy an unusual degree of Party unity. His Southern colleagues held powerful posts in the machinery of Congress with which to make his legislative record a brilliant success—or a dismal failure. They would have no better chance in their lifetimes to place a fellow Southerner in the White House, but this they could insure only by helping Johnson prove that he would be truly a leader of all the people.

REPUBLICAN IMAGE STRATEGY IN 1964

Decisions concerning Republican image strategy in 1964 will obviously depend upon the candidate. Senator Goldwater insists that the Party and its standard bearer in 1964 should offer the American people a choice in contrast to the Democratic Party rather than an echo of it. What looked in November, 1963, like a conscious effort to moderate several of his well-known strongly conservative views had subsided before February and, should he be the convention choice, the nation may well have a clear-cut choice between the parties' presidential nominees. Goldwater's directness, virility, and down-to-earth warmth have given him a very favorable image with Republican stalwarts. The extent to which this symbolic image would overshadow his instrumental image of unyielding conservatism in the eyes of independents, moderate Republicans, and anti-Johnson Democrats is yet to be reckoned.

Governor Rockefeller, on the other hand, feels that a so-called central position on domestic and foreign policy represents the current American consensus. Since the Democratic Party from Roosevelt's time has occupied the center positions in national and international policy, he is driven to take the position that the Republican Party with himself as leader can achieve better than the Democrats the common aims of a majority of the American people. The policy differences, in most areas, between a Rockefeller and a Johnson may be a matter of degree; approaches to implementation would reveal substantial differences between the two men and their parties.

Rockefeller's image as an outspoken champion of the middle-of-the-road course, or "me-too position" as some have called it, has obviously not endeared him to the conservative wing of the Republican Party. But it is his symbolic rather than his instrumental image which constitutes his major problem. His divorce and remarriage have reminded the nation's political leaders of the potent force, positive or negative, that the symbolic image can be in an individual's quest for the American presidency.

Richard Nixon has largely erased the negative aspects of his image because of the 1960 presidential race and because of his responsible and forthright positions on the Birch Society in California in 1961. The fact that he has been a two-time loser, however, now has become the millstone around his neck. If Nixon should be selected as the nominee it is probable that his campaign would be somewhat more hard-hitting than was the campaign in 1960. His statements in New York before a Republican finance dinner on January 22, 1964, seemed to reveal his plans, should he again be nominated:

> We shall not win by resorting to image-making. . . . We shall win and deserve to win by standing on principle on one great issue. That issue is the initiative against communism.

If the New York statement of Nixon reflected his attitude toward the proper image of the Republican Party in 1964, so, perhaps did the statements made that same evening by two other possible nominees reflect their conceptions of what the Grand Old Party's image ought to be.

Governor William W. Scranton of Pennsylvania reminded his Indianapolis listeners that the greatest hour of the Republican Party was when it presented a positive program, not a negative image.

And Governor George Romney of Michigan told an audience in Washington, D.C., that the Republican Party must give new leadership to restore personal responsibility, individual morality, family life, public integrity, and faith in American principles.

The determination of the image strategy of the Republican Party in 1964 must indeed wait upon the selection of the man to mold the image.

MEASURING THE PUBLIC REACTION

Just as television has introduced a dramatic new campaign device into American presidential politics, political opinion polls have given party leaders a new tool with which to measure the response to the campaign effort. The first published American political opinion poll was one conducted by the *Harrisburg Pennsylvanian* in 1824, in Wilmington, Delaware, concerning the contest between Andrew Jackson and John Quincy Adams. However, opinion polls have now been refined to the point that many political leaders use them along with other indices of the political winds to determine the wisdom of adjusting political tactics as the political situation changes.

The 1960 Democratic campaign was supported by three types of opinion measurement. Louis Harris identified "cutting issues" of deep concern to the people by adding Kennedy questions to his statewide commercial polls. Given ready access to John Kennedy, he was able to shape the emphasis in many of Kennedy's speeches.

Dr. George Belknap accompanied the early tours to analyze crowd reaction. Suspecting that jumping and screaming teenagers in the front rows were unrepresentative of the real voters, he would post four or five young Democrats toward the rear of the crowd to talk to people about their reactions. Such responses unfortunately centered on style and mannerisms, which Kennedy neither could nor wished to change, so the tour analysis was dispensed with in mid campaign.

Simulmatics, Incorporated, a group of New York liberals, was employed to undertake public opinion simulation studies and made reports directly to Robert Kennedy.[10]

[10] See Ithiel DeSola Pool and Robert Abelson, "The Simulmatics Project," Chapter 6 in Harold Guetzkow, *Simulation and Social Science* (New York: Prentice Hall, 1962).

Richard Nixon followed the findings of the political analysts closely as he structured the last few weeks of his campaign. Among state party leaders, perhaps Ohio Republican Chairman Ray C. Bliss is best known for his use of a wide variety of polls to ascertain a given strategy and to make such adjustments as are necessary with the progress of the campaign.

Although there has been considerable controversy over the accuracy of political opinion polls, a graver question is concerned with the effect of these polls on the democratic processes, more particularly the popular electoral process. The defenders of polling insist that by separating the issues, by stating them simply and clearly, and by covering the electorate completely and continuously they can help bring our political processes closer to the traditional democratic thought underlying our system.

According to this argument, ascertaining the major concerns and the will of the majority is an invaluable aid to presidential candidates since they are then enabled to address themselves directly to the questions most troublesome to the electorate.

Not everyone agrees that making the voice of a turbulent and changing public more audible in the midst of a presidential campaign is wise. It is held that polls destroy political courage and leadership, that they actually constitute a brake on progress because they give voice to the public tendency toward complacency and conservatism, and that the polls themselves mask the complexities of our decision-making process, hence are based on a misconception of democracy.

Regardless of the theoretical arguments, pro and con, pollsters have assuredly long been at work for several of the potential Republican presidential nominees. President Johnson, too, can be assumed to be deeply interested in what the Gallup polls and others are finding about the public reaction to his administration. The poll findings, tempered by a variety of other indices, will again inescapably play an important role in the strategies of the Democratic and Republican presidential campaigns.

Chapter IX

Meeting the People

WHY GO TO THE PEOPLE?
There is no substitute for meeting the people. The candidate who goes to the people gets the people.

This elementary principle of American politics stems from a small-town tradition in American behavior. Voters give their confidence to leaders whom they know. Television and radio, newspapers, advertisements, magazine articles can acquaint them with the name and qualifications of a candidate. But getting to know him requires meeting him face to face, shaking his hand, asking him a question, and talking to other people who know him.

What is he really like? Does he shake hands firmly, with vigor, or limply like a cold fish? Does he seem really genuinely glad to meet you? Is he interested in what you have to say? Does he think your opinion is important? Or is he aloof, haughty, self-centered, "phony"?

A homely illustration of this basic search for the inner quality of a man has been offered by Senator Paul H. Douglas of Illinois. He reports that the best training he received for a career in politics was milking cows as a boy for he thereby developed a strong and tireless grip.

These questions, trivial as they may seem to those who want a presidential campaign to be a grand debate on policy issues, are at the heart of political decision-making in presidential elections. American men and women prefer to trust their government to a man whom they would trust with their savings, their legal difficulties, and their personal problems. And they don't hesitate to write him about such matters once he is elected.

If he is to meet the people, the candidate must go to them, and in a country as large as the United States this means a grueling tour, state by state, city by city, to meet and shake hands and talk to as many people as he can. And as he does he not only seeks their confidence, he learns from them whether he is winning that confidence. Theodore White eloquently caught the candidate's need to get the people's response in *The Making of the President:*

. . . the candidate, whoever he is, sits at the center of a web of affairs so complex as to be dehumanized; his ideas, his phrases, his finances, his schedules, are all prepared for him by others; wherever he pauses to consult with staff, he must already make the detached executive decisions of a President. Thus only the personal audience, below the level of strategic calculation, can give him the one thing he needs most: the response of warmth or frost, of applause or indifference. Its laughter, its scowl, its silence, its cheers, its yearning, its measuring eyes, are the only clues in the mystic communication between the leader and the led, to tell truly whether he has reached those he seeks to lead. Becoming President is an utterly personal business between the man who offers himself as national leader and the Americans who judge him. The candidate must feel the beat of the people he hopes to lead; their heart is his target. And no public-opinion poll or analysis can tell him half so well whether he has reached that target as can the people themselves, giving him the beat of their response.[1]

Only Warren G. Harding, Republican candidate in 1920, has dared in this century to campaign from his "front porch"—have the people come to him and see but few of them. His managers had judged that if he went to meet the people he would lose the election. So they kept him home and kept him quiet.

Television, radio, and air travel have made the campaign from the front porch obsolete. Both major candidates for the presidency now must "barnstorm"—tour the nation as widely as possible—in their search for votes.

[1] Theodore H. White, *The Making of the President 1960* (New York: Atheneum House, Inc., 1961), pp. 305-306.

As they travel, the candidates reach at least four levels of audiences. The nation as a whole hears their appeals through the reports of 50 or more national press representatives who accompany each candidate. The many and frequent stops in a barnstorming campaign, however, preclude a unique and newsworthy speech each time. The traveling press soon learns to listen for something new and to ignore most of what is said. Most speeches, therefore, go unreported or command relatively slight attention in the press across the land.

The local press, television, and radio, however, see a personal appearance as front-page news or as lead-off material for newscasts. Pictures, film clips, reports of the candidate's remarks, little events which convey his personality, all are presented in volume and eagerly consumed, especially by those who saw him or attended a rally.

The face-to-face audience, the people who gather at airport rallies, in school gymnasiums, on street corners, constitute a third audience level. Having made the effort to come to see the candidate, they usually are his staunch supporters. Their reward, principally, is reinforcement and reassurance that their choice is indeed a good one, although by their enthusiasm they may help sway their fellow townsmen watching on television.

The fourth audience is a selected one, composed of those community leaders who are deemed important enough to be granted a few moments of private conversation with the candidate. In such meetings, many votes may be gained by winning the support of men and women whose judgment will shape the attitudes of others. Sometimes, when a particularly important local figure is unable to come to the candidate, the candidate visits him and thereby gains highly valuable local front-page publicity.

TRAVEL

The 1960 campaign saw both major candidates visit virtually every state, some states repeatedly. In September, both made many widely scattered appearances, daily. By October, both had changed to three or four principal appearances a day, usually in a single state.

A Kennedy September schedule is well illustrated by the two-day swing of Thursday and Friday, September 22 and 23. Starting with a talk at the stockyards in Sioux City, Iowa, just before 9 a.m. on the twenty-second, he spoke twice at Fort Dodge, Iowa; addressed the National Plowing Contest at Sioux Falls, South Dakota; spoke at the Corn Palace in Mitchell, South Dakota; met an airport rally at Fargo, North Dakota; and gave a major speech on electric power policy before a convention of public power groups in Billings, Montana, in the evening before flying to Denver, Colorado, for the night. The next morning, the twenty-third, found him at Frontier Park, Cheyenne, Wyoming. He was back in Denver for an address and luncheon, then made two appearances in Salt Lake City, Utah, one a major address on religious freedom at the Mormon Tabernacle.

Vice President Nixon started his barnstorming proper a week after Kennedy, on Monday, September 12. He spoke first that morning at Friendship Airport, Baltimore, Maryland; then at Monument Circle in Indianapolis, Indiana; at Memorial Auditorium in Dallas, Texas; and finally at Union Square in San Francisco. Swinging north the next day, September 13, he spoke in Portland, Oregon; Vancouver, Washington; and Boise, Idaho; then mounted his Mid-Western campaign on Wednesday, September 14, at Grand Forks, North Dakota, and Peoria, Illinois.

By contrast, October 24 and 25 found both candidates spending two full days each in the pivotal Mid-Western states, Nixon in Ohio, Kennedy in Illinois. Both filled man-killing schedules. Nixon spoke at Marietta, Parkersburg (across the Ohio River in West Virginia), Athens, Chillicothe, Cincinnati, Middletown, Dayton, Springfield, Columbus, Marion, Lima, Deschler, London, and Toledo. Kennedy appeared at Rockford, Champaign-Urbana, Peoria, East Peoria, Moline, Rock Island, Des Plaines, Libertyville, Carpentersville, Elgin, St. Charles, Geneva, Batavia, Aurora, and Elmhurst.

As the campaign advanced, both centered greatest attention on the five pivotal states. Of the 64 days of campaigning from Labor Day, September 5, through Monday, November 7, Kennedy spent the equivalent of 9 in New York, 6½ in Pennsylvania, 4½ in Ohio, 5½ in Illinois, and 6 in California—slightly less than half his time. Nixon allocated 7 to New York, 3½ to Pennsylvania, 3½ to Ohio, 4½ to Illinois, and 5 to California—one-third of his time.

The remaining time was distributed remarkably alike. Each gave major attention to other Mid-Western states. Kennedy spent three days in Michigan, Nixon two. Nixon gave 7 days to the remaining Mid-Western states, Kennedy 6. Kennedy spent 8 days in the South, two of them in Texas; Nixon 6. Nixon traveled 4½ days in the West outside California, Kennedy 3½. Kennedy gave 3½ days, Nixon 2, to New Jersey, Delaware, Maryland, and West Virginia. Both gave but a day and a half to New England, which was clearly to divide between them, three states apiece. In addition, Kennedy made two separate appearances in Washington, D.C. Both had a few open days: Kennedy 5, Nixon 9.

In that period, Kennedy made 340 separate appearances, Nixon 211. Both issued a large volume of separate statements, opinions, and collateral material.

ADVANCE SCHEDULING AND PREPARATION

Barnstorming by a presidential candidate in the 1960's calls for the most elaborate and careful advance preparations.

The candidates of both major parties must now expect to travel with an entourage of nearly 100 persons, two-thirds of them representatives of the press, radio, and television. The count runs up quickly. The candidate himself must have a minimum personal party of eight or ten persons: an administrative assistant to handle delicate political negotiations; a press secretary to prepare news releases, negotiate with the press, set up press conferences, and provide facilities for the press; a campaign scheduling manager to map the trips and make physical arrangements; and at least one good speech writer to assemble and draft material for public presentation. Such a personal crew also requires clerical support.

Courtesy requires the candidate to include his party's key political figures from the state he is visiting. The Governor and the United States Senators and Representatives, or the party's candidates for those offices, expect to appear with the presidential candidate. Protocol also usually obliges the inclusion of the state's party chairman, possibly the national committeeman and committee-woman, and especially the state chairman of the "Citizens" or "Volunteers" for the national ticket. An incumbent President has further to include any cabinet or other key administration officer from the state. Each of the elected officers, moreover, is likely to have a key staff member of his own with him. A minimum of 8 or 10 seats for such very important people is unavoidable.

Local party organizations rarely are prepared or equipped to deal with such a deluge. Being subject to high turnover of leadership and dependent upon volunteer working personnel, they find it nearly impossible to imagine the detailed work and the expense required to prepare for the visit of a presidential candidate.

Even a simple speech at an airport demands fantastically complex arrangements. A platform must be provided in a location inside a permanent fence which can keep the crowd from mingling with the visiting party or invading the press section. A flatbed truck trailer has often proved the most economical type of platform. A second platform, fully wired with many outlets for television and movie cameras and radio broadcasters, must be provided about 30 feet in front of the rostrum and at a slightly higher elevation. The press must have tables and chairs for at least 80 persons in a restricted area immediately by the platform and requires direct access to at least two teletypewriter operators and a dozen long-distance telephones. If the President is involved, a local White House switchboard must be installed somewhere in town and a phone placed just at the foot of the steps to the platform by which he can reach any place on earth instantly.

Security precautions require a system of passes to identify those who will greet the candidate at the aircraft, those who will have seats on the platform, the press, telephone and other workmen, local committee workers, and plain-clothes guards. Police must be instructed to keep all others in the public areas and must know to whom to turn in case of an emergency that might demand an exception.

Bands and other suitable entertainment must be arranged. Since school and college bands are the most frequently used, someone must see to it that they know how to play "Hail to the Chief" or the candidate's theme song. Chairs and transportation must be provided for the bands and agreements made with their schools to excuse them from classes if necessary.

Protocol in seating, suitable decorations, and even instructions for the introduction of speakers are required. Thus, when the President is the speaker, the person introducing him, no matter what his station, is permitted to say only, "Ladies and Gentlemen, the President of the United States."

A speech away from the airport means a motorcade. The local committee will be expected to provide several open cars for the candidate, other dignitaries, and photographers; closed cars for the security personnel and communications men; and at least three buses for the press and staff. When the President is involved, special equipment is provided by the Secret Service. But routing, timing, order of march, and protection of the motorcade call for careful preparations.

If meals are to be taken by the visiting party, or an overnight stop is scheduled, hotel or motel rooms with special telephones must be provided the candidate, other dignitaries, and key staff. Press people usually do not expect individual rooms at a luncheon stop.

The local organization is expected to meet all local expenses. The candidate is at enough expense to bring his party in for the appearance. Thus, even a shoe-string appearance by a presidential candidate will cost the local party organization several hundred dollars.

Advice and suggestions for the appearance of a presidential candidate, therefore, simply cannot be made by long-distance telephone or even be provided in a quick overnight visit by a traveling representative from national headquarters. The only workable solution is for the candidate to send out one of his own team as an "advance man" to work closely with the local party people on arrangements for his visit. A good "advance" requires the full-time night-and-day work of an experienced man for a week to ten days on the scene. The advance man must be in early enough to shape the arrangements and must stay with the show until the candidate's airplane is on its way to the next airport. For large cities, or a visit of several days which includes a variety of activities, a team of advance men may be needed. In late October,

1960, John F. Kennedy had a team of eleven advance men to handle his three-day visit to Philadelphia.

KENNEDY AND JOHNSON IN 1960

In 1960, campaign barnstorming by John F. Kennedy and Lyndon B. Johnson was coordinated, but each managed his own movements separately. Each candidate had his own advance scheduling officer and each his own team of advance men.

The theory governing the sequence of appearances was to move the candidates rapidly about the country so that their presence in any locality would be top news for a considerable area. It was deemed better to make separate return appearances in three or four very important cities in one section of the nation rather than to move systematically from one to the other during a single trip. Each time he returned to a region, the reasoning ran, the candidate could expect headlines in most of the regional papers. Air travel made such scheduling possible, even if it was expensive as well as wearing on the candidates and their assistants.

Kennedy scheduling was entrusted to Kenneth O'Donnell, who accompanied the Senator on his trips. Headquarters scheduling was managed by Richard Maguire, supported by Richard O'Hare and John E. Nolan, Jr., who was Advance Chair. The Johnson schedule was entrusted to James Blundell supported by Wilson McCarthy.

The general schedules were worked out early in the campaign by top-level discussions at Democratic National headquarters, but details frequently were modified. The days to be spent in each state by each candidate were decided and the proportionate time to be given each major city was determined. Representatives of the scheduling office called on key Party leaders in the big states—men like Mayor Richard J. Daley of Chicago, the late United States Representative William Green of Philadelphia, and Governor David Lawrence of Pennsylvania—to learn their wishes before making final allocations of time.

Once the broad outlines were set, representatives of the scheduling offices worked with state Party leaders to establish which less important cities would be visited and how long the candidates would spend at each. In some instances, the detailed schedule was worked out by the advance men after they arrived on the scene. For example, Byrne Litschge and Dan Ogden worked out the Kennedy Kentucky schedule with state Democratic leaders in Louisville about ten days before the Senator's arrival, then cleared it with Washington.

Whatever the requests for appearances, the scheduling offices tried to give both candidates two days' rest each week. The days were juggled, however, so that before each of the four television debates, Senator Kennedy would have two full days free of appearances so he could rest and prepare for the confrontation. Such conservative scheduling paid handsome dividends before the television cameras.

Kennedy barnstorming was conducted almost entirely by air. The Senator and his immediate party used the *Caroline,* the Senator's personal plane. The press and other members of the traveling party flew in two Douglas DC-6's, chartered from American Air Lines. Ordinarily a group of nearly 100 traveled in the three-plane air caravan.

Space aboard the *Caroline* was at a premium. Only twenty seats were available. In addition to the Senator, one of his sisters, Mr. Sorensen, Mr. Salinger, and Mr. O'Donnell, stenographic help had to be accommodated. Six to eight seats always were reserved for state dignitaries. Sometimes another key staff man might be added if he were needed for a particular appearance.

THE ADVANCE MEN

Final arrangements for each appearance were handled by an advance man who flew in about ten days before the Senator's arrival. He was especially instructed to work with the local Party organization and not to do the work himself nor to run the local show.

Each advance man had four basic tasks. First, he was to generate a big crowd. To this end he was expected to promote publicity, set up phoning committees, stimulate attendance from surrounding communities, and use any other device to build interest and enthusiasm in the event. Second, he was responsible for the Senator's personal safety. No Secret Service aid was available. Inasmuch as an advance man rarely was trained in security work, he was expected to make suitable protection arrangements with local and state police. Third, he had to obtain adequate facilities for the traveling party. Specific directions were given him about housing for overnight stays and even for luncheon rest stops; about facilities and telephone and teletype requirements for the press; about the number and order of vehicles in a motorcade; about food (Senator Kennedy avoided dining in public); and even about fanfare upon the candidate's arrival—a band, decorations, buttons, and the like. Fourth, he was to work with local party people to insure united support for the Kennedy-Johnson ticket. Primary scars, local factional fights, and differences over policies and programs were to be smoothed over, especially during the candidate's appearance.

Kennedy forces recruited some 87 young men, mostly volunteers and largely from the legal profession, to be Kennedy advance men. Of this number, 45 helped in only one or two appearances. A basic crew of 23 did most of the work and handled four or more appearances each. Among this group were 13 men who set up five or more appearances and served as team captains from early October to the end of the campaign.

Johnson's advance team totaled at least 28 and leaned heavily upon congressional staff once the special session was over. On both the Kennedy and Johnson teams, those asked to do virtually full-time advance work were added to the National Committee payroll if they had no other means of support.

Training was highly informal. Unlike the Republican National Committee, the Democrats depended upon a 32-page instruction manual and the good sense of the men chosen for the advance team.

Much therefore depended upon the good judgment and practical political experience of individual advance men. Commonly a new recruit would find himself airborne within a matter of hours headed for a strange city with his instruction manual, a cash advance of $200, the name of the local Party leader, and the number of the private telephone line to the scheduling office in Washington. If local politicians chose to play games to outwit him, his life could be made miserable. If he knew enough politics to be sure he had the unreserved support of men with real power in the community where he was assigned, he usually could carry matters off with ease.

When several stops were to be made in one state, a team of advance men would be sent under a team captain. Often a captain would find himself with one or two experienced men and one or two rookies. He would distribute his men as the loads demanded. Ordinarily the inexperienced men were assigned simple jobs such as airport speeches. As a man gained know-how, he drew assignments involving motorcades, then meals, and then overnight stops.

Big teams of advance men were used in New York, Chicago, and Philadelphia. For the three days of appearances in Philadelphia and its suburbs during the next-to-last week-end before the election, a team of eleven advance men was sent in by the Kennedy forces. The team captain appointed lieutenants for each day who in turn were assigned two or three men to handle various segments of the work. On Saturday, for example, the team lieutenant and one rookie assistant ran a 12-hour motorcade through the western suburbs. One experienced advance man handled the morning appearances, another those in the afternoon and evening. Handling three or four appearances simultaneously taxed the powers even of men who had been through six weeks of rugged campaigning. In desperation, they finally had police cars carry them from shopping center to shopping center 30 minutes ahead of the candidate to permit last-minute inspections of facilities.

Each team captain was expected to go over the ground in the stops to be assigned him some five or six weeks before the appearances if possible. He thus could better guide his advance men in the final stages of their work.

Whatever the situation, Kenneth O'Donnell and Richard Maguire backed their men down the line. When the advance man made a decision, it stuck. When the traveling party arrived, the advance man was boss. No one left the planes until he gave the order, and no one changed the order of arrangements after arrival.

LOCAL PROBLEMS

An advance man had to be equal to any occasion. In one city the county jailer, who was a committee chairman for the Kennedy-day rally, proposed that he serve a luncheon to the Senator and his party on the fourth floor of his "hotel." He even displayed three prime country hams he had been curing for the occasion and exhibited the facilities—four cells!

One enthusiastic rally chairman announced to a planning meeting that he had arranged to release a thousand pigeons as Senator Kennedy arrived! A firm "no" from the advance man and a conciliatory discourse on the psychological importance of centering the crowd's attention on the candidate rather than the birds dissuaded him.

Sometimes rivalry spilled over from the primary campaign to complicate the advance man's life. In one city the local Kennedy chairman was planning to exclude Humphrey supporters from the speaker's platform. He couldn't accommodate everyone and felt the workers from the primary deserved to be rewarded. The dropping of a few careful hints by the advance man enabled other local leaders to persuade the chairman that an appearance of Party unity was more important for success than recognition for all the preconvention Kennedy faithful.

Sometimes plans well laid and well executed would go awry. At Fort Dodge, Iowa, Senator Kennedy arrived 45 minutes late because of an unscheduled stop in the previous city. A complicated program, involving a tumultuous ride through the city behind a long parade of floats and high-school bands, a brief address in the city park, and a second address at the airport, was run off in ten minutes less than the scheduled time. Senator Kennedy and his party were hustled back on their planes and the local rally committee congratulated themselves joyfully on a job well done as the caravan taxied for the end of the runway only 35 minutes late. Then came the blow. Clearance for take-off would not be given by the control tower because a scheduled commercial airliner was coming in for a landing! For 30 agonizing minutes the advance man had to "sweat it out" while the planes jockeyed around on the field in an event that had been entirely disregarded in the advance planning because no conflict had been expected with the commercial schedule.

Occasionally the advance man had a stroke of good fortune. Once in the Middle West, when an exceptionally large crowd had wholly blocked Senator Kennedy's return route to the airport, the advance man obtained police permission to use a prearranged emergency back road which required crossing a farm and entering the airport by the landing strip. As the motorcade turned unexpectedly into his yard, the farmer, in overalls and battered hat, stepped out to shake hands with the Senator. The motorcade stopped, the photographers had a field day, and the advance man got special thanks for arranging a good human-interest angle which he had not planned.

Group-work techniques proved especially useful to advance men who knew them. The basic problem was to get volunteer committee chairmen to work as a group in a common enterprise from which they could not be permitted to back out at the last minute. Success turned first on the advance man's making certain that all major tasks had been assigned a responsible person who had adequate numbers of helpers. Then the advance man personally visited each committee chairman to determine just what he had done, what he had left to do, and when he planned to do it. It was at this stage that judicious use of the instruction manual enabled the advance man to shape the course of planning to meet the traveling party's needs. The third step in the process was to assemble the committee chairmen, with the local leader presiding if possible, two or three nights before the candidate's arrival. After a detailed rundown of the timing, procedure on arrival, numbers of people who would be coming, and other basic facts which needed confirmation, each chairman was asked to report. All other committee chairmen were invited to ask questions as he went along to insure that their part of the activities would fit properly. The committee chairman known to be most advanced in his plans and preparations was called on first and a logical sequence of related committees called on thereafter. By the close of the meeting, every committee chairman was fully informed and had made firm commitments of action to all his colleagues, and the group as a whole had developed confidence in the certain success of its endeavors. By such experiences advance scheduling proved its worth.

BARNSTORMING WITH JOHNSON IN 1964

Barnstorming in the 1964 campaign will be heavily influenced by the tragic assassination of President Kennedy on November 22,

1963. The late President was traveling in a typical motorcade in a customary public appearance. The threat of another such attempt upon a President's life must be counted as very real.

The public should therefore expect, and indeed may demand, that the Secret Service provide additional protection when the President travels by limousine. Congress also might well be asked to provide full Secret Service protection for all future presidential and vice-presidential candidates of both major parties from their nomination until the victors are determined.

Such security provisions would protect the public from the destruction of its free choice of candidates for the highest public office by the diabolical whims of conspirators or madmen. It would also ease the advance-scheduling-management problems of the political parties. With security and routing professionally handled by the Secret Service, political advance men could concentrate on crowd turnout, on other physical accommodations, and upon handling local political niceties to insure united support.

Despite the tragedy of November, 1963, a return to front-porch campaigns, even with the advantage of television, seems unlikely. There is no substitute for meeting the people and for an opportunity to talk privately with key local political leaders. Because his opponent will surely barnstorm, President Lyndon B. Johnson must barnstorm, too.

The general outlines of the campaign schedule for 1964 probably will be determined in the White House under President Johnson's personal direction, for he has always taken a keen interest in his campaign appearances. Procedure for scheduling otherwise may follow substantially the pattern of 1960, for the men who handled that campaign are available to President Johnson.

But President Johnson's campaign trips are certain to be strikingly different from those he took as the vice-presidential candidate of 1960. His special appeal to the South and West was promptly revealed by the Harris poll the week after President Kennedy's death. Mr. Johnson surely will tour those areas to reassure them that he understands their economic and social problems. Yet his effort cannot be concentrated there.

The President's appeal in the North and East and to the agricultural Middle West has yet to be established. His knowledge and understanding of foreign policy likewise must be convincingly portrayed to areas where these matters long have been of paramount importance. Thus his basic strategy to win the traditional Democratic strongholds of the North will necessarily involve heavy campaigning there both by the President himself and by a vice-presidential running mate who is likely to be drawn from that section or from the Middle West.

The Kennedy policies, both foreign and domestic, carried vigorously to the Congress as part of his basic strategy to win the North, will necessarily comprise the central burden of President Johnson's appeals. He must journey to New York, Boston, Philadelphia, Cleveland, Detroit, Chicago, and other important cities to speak of civil rights to the racial minorities; of the tax cut to industry and labor; of federal aid to education, medicare, and urban improvements to the liberals. And as he visits and revisits America's northern heartland, he must pledge repeatedly his continued support for the United Nations, for aid to the underdeveloped free nations, and for negotiation with the Communist world from a defense posture second to none. No less is demanded by the times and the circumstances.

NIXON AND LODGE IN 1960

The strategy for the 1960 Nixon-Lodge barnstorming tours was devised by the Vice President and his immediate staff. The Convention promise to visit each of the fifty states reflected Nixon's compulsion to expose himself, in person, to as many people as possible. The wisdom of such an exhausting campaign has been reviewed with serious doubt. The Republican presidential nominee's major efforts to transform his image from the "old" Nixon to the "new" may have suffered because of this too-demanding schedule.

It has been argued, in fact, that overscheduling and at times overexposure were two of the Vice President's worst mistakes in the 1960 campaign. When the campaign pace set for a candidate leaves him wan and weak on the night of a national television debate, for example, the crucial importance of the scheduling function is clearly illustrated.

After Nixon had determined his barnstorming strategy and announced it in Chicago in July, tactical decisions were made. In

some states, such as Ohio, the state organization would select the
places which would be visited and decide the mode of transportation
to be used. In other states, such as California, the Nixon staff itself would set the itinerary. After the staff had established the over-
all field strategy and made at least tentative plans for the visits to
each state, preparations for "advancing" began—plan making for
work in advance of the candidate's appearances.

"Advancing" the Republican national candidates has traditionally been handled by the Republican National Committee. In
1960, however, it was decided that this function, like many others,
would be assumed by the Nixon-Lodge headquarters. The Vice
President's campaign manager, Bob Finch, was well acquainted
with the problems in this field since he had been an advance man
for the Vice President in the 1956 campaign. Jack Drown, Finch's
law partner from Los Angeles, was recruited to help direct the advancing activities.

Shortly after the Convention had adjourned, a selected group of
people from all over the country was brought to Washington for
brief schooling in political advancing. Some were young lawyers,
others had been loaned by industry, still others appeared to be just
out of college. Sponsored by the Nixon-Lodge headquarters, this
school was conducted by men well acquainted with both the technical problems involved in advancing and the political problems
of liaison with state and local regular Party organizations. These
men attempted to impress upon their young students the crucial
importance of establishing and retaining good relations with the
regular state and local Party leaders. As the campaign progressed, more and more people were brought into this activity.
These later advance men spent a short period as apprentices in
the field and then, armed with a manual, were given an assignment
to some city where a Nixon visit was impending.

The advance men's problems with the candidate's movements
may be reviewed under the headings of the kinds of transportation: motorcade, train, and air.

THE MOTORCADE

The instructions to the advance men for all categories of trips
stressed detail. For example, the Nixon-Lodge representatives

were instructed to be very particular about motorcade cars and drivers.

"Brand new cars should be avoided," the manual read, "because of the danger of overheating and the possibility of other mechanical failures. Convertible tops must be checked thoroughly and the cars must be completely decorated before they rendezvous for the motorcade."

Drivers for all except the national candidates' cars were to be young and "fully familiar with the local area and entirely capable of handling their automobile in traffic and in motorcade formation." The driver for the Vice President's car was automatically a Secret Service man and the driver of Ambassador Lodge's car was always to be supplied by the Party headquarters of the host state.

A mid-September telegram to all advance men from H. R. Haldeman (assistant to Jack Drown) instructed the advance man to place his car (in previous practice stationed far ahead of the motorcade) in the motorcade itself. This car was always to contain Haldeman, a police driver, the advance man for that particular visit, and a Secret Service agent, if necessary. In the same telegram the advance men were instructed to make the Nixon car a convertible until further notice. "Schedule top down whenever street crowds are expected, and top up for long highway runs."

Exact provisions for the motorcade lineups were stressed not only in the advance men's manual, but in telegrams sent from Washington, D.C., or from a Nixon staff member traveling with the Vice President's plane.

The plans called for the advance man's car; then a photographer's car (later a flat-bed truck or panel truck was specified); Nixon's car; the security car; a car for the wire services; the press buses and several cars for local office holders and dignitaries; staff cars; and a rear point security car.

By absolute order, the Vice President's car would always contain a Secret Service driver and a Nixon military aide. Only the Vice President and Mrs. Nixon would occupy the second seat. No exceptions were allowed.

Although original orders called for no exceptions to the rule that the press buses must immediately follow the wire-services car, this rule was broken on occasion. Thus, a Haldeman mid-September telegram to all advance men informed them that whenever a candidate for Senator or Governor was riding in the motorcade, his car should precede the press car and follow immediately behind the wire-services car.

Staff men traveling with Nixon rigorously defended this rule on the placement of local and state candidates. They contended that placement of the press bus more than two cars from the Vice President markedly diminished the impact of the crowd enthusiasm, size and general reaction—the very things the press should absorb.

As the advance man's manual put it,

If the press cannot see what is going on they cannot write about it. If the candidate stops, the press must be able to get out to be close to him.

To allow local officials to ride in advance of the press bus may serve their personal interest, admittedly sometimes critically important, but it erodes the Vice President's own critically important interest.

Even the speed of the motorcade was predetermined: never below 15 miles per hour even for large crowds, 15 to 18 miles per hour for scattered crowds and up to, but never beyond, the speed limit for open-country driving.

Press relations were often delicate matters for the advance men to handle. The basic instructions were that regardless of the topic involved—a schedule change, a detail of the local program, crowd estimates, or even a possible news item—only one source should pass the word to the news corps. That source was the Vice President's press secretary. Even the local press chairman was requested not to make news announcements after the campaign party's arrival.

Special events called for special patterns of response. When Mrs. Nixon was available for press coverage the advance men were advised to secure coverage by women reporters, if possible, in preference to men. A customary format for these meetings was developed which included a sit-down for coffee or tea, emphasis on informality, discouragement of photographs after the first few minutes, and an avoidance of the term "press conference" for such affairs. Rather, according to the manual, the language should be "Mrs. Nixon meets the ladies of the press."

Although Nixon advance men were instructed to always check their movements and clear their plans with state and local Party leadership, these instructions were somewhat uncertain in the light of other instructions regarding liaison with the regular Party headquarters. For example, they were told that the local police should thoroughly understand that orders for motorcade position must only come from the Nixon advance man, his designated agent, or the Vice President's press secretary. "A frequent trick," a memo stated, "is for the local official to countermand your order, pull his weight on an officer, and remake the motorcade without your knowing it. It has happened too often."

The general procedures used for Nixon advancing obtained for the 1960 Lodge campaign tours. The differences consisted mainly in small items such as the omission of a security car in the motorcade and the reliance upon local police rather than the Secret Service for the personal security of the Ambassador.

The scores of details listed on the Nixon-Lodge check-off sheets further illustrate the complexity of a presidential campaign tour. Included were such items as: Has the Vice President's room been supplied with copies of all relevant, recent local newspapers? Do the press buses for the motorcade have enough power to keep up with other motorcade cars in hilly and highway driving? Have special phone lines been put in to connect the Vice President's room with his campaign manager and his secretary?

As if these standard check-off items were not enough to plague the advance men and local chairmen, special-order telegrams were often sent immediately preceding the candidate's arrival. The following, for example, was received by one advance man on September 26:

There should be at least six horns of twenty-five to thirty-watt capacity each for all outside speaker requirements during an engagement. There should also be three sixty-watt amplifiers. There should be two microphones on the speakers' platform for the public-address system. These microphones should be of the directional type. Remember we need a platform twenty-five to thirty feet in front of Nixon that will hold a minimum of four newsreel cameramen. Height is such that cameras are at the Vice President's eye level.

THE TRAIN TOUR

A train tour for a presidential candidate is costly and involved, but most effective when it is necessary to make a strong appeal in a large number of small to medium-sized communities. In 1960, Vice President Nixon boarded a fifteen-car train in Washington, D.C., at 10:00 p.m. on Sunday evening, October 23. York, Pennsylvania, was to be the first of 43 public appearances in five states in a period of six days. Included in these 43 public appearances were 15 major addresses and a state-wide television appearance. To illustrate the nature of a train tour, the itinerary for the departure and first day is reproduced on the following pages.

AIR TRAVEL

One of the major problems in advancing a plane tour of various-sized communities is to learn which airport facilities can handle which planes. In addition, information must be obtained on flying times of various types of aircraft under differing conditions. And the question of using military vs. civilian airports must also be resolved.

Perhaps the most difficult of the air-tour problems, however, like the one for motorcades and train tours, is who shall be privileged to accompany the tour. Only a few VIP's can be accommodated on the candidate's plane, and as many newsmen as possible must be carried along.

A political technician like State Chairman Ray Bliss of Ohio solves such problems when any kind of tour comes through his state by using what he calls tour categories.

First there is the *state-wide category,* or what is sometimes termed the *permanent party*—people who ordinarily stay with the tour during its entire tour through a state. This category includes senators, the governor or candidates for these offices, candidates for or holders of the state constitutional offices, state supreme court candidates, the state Party chairman, the national committeeman and committeewoman, the chairman of the finance committee in the state, the chairman of the "volunteers" or "citizens" group in the state, and the state chairmen of the auxiliary groups (farmers, veterans, minority, women's groups, Young Republicans, etc.).

ITINERARY AND SCHEDULE

TRIP OF THE VICE PRESIDENT AND MRS. NIXON

October 23 through October 29, 1960

A. GENERAL INFORMATION

Train will consist of:

1 Pennsylvania Railroad 60′ Baggage Car—RCA to equip for power
1 Pennsylvania Railroad Dormitory Car—Crews
3 Twelve duplex, five bedroom sleepers (N-12, N-11, N-10)
2 Twelve duplex, four bedroom sleepers (N-9, N-8)
2 Three bedroom, one drawing room, 20 lounge seats (Press) (N-7, N-6)
1 Pennsylvania Railroad Diner cleared for Press Room (N-5)
1 Pennsylvania Railroad 48-seat Diner
1 Pennsylvania Railroad midtrain lounge (Reception Car) (N-4)
1 Twelve duplex, five bedroom sleeper (N-3)
1 Twelve duplex, four bedroom sleeper (N-2)
1 Pennsylvania Railroad business car 7504 (N-1)

Total 15 Cars—Capacity 124 in sleepers, based on one person to room.

B. LENGTH OF TRAIN

Each train company has been notified as to the length of the train and will add the length of their engine equipment to that total in order to place a stake for the engineer to line up with.

Sunday, October 23

		NOTES
10:00 PM EDT	Depart *Union Station*, Washington, D.C. for York, Pennsylvania	

Monday, October 24

8:00 AM EDT	Arrive York, Pennsylvania	York pop.: 60,000
	U.S. Senator is Hugh Scott; Candidate for Congress is George A. Goodling (19th District)	
	Remarks by the Vice President from the rear platform	
8:30 AM EDT	Depart York for Harrisburg, Pennsylvania	50 min.—27 mi.
9:20 AM EDT	Arrive Harrisburg, Pennsylvania	Harrisburg pop.: 85,000
	Congressman is Walter M. Mumma (16th District)	
	Rally off train at Market Square	
9:40 AM	Address by the Vice President	
10:10 AM	Depart Market Square for railroad station	
10:15 AM	Arrive railroad station	
10:20 AM EDT	Depart Harrisburg for Lewistown, Pennyslvania	1¼ hr.—61 mi.
11:40 AM EDT	Arrive Lewistown, Pennsylvania	Lewistown pop.: 15,000
	Brief remarks by the Vice President from the rear platform	

193

Monday, October 24 (continued)

11:55 AM EDT	Depart Lewistown for Huntingdon, Pennsylvania	¾ hr.—37 mi.
11:35 AM EST	Arrive Huntingdon, Pennsylvania	**Huntingdon pop.: 8,000**
	Candidate for Congress is Irving Whalley (18th District)	
	Brief remarks by the Vice President from the rear platform	
11:50 AM EST	Depart Huntingdon for Altoona, Pennsylvania	50 min.—34 mi.
1:40 PM EDT	Arrive Altoona, Pennsylvania	Altoona pop.: 70,000
	Congressman is James E. Van Zandt (20th District)	
	Remarks by the Vice President from the rear platform	
2:10 PM EDT	Depart Altoona for Johnstown, Pennsylvania	1 hr.—35 mi.
3:10 PM EDT	Arrive Johnstown, Pennsylvania	Johnstown pop.: 58,000
	Candidate for Congress is John P. Saylor (22nd District)	
	Remarks by the Vice President from the rear platform	
3:40 PM EDT	Depart Johnstown for Greensburg, Pennsylvania	55 min.—48 mi.
4:35 PM EDT	Arrive Greensburg, Pennsylvania	Greensburg pop.: 17,000
	Candidate for Congress is William L. Batten (21st District)	
	Remarks by the Vice President from the rear platform	
5:05 PM EDT	Depart Greensburg for Pittsburgh, Pennsylvania	50 min.—31 mi.

5:55 PM EDT	Arrive Pittsburgh (Pennsylvania Station)	Pittsburgh pop.: 650,000
	Congressmen are James G. Fulton (27th District) and Robert J. Corbett (29th District); candidates for Congress are Arthur O. Sharron (28th District) and Jerome M. Meyers (30th District)	
6:10 PM	Depart station by motorcade for hotel	
6:25 PM	Arrive Penn-Sheraton Hotel	PRESS ROOM: located off lobby
8:00 PM	Depart hotel for Syria Mosque	
8:25 PM	Arrive Syria Mosque	
8:30 PM	Address by the Vice President	
9:30 PM	Depart Syria Mosque for railroad station	
9:45 PM	Arrive Baltimore & Ohio Railroad Station	
10:00 PM	Board train	

The second, or *district category,* covers candidates for Congress, state committeewomen and committeemen, chairmen of the district "volunteer" or "citizens" group and sometimes cochairmen of these groups, chairmen of district Young Republicans, and chairmen of the district "volunteers" youth committee. The *regional category* covers only the regional finance chairman while the fourth, or *county category,* includes county central committee chairmen, county executive committee chairmen, chairmen of the county finance committees, county chairwomen, county "volunteers" chairmen and cochairmen, county farm representatives, county Young Republican presidents, etc.

Insofar as possible, the person in each category accompanies the permanent party only within the category jurisdiction, thus allowing for a maximum effective exposure of the presidential candidate with local and state Party leaders and officeholders.

REPUBLICAN ADVANCING IN THE 1964 CAMPAIGN

The campaign approach, scheduling, and advancing activities, like organization, platform content, and finance, will largely reflect the nominee's desires and the thinking of his immediate staff.

If the Republican National Committee assumes a more direct role in the actual administration of the 1964 presidential campaign, as appears likely, tactical scheduling and the advancing function will revert to Committee control. Decisions of actual campaign strategy, the modes of transportation to be utilized most frequently, and the planning and manning of the motorcades, trains, and aircraft undoubtedly will bear the personal imprint and style of the nominee himself.

Chapter X

Financing the Campaigns

It costs $10 million to run for President. That much, at least, is what both the Kennedy and Nixon forces admit to spending in 1960. Most observers believe a presidential campaign costs much more.

THE COST OF CAMPAIGNS

No one really knows how much it costs to run for President. The reason is simple. No one has ever kept track of all the costs and no law requires anyone to do so. The most diligent research by political scientists has turned up only approximations. This much is known:

In 1960, $25,014,000 was expended by 70 national-level political committees. Of this sum, various Republican committees supporting Vice President Nixon reported total campaign costs of $11,300,000. Democratic committees supporting President Kennedy reported spending $10,587,000.[1]

In 1956, President Eisenhower's reelection cost his Republican committees a reported $8,900,000, while Stevenson supporters expended an estimated $5,500,000.[2]

[1] Herbert Alexander, *Financing the 1960 Election* (Princeton, New Jersey: Citizens' Research Foundation, 1962), pp. 9-11.
[2] U.S. Congress, Senate, *1956 General Election Campaigns* (Washington: Government Printing Office, 1957), p. 42.

In 1952, Republicans spent $6,600,000 to elect General Eisenhower, while Governor Stevenson's backers spent $4,500,000.[3]

These figures represent the reported disbursements plus the known debts only of committees operating in two or more states. Much of the expense of presidential campaigning is borne by state and local party organizations which are not obliged to report their expenditures.

Certain other special committees disbursed large sums that should be added to the total available to the candidates. Most notable among them are the labor committees. In 1960 they reported expending $843,581 directly, but had gross receipts of nearly $2 million. Much of these funds went for registration and get-out-the vote drives, and some funds went to aid Mr. Nixon, but the bulk of the money must be counted for John F. Kennedy.[4] In 1956, labor groups disbursed $540,735 and in 1952, $797,544 largely to the benefit of the Democrats.[5]

It costs at least an extra $1 million to win a contested presidential nomination. Kennedy forces reported spending $912,500 to win the 1960 Democratic nomination. In addition, a family-owned corporation purchased and leased to him a $385,000 airplane.[6] Many costs were picked up by local Kennedy for President preconvention committees. Richard Nixon reported spending $500,000 to win the 1960 Republican nomination, even though he had virtually no serious opposition.[7]

Alexander Heard reports that the 1956 Democratic nomination cost the supporters of Adlai E. Stevenson "at least $1,500,000."[8] Eisenhower preconvention expenditures in 1956 were, of course, unrepresentative inasmuch as there was no contest for the nomination. In 1952, however, Citizens for Eisenhower reported ex-

[8] Alexander Heard, *The Costs of Democracy* (Chapel Hill, North Carolina: The University of North Carolina Press, 1960), p. 20. At least $500,000 to $800,000 of these funds went to congressional campaigns in each year, it appears.

[4] Alexander, *op. cit.*, p. 42.

[5] Heard, *op. cit.*, p. 20.

[6] Alexander, *op. cit.*, p. 16.

[7] *Ibid.*, pp. 21-22.

[8] Heard, *op. cit.*, p. 341.

pending $1,200,000 to win the nomination. Heard estimates that
the Eisenhower nomination effort cost at least $2,500,000 and that
"time, goods, and services contributed without reimbursement . . .
had a dollar value running into additional millions."[9] The Stevenson draft in 1952 was not expensive, however, only $20,000 being
reported. Stevenson himself spent $1,350, most of it during the
Democratic convention. Kefauver, however, who campaigned actively in both 1952 and 1956, spent at least $356,387 in 1952
and nearly $400,000 in 1956.[10]

Why should it take a sizable fortune to win the presidency? The
costs of publicity, travel, and staff support are very high.

The single largest bill in a presidential campaign is for television and radio time. In 1960 this bill ran $3,006,102, divided
$1,900,000 for the Republican candidate and $1,100,000 for the
Democratic.[11] In 1956, the Gore committee reported, the Democrats spent $1,950,000 promoting Stevenson's campaign by tele-
vision and radio, the Republicans, $2,739,000 for Eisenhower.[12]
At least 75 per cent of the money went for television in both elections. For these sums in 1960, the presidential and vice-presidential candidates received an average of 9 hours and 55 minutes of
air time over 429 television stations. These same stations also gave
them 6½ hours of free time, of which 4 hours were for the Great
Debates.[13]

The decline in expenditures in the face of rising costs in 1960
apparently was caused by two major items: the contribution by
the networks of the four hours of prime viewing time for the Great
Debates and the concentration by both candidates upon regional
telecasts of essentially local rallies which were paid for by state
party organizations. In 1956 both candidates had favored 30-
minute national telecasts of major addresses.

The two national committees saved a fortune on the four Great
Debates alone. The networks valued the time at $1,327,520.

[9] *Ibid.*, p. 335.
[10] *Ibid.*, pp. 335-336.
[11] Alexander, *op. cit.*, p. 31.
[12] U.S. Congress, *op. cit.*, p. 9.
[13] Alexander, *op. cit.*, p. 34.

American Broadcasting Company, which estimated the lowest direct cost for its contribution, a total of $250,000, reported that if the revenue sacrificed by affiliated stations and the administrative and advertising costs had been included, the loss would have been an additional $500,000. If such a ratio is generally justified, the Great Debates may have been worth about $4 million! National Broadcasting Company, however, reported its direct cost at $111,130 for each telecast, a total of $444,520. Columbia Broadcasting System reported time and production costs of $633,000 for the four programs.[14]

Other publicity is a heavy consumer of funds. The Democratic National Committee and the National Citizens for Kennedy-Johnson paid at least $2,413,227 to Guild, Bascom, and Bonfigli, the advertising agency handling their account, and $337,500 to Jack Denove Production, Inc., for films and tapes.[15]

Printed materials such as buttons, tabs, and auto bumper stickers add costs. In 1960, the Democratic bill just for those items handled by the Materials Distribution Center totaled $805,303.67. The Gore Committee reported a printing and distribution bill in 1956 of $1,900,076 for the Democratic Party and a $2,187,199 bill for the Republican. The latter figures, however, include costs for senatorial and congressional candidates as well as presidential.

Travel and transportation are large costs. Three chartered airplanes carried the candidates, their traveling parties, and the press to most campaign stops. Keeping an advance man in the field ran at least $40 a day for per diem and transportation alone and each party kept from 20 to 40 men out continuously. The Kennedy tour was estimated to cost $2,500 a day.

Staff salaries at headquarters are large, but not as crushing as might appear. The payroll at the Democratic National Committee ran $50,000 a week during the 10 weeks of the campaign—only about 5 per cent of the total cost. Republican figures were comparable.

[14] *Ibid,,* pp. 34-35.
[15] *Ibid.,* p. 31.

REGULATION OF PRESIDENTIAL CAMPAIGN FINANCE

Presidential campaign finance is regulated in five important ways by Congress.

REPORTS OF EXPENDITURES AND RECEIPTS

Committees operating in two or more states on behalf of candidates for President and Vice President are obliged to report their campaign expenditures quarterly. The Federal Corrupt Practices Act prescribes that the treasurer of each such interstate committee shall file reports with the Clerk of the House of Representatives between the first and tenth days of March, June, and September and before the first day of January each year. In presidential election years, additional reports must be filed between the tenth and fifteenth days before the election and on the fifth day before the election.

The reports must contain the name and address of each person who has made a contribution of $100 or more, in total, during the calendar year; the name and address of each person to whom $10 or more has been paid together with a statement of the sum, date, and purpose of the expenditure; the total sum of all contributions received; and the total sum of all expenditures made. Reports are cumulative from period to period during the year. Thus the final report on December 31 must cover the entire calendar year.[16]

Such reporting does not tell the whole story and really has more nuisance value than utility. Committees operating within a single state are exempted. Thus state and county party central committees and independent state and local citizen committees for presidential candidates can handle very large sums without reporting at all.

The Clerk of the House of Representatives merely keeps such reports on file for two years. He neither publishes nor analyzes them. The welter of detail thus collected has been used by a few scholars who have an interest in political finance, but even they have found the data largely unenlightening. The public has virtually no knowledge of the procedure or the information thus collected.

[16] 2 U.S.C. secs. 241-248.

LIMITATIONS ON SOURCES OF CONTRIBUTIONS

"It is unlawful," reads the Corrupt Practices Act, "for any corporation whatever, or any labor organization to make a contribution or expenditure in connection with any election at which Presidential and Vice Presidential electors . . . are to be voted for, or in connection with any primary election or political convention or caucus held to select candidates for any of the foregoing offices." The same section also forbids "any candidate, political committee, or other person to accept or receive any contribution prohibited by this section."[17]

Public Law 772 of the Eightieth Congress extended the prohibitions to any person or firm which has entered into a contract to sell any sort of goods or services to the United States during the life of the agreement.[18]

Such provisions have invited evasion. The Subcommittee on Privileges and Elections of the United States Senate in 1957 reported that the United States Chamber of Commerce had circulated widely a publication expressing the legal opinion that the following political activities could be undertaken by corporations:

(1) Pay salaries and wages of officers and regular employees while engaged in political activities;

(2) Publish opinions and arguments of a political nature, expressed as the views of the corporation, in any house organ or other printed document circulated at the expense of the corporation;

(3) Purchase radio and television time or newspaper space for the presentation of the corporation's political views;

(4) Use any other means of expressing the political views of the corporate management, publicly or privately;

(5) Encourage people to register and vote, and disseminate information and opinions concerning public issues without regard to parties and candidates.

The Committee reported that testimony had been developed which showed that corporations also:

(1) Make use of the advertising or entertainment funds of trade associations for political contributions;

[17] 18 U.S.C. sec. 610.
[18] 18 U.S.C. sec. 611.

(2) Place advertisements in political publications through public relations firms or advertising agencies;

(3) Make contributions in kind to political candidates (make available to them without pay the use of offices, airplanes, etc.);

(4) Permit the padding of expense accounts with the understanding that political contributions should be made out of the padded amounts; and

(5) Pay or prepay bonuses with the explicit or tacit understanding that part of such remuneration shall be spent in campaign contributions.[19]

Labor unions have taken the same attitude about use of funds from union treasuries. However, the endorsement of Democratic candidates in labor newspapers has led Republican union members to object to such use of their funds. In 1961 the Supreme Court ruled that railway workers, who are compelled by the Railway Labor Act to belong to a railway union, may prevent the union from using their dues for political expressions which they disapprove.[20]

To avoid these restrictions and yet to mobilize the resources of a large organization, the labor unions have developed independent Committees on Political Education which technically are not labor unions, although they usually are headed by labor union leaders. These committees raise funds from their members for avowedly political purposes, make contributions to candidates, solicit votes, and engage in other direct political action.

Federal employees are free to give to political causes, but they may not solicit funds and they may not be asked to contribute on public property. Presidential appointees and employees of the immediate office of the President are exempted from these restrictions. Similar prohibitions do apply to state employees who are paid in part by federal funds.[21]

The purchase or sale of goods, commodities, or advertising which are designed to raise money for a presidential campaign also is prohibited.[22] Political committees therefore simply offer special buttons, hats, ribbons, banners, pictures, and the like as "gifts"

---

[19] U.S. Congress, *op. cit.*, p. 24.
[20] *International Association of Machinists* vs. *Street* 367 U.S. 740 (1961).
[21] 5 U.S.C. sec 118 i and k.
[22] 18 U.S.C. sec. 608.

in return for "contributions" of a suggested amount. Tickets to fund-raising dinners and entertainment programs also are cautiously offered "free" in recognition of generous contributions—usually of $100 or more.

The gift subterfuge has had one benefit for the political parties: excise taxes are not charged on the amounts of the gifts. The political committees thereby enjoy the entire benefits of the proceeds.

LIMITATIONS ON AMOUNTS OF CONTRIBUTIONS

Individuals are limited by the Hatch Act of 1940 to a contribution of $5,000 during any calendar year to each presidential candidate and presidential campaign committee.[23] Intended to reduce the influence of wealthy individuals, the provision has only made bookkeeping more complicated for the political parties. An individual who wishes to give more than $5,000 simply divides his money by having his wife and other members of his family give $5,000 each or by distributing such sums among different political committees backing his candidate. Indeed, inasmuch as there is no limit on gifts to state and local committees, or on their transfer of funds to the national committees, the simplest way to make a very large gift is to turn it over to a state central committee for handling.

LIMITATIONS ON AMOUNTS OF EXPENDITURES

National committees also are limited by the Hatch Act to annual expenditures of $3 million.[24] In ordinary years, when committee operating budgets run from $750,000 to $1 million, the restriction is academic. In campaign years, the restriction is a major handicap to fiscal control.

With presidential campaign costs running more than $10 million, the candidate for President is obliged to establish several other national committees, each of which can spend $3 million. Such an arrangement requires the keeping of several sets of books, the shifting of funds and bills back and forth among committees to

[23] *Ibid.*
[24] 18 U.S.C. sec. 609.

keep each one from spending more than the legal limit, and sometimes even the transfer of personnel from one payroll to another. With several treasurers in the act, central fiscal control becomes unnecessarily complex and unwieldy.

Only a partial solution can be found in using the credit of the regular National Committee. As a continuing body which must meet outstanding debts, the National Committee can postpone paying some bills, for example printing, telephone, and leased transportation, for 60 days after the election. Being then in a new calendar year, it is free to spend an additional $2 million or so to pay campaign bills.

Because the limitations on amounts of contributions and on amounts of expenditures are not only ineffective but are actually an impediment to responsible fiscal control of presidential campaigns, the President's Commission on Campaign Costs recommended in April, 1962, that both provisions be repealed.[25]

LIMITATIONS ON THE PURPOSES OF EXPENDITURES

Prohibition of the bribery of voters is the only federal limitation on purpose of presidential-campaign expenditures. Many states, however, restrict other actions which affect presidential elections. Thirty-two prohibit the furnishing of intoxicating liquor on election day and fifteen prohibit expenditures to transport voters to the polls, although nine of these exempt the sick and the infirm.

Thirty-one states enumerate permissible expenditures. Some state laws are limited to candidates only, others apply only to political committees. The lists of acceptable purposes run the gamut of ordinary campaign activities and include such items as printing, traveling expenses, rent, salaries, and employing counsel.[26] Such state restrictions, if construed to affect presidential candidates, seem not to have imposed handicaps or to have significantly altered campaigning.

[25] President's Commission on Campaign Costs, *Financing Presidential Campaigns* (Washington: Government Printing Office, 1962), p. 17.
[26] See U.S. Congress, Senate, *Final Report of the Special Committee to Investigate Political Activities, Lobbying, and Campaign Contributions* (Washington: Government Printing Office, 1957), pp. 327-337.

FREEDOM FROM LIMITATIONS ON PERSONAL ACTIONS

Candidates for President and Vice President enjoy a unique personal freedom from regulation. Technically, they are not candidates for office. The candidates being chosen by the people are running for the office of presidential elector. Thus, unlike candidates for Congress, presidential candidates need not report contributions they receive or expenditures they make in their own campaigns. They also face no dollar limitations on the amounts they personally can spend. They are, however, prohibited from receiving contributions from corporations and labor organizations and cannot solicit campaign funds if they are receiving compensation for services from the Federal government.

WHO PAYS THE BILLS?

The major political parties get funds for presidential campaigns from the people who have the money: the well-to-do. Small gifts from many people, championed by idealistic political scientists who would like to see the parties freed from dependence upon personal and corporate wealth, are hard to organize and unproductive for the national party organizations.

Two types of small-giver drives have been tried by both parties: mail solicitation of a list of party faithful by the national committee and direct door-to-door solicitation by local party committees which are expected to hand a share of the proceeds to the national committee. Mail solicitations of "sustaining memberships" of $5 or $10 a year have yielded $240,000 for the Democratic National Committee, but door-to-door solicitation has never brought in more than $120,000. Although reports indicate some large sums have been raised door-to-door, most of the money understandably sticks in the treasuries of local and state committees along the way.

Such amounts will not keep a national committee operating in ordinary times. In a presidential campaign, they will not keep the doors open a week. So the committees turn to more easily tapped and more lucrative sources—their own state central committees and those who are able to make large personal donations.

THE GIVING CIRCLE

Those who give big money can raise big money. Few people give big money without being asked. These basic rules underlie use of the "giving circle."

Every large community has a group of leading citizens who are quite well-to-do. Well acquainted with one another, operating in the same social circle, doing business with one another, their families probably intermarried to some extent, these people are the pillars of the local churches, the chairmen of service-organization boards such as the Red Cross and the Camp Fire Girls, the fund raisers for community projects, and the financial angels for their colleges. Their gifts to their several "activities" are tax-deductible and, for those families with very substantial incomes, may even be pro-gramed systematically in order to strengthen their influence and to maximize tax savings.

Every few weeks, someone in the giving circle calls on most of the others on behalf of the charity or service in which he is taking a leading part. For the Community Chest, all will be visited. For each church, only identified members will get a call. A regular season for giving for each charity is long since well established: the Community Chest in October, the Tuberculosis Association in December, the Polio Fund in January, and so on. In the course of a year, many members of the giving circle have called on the others on behalf of a project which they have agreed to support.

In September of presidential election years, another round is made, this time by the members of the giving circle who have offered or been invited to be the fund raisers for the presidential candidates of their political parties. Each knows whose pocketbooks will be open, for his have been open to them, and each knows who will probably be giving to the other candidate and who may even give to both. Thus the Republican fund chairman does not bother his known Democratic colleagues, and vice versa, unless he suspects that defection is in the wind. One does not use up "credit" with a member of the giving circle needlessly, for the next visit may involve renewal of an insurance policy or a loan for a new building.[27]

[27] Heard, *op. cit.,* pp. 78-84 catches the spirit of this point.

Giving circles do not operate just in the $1,000 to $5,000 gift class. Those who give in the $100 to $500 class also operate giving circles and still more modest levels also flourish. At all levels, however, the principle is the same. He who would raise funds must be one of the circle of givers whom he will solicit.

Big giving starts, then, with those who have money and who feel a personal responsibility for the success of the campaign. Such a person may be related to the candidate, be a close personal friend, have a great deal to gain or lose by his success or failure, or feel very deeply about the policies he espouses. Motivation is highly complex.

Giving in a presidential campaign is a personal matter, however. Few big givers do so as a matter of habit. Mr. Kennedy could loosen the purse strings of men who never gave to Mr. Stevenson, while Stevenson opened doors which were closed to Mr. Truman before him. So the members of the giving circle in each city act accordingly, expanding the circle or varying their visits as political intelligence dictates.

The essential first move of a candidate who would raise big money is to secure on his team a member of the giving circle in as many major cities as he can. In 1960, John F. Kennedy had a head start over all his competitors. He had brothers-in-law in Chicago and Los Angeles, and close business associates of his father in New York and Philadelphia. The top giving circles of the major cities of the nation were immediately open to him.

ASSESSMENT OF STATE COMMITTEES

The other major source of funds for a national campaign is assessment of the state central committees. Each will be asked to raise what the national committee regards as a fair share of the campaign cost.

"Fair shares" may be determined in many ways. Sometimes a scientific formula will be used based on population, numbers of party supporters, and per capita income. More often the quota is set by the amount raised in a previous campaign—for proved ability to get money is more important than theoretical capacity.

Both sources of funds—the giving circle and the state committees—will be helped in their efforts by formal affairs in their chief cities aimed at the well-to-do. The most common device is the $100-a-plate dinner at which the presidential candidate is the speaker. In recent years, variations on this theme have raised the ante to $250, $500, and even $1,000 a plate where there were enough rich people to hold such exclusive parties. In Washington, D.C., both political parties repeatedly have packed the District of Columbia Armory with 5,000 guests for $100-a-plate affairs.

WHO THE BIG GIVERS ARE

The big givers are the leading industrial families of the United States, the officials of their industries, professional men who serve them, the men who lead their employees, and the leaders in the law, medicine, entertainment, and advertising. Few farmers are big givers and virtually no career public servants are in that class.

In 1960, twelve leading families gave $646,521; in 1956 the same families gave $1,153,735. Most was given to Republican causes. The Democrats received $78,850 from them in 1960 and $107,109 in 1956.[28] In 1960, ninety-five individuals gave $10,000 each, or more. Of these, 60 contributed to the Republicans, 35 to the Democrats. Yet the biggest single giver in either campaign year, who was not also a candidate for office, was Mr. Lansdell K. Christie of New York, who in 1956 gave $73,164, mostly to the Democrats.[29]

In 1956, 199 officers of the nation's leading corporations gave $1,936,847. In 1952, 92 officers gave $1,014,909. All gifts were of $500 or more. Only 19 labor officials gave $500 or more, however, to total $19,000. As might be expected, most of the corporate giving was to Republican causes, most of the labor to Democratic.[30]

When one family can give more than a national political party can raise in a comprehensive door-to-door drive for small gifts, and two families did so in 1960, the parties may be pardoned for

[28] Alexander, *op. cit.,* p. 61; and U.S. Congress, Senate, *1956 General Election Campaigns, op. cit.,* p. 12.

[29] Alexander, *op. cit.,* p. 59.

[30] U.S. Congress, Senate, *1956 General Election Campaigns, op. cit.,* pp. 12-15.

seeking the money where it can be found. Neither party is now or is likely to be well enough organized or sufficiently centralized to be able to raise through small-giver drives enough money for a presidential campaign. Both parties in 1964 are certain to rely upon the giving circle and the assessment of state central committees and, thus, upon those who are affluent enough to give generously.

REPUBLICAN FINANCIAL ORGANIZATION

Since 1937 the Republican National Finance Committee has served as the central financial organ for the Party. It was obvious after the debacle of 1936 that a major rebuilding job was necessary if the Republicans were to come back. Rebuilding a national institution is a costly process. Thus it was that the Republican Finance Committee was created to coordinate financial planning for the National Committee, the Senatorial Campaign Committee, and the Congressional Campaign Committee.

Selected for the job of restructuring the financial apparatus of the Republican Party was Carlton G. Ketchum of Pittsburgh. His role in the rebuilding process emphasized the early recognition of the need for professional staff men in the financial phase of Party political work. For Ketchum, though a dedicated Republican, was not a politician per se. He was, rather, an eminently successful fund raiser.

THE REPUBLICAN SYSTEM

Under Ketchum's direction the Republican National Finance Committee assigned to individual state finance committees annual quotas which they were expected to raise and send to the National Finance Committee. The actual quotas assigned to a given state were based on the electoral vote of the state, the population, the Republican vote in the last election, the personal income tax paid by the state's residents, the number of occupied dwellings, and the purchasing power of the state's population.

Having learned how much it owed the National Party organization, the state Party leadership was to determine its own needs for the next year and add this amount to the national figure. Each county finance committee was then assigned by the state finance committee an equitable share of this combined state-national figure. To this figure it would in turn add the costs of its own local operation in order to compute the total amount it must raise to meet its obligations.

Ideally, all Republican fund raising in a county was to be undertaken by that county's finance committee. The fund-raising program became, under Ketchum's plan, similar to the annual United Fund drives for support of various social agencies in most large cities.

The unified nature of the campaign theoretically eliminated the possibility of a given party member being asked to donate more than once to the Republican Party during any given year. The state finance committee was to function as the centralized control center not only to set county quotas and work out agreements with county finance committees, but also to provide assistance in the form of professional fund raisers working out of the state finance committee.

A third cardinal feature of the Republican program was the separation of the fund-raising function from the "political" activities of the Party. There were good reasons for this separation. Experience over the years had clearly indicated that good "political" leaders are often not good money raisers; conversely, good money raisers may not be the best public spokesmen for a party. Thus the political leaders of the operating units of the Party were instructed to submit an estimate of their needs for a given year and, subject to negotiation with the finance committees (county, state and national), a final budget was to be arrived at which the finance committees then undertook to provide.

These innovations wrought by Ketchum set the pattern for Republican fund raising from 1937 on. They introduced professionalization in the political fund-raising area and provided for continuous, year-round programing of the Party's finance efforts.

Failures were bound to occur in such a neat system. The extent to which Republican fund raising approached the Ketchum ideal has varied from state to state and in some states from year to year. In few states do all of the counties agree to accept the "united giving" program. Some state finance committees cannot raise the necessary funds to pay their quota to the National Finance Committee or to meet their commitment to their own state Party executive committees.

Another problem encountered in the administration of the unified fund drive is the independent fund drive for a particular candidate. Such drives sabotage, in effect, the Party's attempt at a united effort, but the Party can do little about them. During a presidential year, volunteer or citizen committees are especially likely to be in the field raising money in competition with the regular finance committees, although they are formed primarily to attract funds and votes from citizens not likely to respond to a purely partisan approach.

FINANCING, 1960-1963

Despite these unavoidable variations, the Republican fundraising plan has worked well and the Republican national committees entered the presidential campaign of 1960 in a fairly strong financial position. Their treasury had a small surplus left over from their 1959 budget, and they benefited handsomely early in the year from a series of highly successful fund-raising dinners honoring President Eisenhower. When all the bills were in, however, and all the figures tallied, the Republicans discovered at the end of the campaign that they had amassed a net debt of slightly over $700,000. Excluding state and local committee expenditures, costs for the national Republican presidential campaign amounted to $11,300,000 in 1960. Where did the money come from to pay this large a bill?

Unlike so many of the 1960 Republican presidential campaign operations, Republican fund-raising was centered at the Republican National Committee Headquarters, more precisely in the Republican National Finance Committee. Setting an original campaign goal of $7,800,000, the Finance Committee actually raised over $8,000,000. Added to this was $500,000 raised by national Nixon-Lodge Clubs, $2,300,000 raised by the Volunteers for Nixon-Lodge, and almost $375,000 raised by miscellaneous Republican committees. The grand total was $11,180,000.

Two sources supplied most of this $11,180,000. *Large individual gifts* to the Republican National Committee, the Congressional

Campaign Committee, the Senatorial Campaign Committee, and the Independent Television Committee totaled $6,213,766. *Fund-raising dinners* supplied most of the rest. Eighty-three "Dinners with Ike" netted the national Party $1,800,000; thirty-six "campaign dinners" yielded $1,200,000 for the presidential campaign; and twenty-three additional fund-raising affairs turned in an estimated $1,250,000.

Despite their $700,000 campaign deficit, the Republicans started 1961 with cash balances amounting to roughly $500,000 distributed among the three national committees. Their plans called for a 1961 fund-raising goal of $2,500,000 which would retire their debt and allow them ample funds for the upcoming 1962 congressional campaign.

To raise this money the Republicans concentrated on a program which gave associate membership in the national Party to every $1,000 contributor. A congressional dinner, again featuring Eisenhower, was also used in June of 1961. It netted roughly $450,000 for the 1962 congressional election campaign.

But the heavy reliance on these emergency devices, such as the Ike dinners, had provoked the long-time advisor to the Republican National Finance Committee, Carlton Ketchum, to insist that extra effort be placed on improving the unified fund drives at the state and county levels. He argued against what he thought was an overemphasis on direct national solicitation. But many states were not meeting their national quotas. Where could the national Republican Party turn?

One direction pointed clearly toward broadening the financial base of the Party. Both major parties had spent considerable time with such programs as Dollars for Democrats and Neighbor to Neighbor during the 1950's; and there had been some local successes (Hennepin County, Minnesota, for example, had set a Neighbor to Neighbor goal of $60,000 in 1960 and raised $94,000). But since a relatively small percentage of these funds reached Washington, this program did not seem to offer promise of substantial funds. Some national Party leaders began to look toward the use of a direct-mail solicitation from the National Party Headquarters.

Such a plan had been used by the Democratic National Committee since 1957 and by some state Republican committees as well. It was not entirely new to the Republican National Finance Committee either, for late in 1959, Spencer T. Olin, then Chairman of the Republican National Finance Committee, experimented with the idea of a direct-mail solicitation campaign from the national Party headquarters. The experiment was a request for a small contribution from those who could not participate in a "Dinner for Ike." Though it had only a limited financial success, Olin was helping to set the stage for a national Party sustaining-membership program. In an extremely interesting and informative interoffice memorandum, Olin outlined the problems and prospects for such an effort. He reported encouraging returns from a test mailing but commented on two problems. First, many people got two or more appeals. Such duplication is inevitable, since many people are on more than one mailing list, especially commercial mailing lists. It would be costly and it is impossible to eliminate these duplications. Second, all but a few mailing lists are mixed—Democrats, Republicans, and what not—and cannot be sifted. So prominent Democrats inevitably get Republican fund appeals; and quite often they use them in public ridicule of the Republicans. Olin was not disturbed by either problem.

A program of solicitation by direct mail for sustaining memberships ultimately was established in 1962, with the joint support of the Republican National Committee, the Republican Senatorial Campaign Committee, the Republican Congressional Campaign Committee and the Republican National Finance Committee. A contribution of $10 entitled the donor to a year's subscription to *Battle Line,* the National Committee's regular publication, and a sustaining-membership card issued from the Republican Party national headquarters.

The success of the Republican sustaining-membership program was much greater than expected. In the first year of its operation more than $900,000 was raised in this way. In 1963 it brought to the National Headquarters slightly more than $1,000,000. And in 1964 receipts from the early months indicate contributions are running substantially ahead of the similar period in 1963.

But these funds have been used mainly for National Party current expenses. A series of major fund-raising dinners in January was necessary to finally retire the last $225,000 of the 1960 campaign debt. With no debt and a small surplus, the Republican National Headquarters then looked forward to the 1964 campaign.

FINANCING, 1964

What it saw was not entirely reassuring. Fund raisers around the country opined that too much emphasis was being placed on the prospective presidential candidates. Frank Kovac, formerly an executive in the Republican National Finance Committee, had assumed the executive directorship of the finance committee of the Goldwater for President Clubs. He indicated that Goldwater was receiving tremendous financial support at the grass roots and that much "contingent" money was available across the land. (Contingent money here means that a check is good only if Goldwater receives the nomination.) It was assumed by some observers, however, that Goldwater would not get the so-called Eastern "big money" that a more moderate candidate could readily command.

These same fund raisers suggested that if Rockefeller were to be the nominee substantial amounts of money from large contributors would be available for the national campaign but some feared that such a candidacy would dry up sources usually counted on for state and local support. (This problem was one experienced in the 1960 campaign, where record-breaking sums were raised for the national election but where many state and local Party organizations were hard-pressed for campaign funds.)

A moderate or compromise candidate such as Scranton, Morton, or Romney would probably have less money available than either Rockefeller or Goldwater but more of it would be from the regular contributors who are party-oriented rather than candidate-oriented.

DEMOCRATIC FISCAL IMPROVISATION

The Democratic Party has never developed a separate, systematic fund-raising system comparable to the Republican. In part, the failure has been deliberate. Observing the power which the fund chairmen wielded within the Grand Old Party, Democratic leaders avowed preference for a system which kept authority in the hands of the duly elected county and state chairmen. In part, the failure was due to the Democrats' special problems in raising funds. In the South, the Party could seek money from the general business community which the Republican finance system taps in the North. Elsewhere, it depended upon lone Democrats among the businessmen, on labor, on special industries such as entertainment and beverages, and on public employees. Systematization of such sources did not promise to be greatly more productive than the old order.

· THE POVERTY OF THE DEMOCRATIC NATIONAL COMMITTEE

In 1960, a $750,000 debt from the 1956 presidential campaign still hung over the Democratic National Committee. Every effort to erase it had been insufficient. Although some old bills had been paid, most incoming funds had been used, in effect, to keep the National Committee going.

National Chairman Paul M. Butler, in an effort to develop independent sources of finance for the National Committee, had established a Finance Director and had asked him to seek new sources of revenue in small-giver drives. Two promising efforts had been mounted. The Dollars for Democrats Drive, a door-to-door solicitation by county central committees, had operated yearly beginning in 1957 and had raised from $45,000 to $106,000 each year. The Sustaining Membership Program, also inaugurated in 1957, solicited $10 contributions to the National Committee by mail. By 1960 a list of 600,000 Democrats had been compiled who annually gave nearly a quarter of a million dollars.

A further effort was made to raise money by assessment of state central committees. Income from assessment, set up at $1,187,500 per year, was designed to pay committee bills and retire the campaign debt by 1960. Early in 1960 a new quota formula was announced, based upon the number of Democratic voters, the number of Democratic incumbents, and other acceptable criteria.

Assessment became increasingly a failure. On June 30, 1960, Chairman Butler published a very revealing report on state quota payments from 1957 through 1960. Only eight states and territories had paid in full: Maryland, Virgin Islands, South Dakota, Wyoming, District of Columbia, Delaware, New Jersey, and Florida. Maryland's 164 per cent of its share had been paid almost wholly by Montgomery County, adjoining the District of Columbia, with the proceeds from its extraordinarily successful Dollars for Democrats Drives. However, on the basis of quarterly installments, half of the states were virtually up to date. Seventeen states had paid less than half. Three states, with a long record of nonpayment, were listed at the bottom: Mississippi at 8.6 per cent, Puerto Rico at 10.6 per cent, and South Carolina at 11.6 per cent. Worst offenders among the big urban states were Illinois, ranking forty-eighth with but 34.4 per cent paid, and New York, ranking fortieth with 44.9 per cent in. Six southern states were in the group most in arrears.

Butler rewarded the faithful states by assigning them front seats at the convention and by giving them the best Los Angeles hotels. The Illinois delegation, by contrast, found itself in the back of the Sports Arena and consigned to a hostelry without air conditioning "just off skid row."

In a last desperate effort to bail the National Committee out of debt by convention time, Butler announced a special "750 Club" which was to enjoy special facilities and special privileges at Los Angeles. Membership in the club was obtained by a $1,000 donation to the National Committee. Hard work on the 750 Club program and last-minute quota payments, encouraged by the assignment of housing and seats at the convention, reduced the debt somewhat by the opening of the campaign.

KENNEDY FUND RAISING IN 1960

Fund raising for the Kennedy campaign used three basic sources: the giving circle was tapped in as many cities as possible, state central committees were assessed quotas double their 1956 contributions, and the regular small-giver efforts were carried through.

Before the Convention, Paul Butler had established a National Finance Committee which was to raise funds for the campaign. Chairing it were Roger Stevens of New York and Sydney Solomon of St. Louis. Each state chairman had been asked to appoint one or two persons to represent his state on the Finance Committee and most had done so. On the Saturday following the nominations, the Finance Committee met for the first and only time in the Biltmore Hotel in Los Angeles. Thirty-seven persons showed up and agreed to bend every effort to raise funds. Illinois enthusiastically proposed a very large fund-raising dinner in the near future. Beyond the individual efforts of the Committee members, however, the Finance Committee itself did not function further in the campaign.

Retained as National Committee Treasurer, Matthew H. McCloskey promptly undertook to assess the states. He and Finance Director Dennis Jensen arranged eight regional meetings, to each of which were invited the National Finance Committee members, National Committee members, state chairmen, and Dollars for Democrats chairmen of several states. Representatives from all but eight or nine states attended one of the meetings. Quotas were agreed upon. The new formula was set aside and McCloskey instead asked each state to raise twice the sum it had contributed to the Stevenson campaign in 1956. Under this plan, little would be expected of states which had done little for Stevenson. McCloskey therefore judiciously raised the sights for those states which had obviously not done what they could.

To follow up the regional fund-raising conferences, a meeting was held at the Mayflower Hotel in Washington, D.C. which Senators Kennedy, Johnson, and Jackson, Adlai Stevenson, and former President Truman attended. Agreement was reached to promote a series of $100-a-plate dinners in key centers across the country as a major fund-raising device.

Small gifts were encouraged by the Sustaining Membership Program and Dollars for Democrats. Six hundred thousand requests for $10 sustaining contributions were mailed out and $240,000 received.

The Dollars for Democrats Drive officially yielded $121,059.92 which the Democratic National Committee was able to identify, making the 1960 Drive the largest and most successful such effort.

Nearly twice the previous volume of certificate books, 400,000, was distributed. Forty-eight states and territories organized statewide Drives and county Drives were used in at least two nonparticipating states.

Total yield of the Dollars for Democrats Drive will never be known because county and state organizations did not send forward one-third of their gross receipts to the National Committee, as the division of proceeds presumed, and because the National Committee did not identify special accounts carefully as the funds came rolling in. Some state and local committees argued that inasmuch as they had paid their quotas they had no further obligation to contribute to the higher units. Some money which states sent to the National Committee was not identified as coming from their Dollars for Democrats Drive and thus was not credited to it. Arkansas, for example, raised a large sum by its door-to-door canvass but lumped the proceeds in with other money in submitting its quota payments. Clerks at the National Committee often failed to identify Dollars money as such at the time of receipt and thus it was not picked up by the tabulating system. Moreover, after the middle of October, all major checks were put through the Citizens for Kennedy-Johnson finance system, which did not distinguish among sources of contributions.

One other effort to reach small givers—a souvenir-check campaign—failed. Thousands of blank souvenir checks were printed up in $1, $5, and $10 denominations and distributed ahead of the candidates on the tour. On one side the check was a business-reply card. On the other, a check to the Democratic National Committee ready to be signed. All the well-wisher had to do was name his bank and sign, then drop it in the mail. The Committee received very few souvenir checks and did not even recover expenses.

At the height of campaign pressure early in November, the National Committee discovered that it had been getting money from an unexpected source: a forger in Spokane, Washington. With a fine impartiality, he had sent generous checks to both the Democratic and Republican National Committees and had signed the names of prominent local party leaders whom he apparently thought were not being generous enough. On one $700 check, simulating the victim's handwriting, he even added, "Pour it on!"

THE HUGE DEBT: ITS CAUSE AND ITS REPAYMENT

The unparalleled campaign debt of $3,820,000 piled up because the Kennedys campaigned to win and realized they had to match their opponents nearly dollar for dollar. Their credit was good because they were known to have money. The 1960 campaign cost as much as both Stevenson campaigns combined! The funds didn't come in fast enough because the Democratic Party was not geared to raise $10 million in three months.

From the beginning, both Matthew McCloskey, Treasurer of the National Committee, and Stephen Smith, the effective Treasurer of Citizens for Kennedy-Johnson, knew they would have to divide the costs between them and that both would probably spend to their legal limits. McCloskey started with the added handicap of having used nearly a third of his limit to pay the debts and run the preconvention affairs of the National Committee. Thus at least one other major committee would have to handle part of the expenses.

The basic steps in preventing a campaign deficit are to impose budget and accounting controls centrally and to enforce rigid economy. In an effort to simplify procedure and to maintain some vestiges of central control, the Comptroller's office of the National Committee installed a form of automatic data processing which was made available to Citizens for Kennedy-Johnson. Early receipts and expenditures were run through the National Committee's books. In mid-October, as the National Committee approached its spending limit, everyone on its staff was fired and immediately retained by the Citizens for Kennedy-Johnson. All incoming contributions of any size were signed over to Citizens by National Committee Treasurer McCloskey. Bills similarly were redirected. The Citizens accounting team was moved from the Esso building to the fifth floor at 1737 L street and processed its receipts and expenditures through the National Committee's machines.

To control budgets, Ralph Dungan and Richard Donohue tried to set spending limits for each unit of the Committee. Successful to a degree with the new auxiliary units, they faced the problem of having several units with separate treasuries and several old units of the Committee which expected to clear expenditures through the Chairman's office.

On September 21, Chairman Jackson also sought to impose central budgetary controls by assigning William H. Perkins the task, but recognized the organizational dilemma he faced by confining Perkins' function to "the orderly and economic use of the Committee's funds."

Both National Committee Treasurer McCloskey and Citizens Committee Treasurer Smith appear to have exercised independent judgment about clearing expenditures. McCloskey seems to have taken the position that he should pass on expenditures inasmuch as the National Committee ultimately would have to meet all unpaid bills. Smith also appears to have believed that he should pass judgment as long as Citizens for Kennedy-Johnson was paying the bills. As a result, some projects were approved by one man only to be disapproved by the other.

The National Committee itself compounded the financial problems. Many persons were able to spend money without having to worry about where it came from. For example, because there was no central personnel system, department heads were permitted to set salaries independently. Stipends for clerical help were kept within reason, but professional salaries in several instances reached the absurd—with a few persons even being granted $500 a week until review by the Finance Department ended the practice. Also, although cash advances were used for men sent out of Washington on Committee business, credit cards for airlines, telephones, and food also were issued. Abuse followed. The Committee received food bills charged to a restaurant across the street from headquarters and discovered that a few of its irresponsible representatives had occupied extremely expensive hotel rooms to which they had ordered generous quantities of food and drink. One man even sent the Committee a doctor bill!

Sometimes just poor planning ran up bills needlessly. In Philadelphia, nearly 70 members of the press were permitted a $5 dinner at National Committee expense, although all had their own expense accounts, because no one had arranged with the restaurant's manager to collect from them as they arrived.

Other slips might be noted. The supply of buttons and lapel tabs purchased totaled 67,982,652, just about two for every vote Kennedy received! Yet the Committee's supply was exhausted when the campaign closed.

Miscalculations and needless expenses probably account for a very minor portion of the debt. The debt came because campaign costs were up. It came because the Kennedys were determined to conduct a thorough campaign, better advertised than in 1956, better advanced, better staffed, and better supported with auxiliary efforts.

A $3,820,000 debt gets on the books because some companies extend credit. Television and radio stations give no credit. Cash must be paid to the station 48 hours before air time or the show doesn't go on. Credit in 1960 came especially from printing concerns which enjoyed generous contracts, from airlines which rented airplanes and crews to the Committee, and from the telephone company which tolerated an intolerable bill.

A winner has a much easier time paying his bills than a loser. The first big step for the National Committee was to hold an inaugural eve "Gala" starring Frank Sinatra; Peter Lawford, the President's brother-in-law; and many other stars of stage and screen. Seats at the District of Columbia Armory were given those who contributed $100 or more. Nearly one-quarter of the debt was erased in one night.

There followed a series of $100-a-plate dinners across the land in celebration of Jefferson's birthday. The following January, a whole series of $100-a-plate victory dinners marked the inaugural anniversary. Another $100-a-seat Gala in 1963 on the second anniversary of inauguration virtually erased the debt.

DEMOCRATIC PREPARATIONS FOR 1964

Somehow the Democratic Party must gear up for a $10-million campaign in 1964, for no organizational overhaul of Party finance has been undertaken. The first steps were taken before President Kennedy's death with a plan for another inaugural-anniversary celebration. The tragedy of November 22 postponed the kickoff until May, 1964, when a series of $100-a-plate dinners across the nation was scheduled to start the building of the campaign chest.

The two small-giver drives have been continued by the new regime, not so much for the revenue they produce as for the opportunity they afford persons of modest means to feel they have a real stake in the success of the Party. Both Dollars for Democrats and the Sustaining Membership drives were scheduled for 1964 and could be expected to surpass previous efforts.

Thus traditional use of the giving circle and assessment of the state central committees appeared likely to be the main stay of Democratic fund raising in 1964. With an incumbent President seeking reelection, however, the odds seemed good that pocketbooks would open generously.

Chapter XI

Campaign Sidelights

Presidential campaigns have many minor facets. Speakers have to be found to fill the requests of thousands of organizations. Absentee voters need to be assisted in exercising the franchise. Pamphlets about the candidate and his ideas are demanded by special-interest groups, school and college classes, service clubs, churches, and local party organizations. Buttons, auto bumper stickers, banners, and window cards are distributed. Thousands of letters must be answered.

BANNERS, BROCHURES, BUTTONS, AND AUTOMOBILE BUMPER STICKERS

No one know whether banners, brochures, buttons, and bumper stickers do any good in a presidential campaign. All are forms of advertising, and all candidates operate on the assumption that it pays to advertise. Even unopposed local candidates distribute campaign cards, put up signs, and buy space in weekly newspapers.

Name familiarity is the basic objective of campaign advertising. Buttons, window cards, and bumper stickers, however, have the added virtue of creating the impression of widespread support for the candidate. A voter becomes an advocate when he wears his candidate's button in his lapel, displays his candidate's bumper sticker on his car, or places a window card in his shop. His choice may influence his friends.

Most political advertising also conveys ideas beyond the candidate's name. Party identification is the most common. A slogan or a promise also is usual. The candidate stands for "peace and prosperity," or reminds the voters that "he gets things done," or asserts that "there is no substitute for experience." The candidate's picture helps tell the story.

Most costly and probably least useful are the pamphlets and brochures. Quantities of staff time are burned up grinding out a wide variety of these gems of partisan propaganda, although it is doubtful that many are actually read by anyone but convinced partisans. In 1960, for example, Kennedy put out more brochures than buttons and paid three times as much for them.

DEMOCRATIC CAMPAIGN MATERIALS IN 1960

In 1960, $805,303.67 worth of materials were processed for the State Central Committees by the Materials Distribution Center of the Democratic National Committee. The bulk of that bill, $519,718.72, was paid by the National Committee. The remainder, $284,483.95, was in the form of paid orders for materials which the Distribution Center forwarded to the John C. Dowd Company of Boston, Massachusetts, the central supplier of materials.

A total of 139,962,903 items was purchased either by the National Committee for free distribution or by the State Central Committees. The three largest groups of items were ten varieties of brochures totaling 37,457,720 units; Kennedy, Kennedy-Johnson, and Viva Kennedy buttons, 33,718,254; and three varieties of lapel tabs, 34,264,398. In addition, the distribution included 13,329,611 bumper stickers in six different varieties; 18,192,910 window shields of three varieties; 2,153,438 picture sheets of Kennedy, of Johnson, and of both; 31,987 plastic picture posters; 375,004 window cards in three varieties; and 356 banners.

The supply was generous, but if the wails of the local organizations were to be believed, not generous enough. For each of Kennedy's 34 million voters there was a brochure, a button, and a lapel tab. Assuming that some families had only one car, there was also a bumper sticker or a window shield for all as well.

The problem in any system of materials distribution is getting the supplies out to the voters. In 1960, the Democratic National

Committee started early and decentralized its effort. On July 25, each Democratic State Central Committee was asked to appoint a State Coordinator of Materials Distribution. By August 10 all fifty states and the District of Columbia, the Virgin Islands, and the Canal Zone had done so. Illinois even designated a separate additional Coordinator for Chicago. Some state Citizens for Kennedy-Johnson organizations also appointed materials coordinators.

To handle the demand, three distribution centers were set up. Twenty-three Eastern and Southern states and the territories were served out of Democratic National headquarters in Washington, D.C. Thirteen Midwestern states were handled from Chicago. The 13 Far Western states and Texas received supplies from San Francisco.

Free materials were sent out in five categories. By August 31, each State Central Committee was sent an initial free allocation of materials based on its total population. No state received less than ¼ per cent of the total amount sent. New York got 10 per cent, California 8 per cent. A total of 31,854,030 items was sent free to the States.

Individual requests were filled free for persons who wrote to the Committee. Volunteers prepared some 50,000 kits containing several basic campaign items such as a button, a bumper strip, a window sticker, and a brochure, depending upon the request. Individual requests of all kinds consumed an astonishing 18,831,881 items!

As part of advancing the candidates, additional materials were shipped free to cities where John Kennedy and Lyndon Johnson were to appear. The day of the speech, buttons and lapel tabs would be distributed on downtown street corners by girls wearing Kennedy hats and large Kennedy buttons, posters would be put on lamp posts, and cards would be placed in store windows. Some 3,361,081 items were distributed as part of the advance work. Of that amount, 2 million were buttons and tabs and 600,000 were automobile stickers.

Ten per cent of the free materials were made available to labor organizations. State Citizens for Kennedy-Johnson organizations also received quantities of free materials from the Democratic National Committee.

After September 1, State Central Committees were expected to buy any additional materials they needed. Orders were sent to the nearest Materials Distribution Center and then were forwarded to the John C. Dowd Company. Orders usually were filled within 24 hours of receipt.

Small Kennedy or Kennedy-Johnson buttons—the one-inch size—in three colors, cost $7.55 per thousand. Lapel tabs, in one color, were cheaper—$1.75 per thousand. Bumper stickers ranged in price from $20 per thousand to $35. Auto window shields, in three colors, cost $8 per thousand. Posters were less popular. The 28 × 45 inch Kennedy or Johnson one-sheet posters cost $101 per thousand—10 cents each. Window cards ran $71.50 per thousand. Brochures, heaviest in demand, cost $22.50 per thousand.

Certain other materials could be purchased directly from the United Publishing Company in Washington, D.C. Copies of the Democratic Platform were 10 cents each. The 1960 Democratic Fact book cost a quarter. A quarter also would buy the Big Issues kit containing a series of pamphlets.

REPUBLICAN HANDLING OF MATERIALS IN 1960

Long before the presidential contest actually gets underway, the two National Party Committees try to attract supporters and voters through publication of general materials which help set the stage for the campaign itself.

The Republican National Committee eulogies of the Eisenhower administration, early in 1960, are instances in point. Small pamphlets produced by the Public Relations Department examined the recent Republican record in education, the living standard, national wealth, foreign policy, farm policy, civil rights, savings, labor, and other fields, comparing that record with similar records under past Democratic administrations.

A second kind of preconvention literature, designed to attract potential Party workers, stressed the importance of getting into politics, and urged young people who were to vote for the first time in 1960 to join the Republican ranks. Since the Party enjoyed the advantage of the White House, the Eisenhower prestige as the incumbent President added effect to such invitations.

Faithful Party members were recipients of still another kind of early campaign literature. In January of 1960 National Committee Chairman Thruston Morton sent an open letter to Republican neighborhood workers in which he stressed their vital role in the over-all campaign effort, outlined the major campaign issues as he saw them and asked the workers for extra effort in the months ahead.

While these special election-year publications were being put out, the Public Relations Division continued to issue a monthly *Chairman's Fact Memo* to roughly 20,000 of the upper echelon Party leaders across the nation. A daily handout called *Battle Line* went to 500 Republican members of the executive branch, Congressmen, and state Party officials. In October, *Battle Line* was transformed from a daily "scoop sheet" to a fifteen-page magazine. It was then mailed to approximately half a million Party workers ranging from the highest officeholders to precinct committeemen and committeewomen across the nation.

Large though the quantities of such publications are, they are rather intraparty than all-voter materials. Procurement and distribution of these latter materials by the National Committee have been sharply reduced in recent years. Influential Committee staff members have determined that extensive expenditures on such items are unwise when total presidential-campaign spending for the Committee is limited by law to not more than $3,000,000. Hence they distribute relatively little; instead, they give guidance to state and local party organizations. It is customary for the Republican National Committee Public Relations Division to prepare "campaign packets" containing samples of the major items available.

Such packets, called "Official 1960 GOP Campaign Victory Kits," included copies of the abbreviated platform, biographies of the candidates, and subject-matter pieces on labor, agriculture, senior citizens, civil rights, foreign policy, etc. If it went to a Party organization or official, such extra items were included as sample placards, the *Speaker's Manual* and a forty-five page catalog which listed all known companies that produced Republican and Nixon campaign material.

The articles listed in this catalog give some indication of the size of the "political-items" business: arm bands, ash trays, attaché cases, auto antenna flags, auto emblems, license plates, balloons, bells, bottle caps, calendars, candy, coasters, combs, cookie cutters, door hangers, fans, feathers, flags, flower seeds, handkerchiefs, head scarfs, hosiery, and more and more.

Although the Research Division assisted the Public Relations Division by preparing much of the content for its various publications, its major election-year job was to develop the *Speaker's Manual,* entitled "The GOP Record of Progress," a sixty-three page examination of the Eisenhower administration's accomplishments, the major 1960 issues, answers to leading Democratic charges, brief Nixon and Lodge biographies, and a statement concerning the importance of giving a Republican President a Republican Congress. In addition, Dr. William Prendergast and his staff compiled a detailed comparison of the Democratic and Republican platforms, produced a brief summary of the contents of the 1960 Republican platform, and prepared memos on certain questions for Nixon and Lodge.

Research and Public Relations were not the only departments at the Republican National Committee concerned with issuing campaign materials. As the campaign progressed, an Answer Desk was set up specifically to prepare and issue immediate answers to statements made by the opposition the day before. Manned by Oliver Gale, a special assistant to Neil McElroy when McElroy was Secretary of Defense, it not only served campaigners in the field but also released such answers to magazines and newspapers. Gale, a brilliant writer, received assistance from the Research Division and from time to time from friends in the White House.

The Women's Division produced campaign materials of its own. One was a set of ten 4 × 6 inch cards. Entitled "Let's Tell the People," these cards covered all of the major issues and were designed for use by speakers.

Chairman Morton himself initiated a chain-letter operation during the last two weeks of the campaign. This letter device, which had been used in 1952 and 1956, involved writing to ten friends and enclosing a copy of a letter from President Eisenhower which urged extra efforts in the final days of the campaign.

While all of the above represented much manpower and time, the major effort in distributing presidential-campaign literature was not centered at the National Committee but in the Nixon-Lodge distribution headquarters, a block away at the Solar Building. Here huge shelves were loaded with a vast amount of campaign literature, some produced early in the year by the National Committee, most developed after the Convention for the Nixon-Lodge campaign, tons of such basic mailing pieces as the large tabloid, "Meet Richard Nixon," and the materials that went into the SNAP Pack. In addition, there were copies of the "issues" papers, various kinds of banners, buttons, and portraits of the presidential and vice-presidential candidates.

Buttons and badges were issued by both the National Committee and the Nixon headquarters in small quantities. Such larger items as the three-by-five-foot color photographs of the candidates were given only to official Party or volunteer organizations; others who requested them received the name of the publisher.

WHAT TO EXPECT IN 1964

The major tasks involved in campaign propaganda and distribution will revert to the Republican National Committee in 1964. Chairman William Miller has talked to the leading candidates for the nomination, and they have assured him that the waste and inefficiencies of the dual development and distribution system should not reoccur this year.

What will the 1964 campaign materials be like?

On February 14 the first of a series of studies of the past record of President Johnson was issued by the Research Department of the Republican National Committee. This study considered the pronouncements of the President in the area of civil rights both when a candidate for Congress and the senate and when a candidate for the vice presidency. Johnson's statements while a senator are also compared with his statements as Vice President and President. Subsequent reports will cover his statements and record on education, labor, and taxation. The pattern by early March seemed clear. One of the basic charges brought against the Johnson administration will be that his administration has been more concerned with press agentry than with action.

By March of 1964 the traditional Party-oriented noncandidate propaganda was starting to take shape and material for the *Speaker's Manual* was being gathered.

CORRESPONDENCE AT DEMOCRATIC HEADQUARTERS

Presidential candidates get bags of mail every day. Someone has to answer them, for the candidates never have time. In 1960, both political parties worked out very similar systems for handling the flood of mail.

The Democrats centered their correspondence section at 1106 Connecticut Avenue in the ballroom of a former dance studio. Mirrors around the room added to the impression of intense activity.

Processing of mail fell into three main steps: screening and reference, preparation of replies, and typing and signature.

Incoming mail was first opened, read, and referred. If a letter was primarily devoted to a subject of concern to an auxiliary unit, such as Farmers for Kennedy-Johnson, it was immediately referred to that unit for reply. If it was a routine request for campaign materials, the letter went to the Materials Distribution Section; if a request for a speaker, to the Speakers Bureau; if an inquiry on voting, to the Voters Service Bureau.

Many letters, however, could not be thus referred and were very much alike or asked the same questions. For example, after John F. Kennedy, Jr. was born, many thousands of letters of congratulations poured in to the National Committee. When a particular type of letter kept turning up, a stock reply was prepared. Several such stock replies were used.

To handle the volume of such routine inquiries, several large bins were set up with labels to identify the type of letter they contained. When a routine letter came in, it was promptly identified and dropped into its proper bin. Periodically a messenger would make the rounds of the bins and deliver the contents to the robot-typing room for final processing.

Stock replies were cut on robotype tapes for three or four machines, depending on need. All letters were kept to one page if at all possible. A single typist would sit in the center of three or four machines. Taking a routine letter, she would insert letterhead stationery into a typewriter, type in the sender's name and address, insert the salutation, and start the robotype. While the first machine was typing the letter, she would start other similar letters on the second, third, and fourth machines, returning to the first by the time it had completed its task.

The letter was then ready for the signature machine. A battery of three machines continuously signed "John F. Kennedy" or other appropriate signatures. The newly typed letter would be delivered to the proper signature machine operator, who in a matter of seconds would run it through the process. It was then ready to fold, seal, and mail.

Complex letters had to be specially handled. One crew did nothing but tackle the unusual or difficult requests. Sometimes the Research Division had to be called for help and occasionally policy issues were raised which required a letter to be cleared by Myer Feldman. At any event, special letters had to be individually typed so that the complex-letter operation consumed proportionately the greatest amount of staff time in processing.

WHO WRITES LETTERS AND WHY—SOME REPUBLICAN EXAMPLES

Although distribution of materials takes much of the time of the Public Relations Division during a presidential campaign, answering letters and responding to offers of help is almost as time-consuming. What do people write about and what do they ask from the National Committee during a presidential campaign? An inventory of the mail received by the Republican National Committee during two weeks of the campaign is illustrative.

During what was virtually the first week, August 1-8, two hundred letters came in, most of them from well-wishers with suggestions, songs, and slogans. The slogans ranged from the obviously unusable "Don't be a Jack Ass—vote Republican" to the questionable "I Pick Dick." One gentleman suggested, "Why elect a boy to do a man's job, and a man to be the understudy? Vote Republican."

A well-meaning lady from Boston felt "Blessed are the peacemakers" should be the Republican "battle cry." An eighty-five-year-old man submitted a carefully hand-printed, lengthy verse which included: "Follow on—Follow on, March on—March on, is there a better man to lead us on than Nixon? The GOP says No."

The songs were of similar variety. Many came recorded on tape or disk. Several from the South used famous hymn tunes with new words. Thus "Bringing in the Sheaves" became "Bringing in the GOP" for one composer, while another zealot changed "Sitting in the Sunshine" to "Voting in the Morning."

Some of the suggested songs were handwritten with original tunes and verses. Others were published; many were fully orchestrated. One company sent a letter criticizing the Committee for not using their song, "Click with Dick," at the National Convention. A majority of the songs and slogans were written by retired people.

The second largest category of mail sent to the Republican National Committee in this week was requests from state, county, and ward campaign committees. These committees requested campaign materials such as copies of speeches, platforms, pictures, campaign buttons, and candidate biographical information. Several letters from individuals came from areas where campaign materials were not readily available even at Republican Party Headquarters.

A third category of mail included the letters commenting on a particular aspect of the campaign, or mentioning a particular issue on which the writer wished the Party to take a stand. It is interesting to note that of the two hundred letters received during the first week of August, only fifteen expressed these particular concerns. One man wrote to criticize Mrs. Lodge's public appearance. In his estimation she appeared "too much above" the common people. Another serious voter suggested that more humorous television scripts should be used for Mr. Nixon. A woman wrote to criticize the constant interruptions of the newscasters during the Convention, and a lawyer suggested using barber shop quartets "at all big meetings of the campaign."

Letters from people seeking employment in the campaign were rare. One from a woman seeking to be a speech writer gave a lengthy description of her ability to foresee political happenings. Another from a retired Presbyterian minister offered his special talent for writing epigrams, and suggested that he could act as consultant and give Nixon's ideas a little more punch. The only payment he sought was the use "of a couple of light housekeeping rooms in Washington until election eve." Other letters came from radio and television stations, voting officers of the armed forces, and from students and teachers. Most of these correspondents requested information for public use or for teaching purposes.

During the last week of the campaign, October 26-31, by far the largest number of letters came from students, both elementary and college, their teachers, and librarians. Most of these requested "The History of the Republican Party," pictures of the candidates and information on their backgrounds as well as general background material for the campaign. Younger children often asked for buttons and stickers. One student openly resented her treatment at the local headquarters when she went to get buttons for herself and her mother. Because they wouldn't give them to her since she was not old enough to vote, she wrote, "Some day soon I will be old enough. Do you think this is any way to treat a future voter?"

Relatively few of the letters contained requests for material on the issues. Platforms were frequently requested, however, and there was some demand for pamphlets on the farm issues, civil rights and foreign affairs.

Criticisms from interested Party members and voters mainly concerned three items: the debates, civil rights, and suggestions for posters and flyers. One lady wrote, "If prayers are meant to be answered Nixon will be our next President. But please do some thing more than what has been done and God forbid any more TV debates." A door-to-door campaigner for the Republicans said, "The debates have not been helpful. People generally say they were confusing."

A letter from Huntington, New York emphasized a point mentioned earlier, namely, Nixon's reluctance to delegate authority to other members of his campaign staff. Enclosed in the letter was a leaflet concerning the Statement of Presidential Candidates on Operation of the Federal Aviation Act of 1958. Its publisher had requested policy statements from both candidates on the current operation of the Federal Aviation Act. Kennedy's reply was in the leaflet, but Nixon's had not been available at the time of the printing. The comment on the leaflet: "Lets have a reply . . . I feel we need the Airline vote, some 8,000 plus. Don't you?"

There are always letters from those who have a special reason for writing. One staunch Nixon supporter proposed a novel task for the next President.

I am locked up in the New York Insane Asylum almost 21 years without due legal cause . . . and apparently no one cares. I've been writing letters all these years to public officials. . . . The God appointed task of stopping the insanity racket which flourishes in the U.S.A. is the lot for the next President of the U.S.A. and I know of no man better qualified for it than Richard Nixon.

Other common requests during the last week were for platforms, the acceptance speeches, and copies of *Battle Line*. Political Committees continued to ask for the *Speaker's Handbook,* the *Worker's Manual* and the *Campaign Manual.* One prophetic letter writer stated she was "terrified at the thought of Johnson ruling the country if Kennedy should lose his life at the hands of a religious madman."

The following gives the exact number of requests and their source for the week of October 25.

Requests from Schools, Teachers and Students

Pictures—33
Republican Background Information—107
Portfolio of Candidates—126
History of Party—91
Platform 1956—2
Platform 1960—49
Buttons, Pins, and Stickers—38
Issues Pamphlets:
  Defense—5
  Housing—2
  Education—2
  Commerce—1
  Foreign Policy—4

Civil Rights—6
Farm—8
Electoral College—1
Economy—2
Judd's Keynote Speech—3
Candidates' Speeches—5
Speaker's Handbook—2
Worker's Manual—1
Lodge's UN Speech—2
Meeting the Challenge of the '60's—2
Building a Better America Platform—4
Battle Line—4
White Paper—2
Kit—1
Kennedy's Voting Record—2

Requests from Citizens

Pictures—6
Candidate Information—4
Candidates' Speeches—2
History—5
Background Material—6
Battle Line—15
Platform, 1960—15
Absentee Voter's Manual—2
Nixon's Voting Record—1
Debate Copies—2
Republican Stand on:
  Foreign Policy—1
  Farm—1
  Civil Rights—1
  Education—1
  Communism—1
Campaign Manual—4
Worker's Manual—4
Speaker's Handbook—2
White Paper—2
Judd's Keynote Speech—1
"What the Democrats think"—4

THE UNBORN DEMOCRATIC CAMPAIGN

The elaborate plans of a preconvention Campaign Planning Committee, established in March, 1960, by Democratic National Chairman Paul M. Butler, went largely unused. Although it was composed of top Party leaders, had representatives of each of the major candidates for the Party's presidential nomination, established eight subcommittees, and held four major meetings, the Committee proved unable to produce plans which could be carried into the campaign. The candidate had his own ideas and plans, and once he had won nomination, he called the plays—as might have been anticipated.

The initial meeting of the Committee, March 14, 1960, ran headlong into the generous plans of the advertising agency which had been retained by the National Committee. At a cost of $3,500,000 to $4,000,000, the agency proposed both preconvention and postconvention advertising programs.

A $400,000 four-week preconvention advertising program was supposed to project the image of the Party by using animated cartoons which had a humorous pitch. One-minute spot telecasts were to portray the Republican elephant in a petulant, negative mood when asked about medical care for the aged, federal aid for education, resource development, family farms, and the like. With a condescending look and a wave of his trunk he would finally declare, "If they want a change, let 'em vote Democratic."

Although the suggested cartoons provoked hilarity from the partisan Planning Committee when exhibited at its second meeting, they also proved sobering. The realistic Committee members knew that abusing their opponents' symbol would be regarded as foul play and would lose votes, not make them. Inasmuch as the National Committee was still in debt, the cartoons were quietly buried.

Postconvention television programing was a more serious matter, however. Only 18 opportunities were available for five-minute spot broadcasts in the evenings because there were only that many live television shows during the campaign period. The Committee therefore recommended purchase of as many of them as possible. In addition, 12 thirty-minute nationwide telecasts were proposed, of which at least six would be single-network shows. Special spot telecasts in key states and in the farm states also were recommended, as was advertising in the Negro radio and press.

The purchase of newspaper advertising was opposed, however. Instead, the Committee recommended that kits be prepared with copy, layout, and mats for use by state and local organizations in newspaper advertising. Billboards and advertising cards in buses were to be used only if adequate funds were available—a polite way of rejecting those media.

The subcommittees which were established reveal the range of interests which the Campaign Planning Committee explored: Coordination with Congressional Campaigns, Media, Cooperation with Friendly Organizations, Political and Campaign Organizations, Research Materials, Voting Research and Utilization, Fund Raising, and Campaigning Techniques and Plans.

Other than the Media subcommittee, the most creative group was the Subcommittee on Campaigning Techniques and Plans under the chairmanship of Neil Staebler of Michigan. Among the ideas advanced were a recruitment and training school for campaign advance men; a systematic series of regional meetings between the candidates and key party leaders in early August; a neighborhood discussion program with flip charts on selected issues; a system of strategic planning; the establishment by the state and local Party committees of unified campaign committees wherever possible; the establishment of a Materials Distribution Section at the National Committee; the preparation of a simple national-issues pamphlet for widespread use by precinct workers; recognition for rank-and-file political workers who do an outstanding job in organization, fund raising, registration, voter turnout, and similar projects; and "that meetings for energetic delegates and alternates to the National Convention be organized during the mornings of July 12, 13, 14, and 15 to present materials of use in local political organization and campaigning."

With the change of National Committee leadership, the Campaign Planning Committee simply was not called to meet again. No effort was made to draw upon the ideas it had assembled nor to implement its suggestions. Some of the creative recommendations, however, popped up during the campaign, for many of the individuals who had served on the Committee were very active in helping to elect John F. Kennedy.

Chapter XII

The Meaning of the Election

 Electing a President in the United States is boisterous, expensive, exhausting, and contentious. Sometimes, in the past, it has been bitter and even crude. Observers from other lands often find it bewildering and dismaying.

Great leaders are bombarded by their opponents with whispered ridicule and extravagant criticism. They are promoted by their followers with lavish phrases and exaggerated claims. The voters are reminded of their own discontents and prejudices as well as of their own ideals and legitimate desires.

The presidential election itself can fall at a time when issues must be invented for debate or in the midst of war when division at home is a luxury the nation can ill afford. On the other hand, the election can precipitate a great decision, as in 1860, or enable the nation to chart a new course in grappling with human problems, as it did in 1932.

Despite their noise and evident tumult, American presidential elections have been regular, orderly, and free. Every four years since the adoption of the Constitution in 1789, on the first Tuesday after the first Monday in November of years which are divisible by four, the United States has held a presidential election. The election on Tuesday, November 3, 1964 will be the forty-fifth.

Thirty-five different men have served as President. Twenty-seven were elected to the office directly. Eight were elected Vice President and became President upon the death of their predecessors. Of the latter, three subsequently won election as President in their own right. Eleven Presidents were elected to two terms, the constitutional limit since 1951. Only one, Franklin D. Roosevelt, was elected President four times, in 1932, 1936, 1940, and 1944. Roosevelt died in April, 1945, after serving 12 years and one month. The briefest service was by William Henry Harrison, who died April 4, 1841, just one month after taking office.

Some Presidents have changed the course of American history and left a memorable mark in the development of world freedom. Among them were George Washington, Thomas Jefferson, Andrew Jackson, Abraham Lincoln, Theodore Roosevelt, Woodrow Wilson, and Franklin D. Roosevelt. Others have preferred to let history take its course and have gone largely unremembered. Party label has been no guide to greatness. Distinguished Presidents have been Federalists, Democratic Republicans, Republicans, and Democrats.

The election of a President of the United States is the largest free electoral decision taken regularly in the world. In the election of 1964, more than 70 million Americans will decide which of two men will hold the office. They may decide that power should remain in the hands of the man who only a year before had the office thrust upon him by the act of an assassin. They may, instead, prefer to pass power to his opponent with the mandate to follow different policies or to use different methods of administration.

Either decision will once again demonstrate that a free people can entrust the greatest political power and the most overwhelming military might the world has ever known to an elected leader who will wield his authority constitutionally and responsibly and surrender it in course when his term expires. It will also confirm the continuing ability of a free people to chart the course of government. Such demonstrations of human capacity to organize and direct a stable society and at the same time to preserve the rights and dignity of individuals have been the hope of the world for nearly two centuries.

One hundred seventy-five years ago, when George Washington

was chosen first President of the United States, democracy was a daring experiment in a small new republic, a collection of former British colonies that clung along the eastern shores of the vast and largely uninhabited North American continent. Across the Atlantic, the glittering capitals of Europe were controlled by hereditary monarchs who viewed the new nation and its democracy with suspicion, distrust, and open hostility. Among them, the wise and shrewd knew enough of history and of men to suspect that its survival and its success would some day bring an end to absolutism and colonialism.

Yet the little nation, with its brand new written Constitution, the first in the political history of the world, was also part of all that had gone before. It did not wish to withdraw from the western world in which it had so recently won its freedom or to repudiate the civilization it had acquired. Its representative legislature, its many religious beliefs, its concept of due process of law, its freedom of speech, its beliefs in the rights of man—all the basic ideals of the new democracy—were drawn from the long struggle for freedom which was still being waged in England. The speech, the literature, the art, and the music of the new Americans also tied them with their ancestral Europe.

The firm establishment of an effective national government for the American states and of a workable democratic method for the free and orderly change of political power in a republic marked a turning point in world history. Henceforth, mankind would be "yearning to breathe free," to follow the trail which Washington and Adams and Jefferson would blaze. The demand for independence and freedom would not wait long. The spark would fall later that year in France and the flame of freedom would spread on and on until, a century and three quarters later, more than one hundred free and independent nations would sit in council at the United Nations in New York.

Successive American presidential elections have reflected the struggles of a growing nation as it developed the natural resources of its continent, battled slavery and secession, built an unparalleled industrial system, wrestled with the social and economic problems of an urban society, and tried to shoulder the frustrations of a world leadership it had not sought. Today the presidency and the system by which it is filled stand as a monumental achievement in the development of human freedom. For the nation which created the office of President, assigned to it the great powers it possesses, and supported it with the political, economic, and military might of the greatest of world powers, did all these things to preserve its revolutionary ideals of freedom and independence. These ideals have become not only America's ideals, but the ideals of free peoples everywhere.

Consequently, the presidential election of 1964 can be said to represent more for the United States and for mankind than a mere partisan contest for control of the executive branch of government in one nation. Although the nomination and the campaigning will be cast in a partisan and nationalistic mold, and the outcome will be interpreted as a victory for one candidate and his policies, the election will, in its deepest meaning, demonstrate the continuing ability of a free people to allocate great power by orderly constitutional means. Presidential power, thus determined and thus controlled, is freedom's guardian, for Americans and for free men everywhere.

Selection of Delegates to the National Conventions

State	Method of Selection
Alabama	Democrats at Presidential Primary; Republicans at State and District Conventions
Alaska	State Convention
Arizona	State Executive Committee
Arkansas	State Committee
California	Presidential Preference Primary
Colorado	State and District Conventions
Connecticut	Democrats at State Convention; Republicans at State and District Conventions
Delaware	State Convention
District of Columbia	Presidential Preference Primary
Florida	Presidential Preference Primary
Georgia	Democrats by State Committee; Republicans at State Convention
Hawaii	State Convention
Idaho	State Convention
Illinois	State Conventions for At Large Delegates; Presidential Preference Primary for District Delegates
Indiana	State and District Conventions
Iowa	Democrats at State Convention; Republicans at State and District Conventions
Kansas	State and District Conventions
Kentucky	Democrats at State Convention; Republicans at State and District Conventions
Louisiana	State Central Committees
Maine	Democrats at State Convention; Republicans at District Conventions
Maryland	State Convention (delegates not chosen at Presidential Preference Primary)

State	Method of Selection
Massachusetts	Presidential Preference Primary
Michigan	State and District Conventions
Minnesota	State and District Conventions
Mississippi	State Convention
Missouri	Democrats at State Convention; Republicans at State and District Conventions
Montana	State Convention
Nebraska	State Convention for Delegates at Large; Presidential Preference Primary for District Delegates
Nevada	State Convention
New Hampshire	Presidential Preference Primary
New Jersey	Presidential Preference Primary
New Mexico	State Convention
New York	State Convention or State Committee for At Large Delegates; Primary Election for District Delegates. No Presidential Preference Voting
North Carolina	Democrats at State Convention; Republicans at State and District Conventions
North Dakota	State Convention
Ohio	Presidential Preference Primary
Oklahoma	State and District Conventions
Oregon	Presidential Preference Primary
Pennsylvania	State Central Committee for At Large Delegates; Presidential Preference Primary for District Delegates
Rhode Island	Primary Election. No Presidential Preference Voting (optional with the political parties)
South Carolina	State Convention
South Dakota	Presidential Preference Primary
Tennessee	State and District Conventions
Texas	State Convention
Utah	State Convention
Vermont	State Convention
Virginia	Democrats at State Convention; Republicans at State and District Conventions
Washington	State Convention
West Virginia	Presidential Preference Primary
Wisconsin	Presidential Preference Primary
Wyoming	State Convention
Canal Zone	Democrats only at Territorial Convention
Puerto Rico	Commonwealth Convention
Virgin Islands	Territorial Convention

Source: Richard D. Hupman and Eiler C. Ravnholt, *Nomination and Election of the President and Vice President of the United States* (Washington: Government Printing Office, 1964).

Electoral Votes: 1956, 1960, 1964

State	1956 Dem.	1956 Rep.	1956 Other	1960 Dem.	1960 Rep.	1960 Other	1964
Alabama	10		1	5		6	10
Alaska					3		3
Arizona		4			4		5
Arkansas	8			8			6
California		32			32		40
Colorado		6			6		6
Connecticut		8		8			8
Delaware		3		3			3
District of Columbia							3
Florida		10			10		14
Georgia	12			12			12
Hawaii				3			4
Idaho		4			4		4
Illinois		27		27			26
Indiana		13			13		13
Iowa		10			10		9
Kansas		8			8		7
Kentucky		10			10		9
Louisiana	10			10			10
Maine		5		5			4
Maryland		9		9			10
Massachusetts		16		16			14
Michigan		20		20			21
Minnesota		11		11			10
Mississippi	8					8	7
Missouri	13			13			12
Montana		4			4		4

State	1956 Dem.	1956 Rep.	1956 Other	1960 Dem.	1960 Rep.	1960 Other	1964
Nebraska		6			6		5
Nevada		3		3			3
New Hampshire		4			4		4
New Jersey		16		16			17
New Mexico		4		4			4
New York		45		45			43
North Carolina	14				14		13
North Dakota		4			4		4
Ohio		25			25		26
Oklahoma		8			7	1	8
Oregon		6			6		6
Pennsylvania		32		32			29
Rhode Island		4		4			4
South Carolina	8			8			8
South Dakota		4			4		4
Tennessee		11			11		11
Texas		24		24			25
Utah		4			4		4
Vermont		3			3		3
Virginia		12			12		12
Washington		9			9		9
West Virginia		8		8			7
Wisconsin		12			12		12
Wyoming		3			3		3
Totals	73	457	1	303	219	15	538

Popular Votes Cast for President in 1956 and 1960

	1956		1960	
State	Democratic	Republican	Democratic	Republican
Alabama	280,844	195,694	324,050	237,981
Alaska	—	—	29,809	30,953
Arizona	112,880	176,990	176,781	221,241
Arkansas	213,277	186,287	215,049	184,508
California	2,420,135	3,027,668	3,224,099	3,259,722
Colorado	263,997	394,479	330,629	402,242
Connecticut	405,079	711,837	657,055	565,813
Delaware	79,421	98,057	99,590	96,373
Florida	480,371	643,849	748,700	795,476
Georgia	441,094	216,662	458,638	274,472
Hawaii	—	—	92,410	92,295
Idaho	105,868	166,979	138,853	161,597
Illinois	1,775,682	2,623,327	2,377,846	2,368,988
Indiana	783,908	1,182,811	952,358	1,175,120
Iowa	501,858	729,187	550,565	722,381
Kansas	269,317	566,878	363,213	561,474
Kentucky	476,453	572,192	521,855	602,607
Louisiana	243,977	329,047	407,339	230,980
Maine	102,468	249,238	181,159	240,608
Maryland	372,613	559,738	565,808	489,538
Massachusetts	948,190	1,393,197	1,487,174	976,750
Michigan	1,359,898	1,713,647	1,687,269	1,620,428
Minnesota	617,525	719,302	779,933	757,915
Mississippi	144,453	60,685	108,362	73,561*
Missouri	918,273	914,299	972,201	962,221
Montana	116,238	154,993	134,891	141,841

State	1956 Democratic	Republican	1960 Democratic	Republican
Nebraska	199,029	378,108	232,542	380,553
Nevada	40,640	56,049	54,880	52,387
New Hampshire	90,364	176,519	137,772	157,989
New Jersey	850,337	1,606,942	1,385,415	1,363,324
New Mexico	106,098	146,778	156,027	153,733
New York	2,750,769	4,340,340	3,830,085	3,446,419
North Carolina	590,530	575,062	713,136	655,420
North Dakota	96,742	156,766	123,963	154,310
Ohio	1,439,655	2,262,610	1,944,248	2,217,611
Oklahoma	385,581	473,769	370,111	533,039
Oregon	329,204	406,393	367,402	408,060
Pennsylvania	1,981,769	2,585,252	2,556,282	2,439,956
Rhode Island	161,790	255,819	258,032	147,502
South Carolina	136,372	75,700	198,129	188,558
South Dakota	122,288	171,569	128,070	178,417
Tennessee	456,507	462,288	481,453	556,577
Texas	859,958	1,080,619	1,167,932	1,121,699
Utah	118,364	215,631	169,248	205,361
Vermont	42,549	110,390	69,186	98,131
Virginia	267,760	386,459	362,327	404,521
Washington	523,002	620,430	599,298	629,273
West Virginia	381,534	449,297	441,786	395,995
Wisconsin	586,768	954,844	830,805	895,175
Wyoming	49,554	74,573	63,331	76,551
Totals	26,027,983	35,609,190	34,227,096	34,107,646

* State carried by third-party electors in 1960 with 116,248.

Appendix IV

Bibliography

Electing the President: 1964 is based primarily upon the direct experience of the authors in the 1960 presidential campaign and upon their continuing close contact with the national political parties. Footnotes have been restricted to references to sources of information beyond their direct experience or to confirmations of their reports.

A growing body of literature is available on several phases of the process of electing the President. To aid those who desire additional information about particular aspects of presidential campaigns, the following selected annotated bibliography is provided:

Alexander, Herbert E. *Financing the 1960 Election*. Princeton: Citizens' Research Foundation, 1961. Only available analysis of 1960 campaign finance. Contains useful charts and tables.

Alexander, Herbert E. *Responsibility in Party Finance*. Princeton: Citizens' Research Foundation, 1963. Very useful analysis of national party fund raising since 1960. Contains materials on state and local fund raising as well.

Bain, Richard C. *Convention Decisions and Voting Records*. Washington: Brookings Institution, 1960. Compilation of basic data on national convention proceedings.

Campbell, Angus, *and others. The American Voter*. New York: John Wiley and Sons, Inc., 1960. Comprehensive analysis of voting behavior based upon the findings of the Survey Research Center of the University of Michigan. Data drawn principally from the 1952 and 1956 presidential campaigns.

David Paul T., *and others. Presidential Nominating Politics in 1952*. 5 vols. Baltimore: Johns Hopkins Press, 1954. Comprehensive report of the Cooperative Research Project on Convention Delegations sponsored by the American Political Science Association. The process of delegate selection and delegation behavior at both national conventions in 1952 was systematically surveyed for every state.

David, Paul T., *and others. The Politics of National Party Conventions.* Washington: Brookings Institution, 1960. A comprehensive study of national conventions as a nominating device. Regarded as the definitive work in the field.

David, Paul T., *editor. The Presidential Election and Transition, 1960-1961.* Washington: Brookings Institution, 1961. A collection of essays on the 1960 campaign and transition.

Heard, Alexander. *The Costs of Democracy.* Chapel Hill: University of North Carolina Press, 1960. The definitive work on political party finance.

Hennessy, Bernard. *Dollars for Democrats, 1959.* New York: McGraw-Hill Book Company, Inc., 1960. An analysis of the Democratic Party's door-to-door drive for small gifts by the man who headed the national drive effort in 1959.

Hupman, Richard D., and Ravholt, Eiler C. *Nomination and Election of the President and Vice President of the United States.* Washington: Government Printing Office, 1960. An official compilation of the laws affecting the nomination and election of the President and Vice President, compiled by the Legislative Reference Service of the Library of Congress under the direction of the Secretary of the United States Senate.

Polsby, Nelson W., and Wildavsky, Aaron B. *Presidential Elections.* New York: Charles Scribner's Sons, 1964.

Pomper, Gerald. *Nominating the President.* Evanston, Illinois: Northwestern University Press, 1963.

Thomson, Charles A. H. *Television and Presidential Politics.* Washington: Brookings Institution, 1956. An analysis of the development of television and its use during the 1952 national conventions and presidential campaign. Raises problems for the 1956 campaign.

Thomson, Charles A. H., and Shattuck, Frances M. *The 1956 Presidential Campaign.* Washington: Brookings Institution, 1960.

Tillett, Paul, *editor. Inside Politics: The National Conventions, 1960.* Dobbs Ferry, N.Y.: Oceana Publications, Inc., 1962. A collection of articles by the National Convention Faculty Fellows of 1960, a program sponsored by the National Center for Education in Politics.

U.S. Congress, Senate. *Final Report of the Special Committee to Investigate Political Activities, Lobbying, and Campaign Contributions.* Washington: Government Printing Office, 1957. Contains detailed report on all federal and state laws which regulate campaign finance.

U.S. Congress, Senate. *Freedom of Communications.* 2 vols. Washington: Government Printing Office, 1961. The complete speeches of John F. Kennedy and Richard M. Nixon delivered during the 1960 presidential campaign. Printed by the Committee on Interstate and Foreign Commerce.

U.S. Congress, Senate. *1956 General Election Campaigns.* Washington:

Government Printing Office, 1957. A report of the Subcommittee on Privileges and Elections of the Committee on Rules and Administration. Contains detailed tables on contributions and expenditures in the 1956 campaign.

White, Theodore H. *The Making of the President 1960.* New York: Atheneum House, Inc., 1961. The story of the 1960 campaign as seen by a talented newsman who accompanied both candidates. Excellent interpretation and good detail.